I0055870

Switched-Mode Power Supply Design with SPICE

Steven M. Sandler

Switched-Mode Power Supply Design with SPICE

Other books by Steven M. Sandler

*Power Integrity: Measuring, Optimizing, and Troubleshooting Power
Related Parameters in Electronics Systems
SPICE Circuit Handbook
Measuring Power: Application Notebook*

© 2018 Steven M. Sandler All Rights Reserved
Print ISBN 978-1-941071-84-7

This book is sold subject to the condition that it shall not, by way of
trade or otherwise, be lent, resold, hired out or otherwise circulated
without the publisher's prior consent in any form of binding or cover
other than that in which it is published and without a similar condition
including this condition being imposed on the subsequent purchaser.

Cover Design by Guy D. Corp, www.GrafixCorp.com

www.FaradayPress.com
1000 West Apache Trail—Suite 126
Apache Junction, AZ 85120 USA

Dedication

This book is dedicated to my wife Susan for encouraging me to challenge myself and for her love that provides me with the strength, energy and support that I need to accomplish it.

Acknowledgments

WRITING A BOOK, as with any other large project, requires the coordinated efforts of many people. I would like to thank the people listed below—without their efforts this book would never have been completed.

Charles Hymowitz is a world renowned authority on SPICE and is currently the Managing Director of AEi Systems, LLC. He was one of the founders of Intusoft and has authored or co-authored three books on SPICE and was the editor-in-chief of the Intusoft Newsletter. He spent endless hours supporting this book and without him it would not have been possible.

Christophe Basso is a world renowned authority on SPICE modeling and also has specific experience with IsSpice. He is the author of *Switch-Mode Power Supply Spice Cookbook*. He is a good friend and always offered his time to discuss power electronics, SPICE and modeling.

Rudy Severns is a world renowned authority on magnetics design. He is President of Springtime Enterprises Inc., and consultant in the design of power electronics and power conversion equipment. I graciously thank Rudy for contributing significantly to the chapter on Modeling Magnetics.

The author and publisher thank Tammie Bard of Intel for her dedicated assistance with capturing code and reviewing the manuscript of this reprinted edition.

About the Author

STEVEN M. SANDLER has been in the power conversion business since 1976. He has worked for companies such as Acme Electric, Lambda Electronics, Venus Scientific, Transistor Devices, Keltec-Florida and Signal Technology. The majority of his work has been involved with the development of power conversion products for commercial, military and space platforms. He was the founder of AEi, a company specializing in the computer simulation and worst case analysis of power electronics. AEi performed a great deal of the computer simulation of the power electronics used on the International Space Station as well as many other platforms.

In 2010, Steve founded Picotest.com, a company dedicated to providing instruments, accessories and training to support electronic test and measurements, with an emphasis on power integrity solutions. Picotest is headquartered in Phoenix, AZ.

For more information on Picotest, please contact the company at 1-877-914-PICO or visit www.Picotest.com.

Publisher's Note

THIS BOOK IS an updated reprint of Steve's historic book *SMPS Simulation with SPICE 3*. Due to the way the book was assembled, many compromises were made in formatting and page composition. We are proud to bring this book back to print and are confident in its value and utility to the practicing engineer; however, we apologize in advance for any oddities that might trouble your eye.

We think all the code fragments will work with the major SPICE versions, including PSPICE, LTSpice and Tina, but we did not try every program and combination. If you find an error, please let us know. Even better, if you find a solution or work-around, please share it so we can help other engineers. If your contribution warrants and our budget permits, in return, we might offer an honorarium or contribution to a favored charity.

The source code is available and on request to the address below, we will email a zipped version to you.

Steve has been selfless in contributing his knowledge to the power supply community. If you have tips or tricks to share, please let us know. Our mission is simple: to improve the quality and performance of all the power supply designs in the world. That's a lofty goal and we can't do it alone—we need your help.

Now, go forth and do great work.

Ken Coffman

Ken@StairwayPress.com

Introduction 7

Buck Topology Converters............................. 132

Chapter 1

Introduction

THE TECHNOLOGY IN the area of computer modeling and simulation is growing at a rapid pace. As computers become faster and more capable, new software provides greater capability. This progress in technology is of great benefit to design engineers and to the companies that employ them. This book is intended to show how to harness the capability of computer modeling and the simulation of power circuits.

Why Simulate?

On more than one occasion, I have been asked (usually by my upper management) why there always seems to be a quest for newer, faster computers, and software. Why are so many precious budget dollars requested for conferences and training seminars? After giving this question a great deal of thought, I came to the following conclusions:

Simulation Saves Money Design flaws that are not detected until the production cycle may delay schedules and significantly increase production costs. Simulation is an aid to the early detection of these errors. Monte Carlo and worst-case simulations help to insure maximum production yield. With the help of simulation, expensive parts and systems can be effectively debugged without the possibility of destroying them.

Simulation Saves Time Circuits can be simulated on a computer much more quickly than they can be built and evaluated.

Simulation Measures the Immeasurable Computer simulation allows engineers to evaluate a circuit with the worst-case values or difficult environmental conditions. It would be quite a challenge to build a circuit that encompasses all worst-case component values, or to measure the effects of solar flares on circuit performance. Simulation allows these types of conditions to be easily evaluated.

Simulation Promotes Safety Simulation allows the evaluation of fault conditions, which may be dangerous to human life. Airline pilots spend a considerable amount of time simulating emergency conditions, of course, rather than practicing them.

Keep in mind that simulation does not—and never will—replace actual circuit testing. Simulation is great for trying out ideas and changing circuit parameters that would be difficult in a real circuit. The only way a simulation can be trusted is if it is verified by actual circuit operation. There are endless examples of engineers who did not heed this lesson—creating a CLM[1] situation for the engineer.

About the SPICE Syntax Used in This Book

This book assumes that you already have a working knowledge of SPICE, in particular PSpice® from Cadence Design Systems. If this is not the case, it is suggested that you review the manuals that accompany your SPICE program before proceeding. A demonstration version of PSpice is available from Cadence Design Systems at www.orcad.com or www.ema-eda.com. The syntax used in this book is generally SPICE 2 or SPICE 3 based, however,

---

[1] Career-Limiting Move

several key PSpice extensions to the SPICE language are utilized in the modeling process. These extensions greatly enhance the simulation efficiency and ability to model various aspects of a power ICs operation. (See the PSpice, SPICE 3, and Other SPICE Extensions section.)

This book is intended to assist you in using SPICE during the design and analysis process. I strongly encourage you to run the example simulations in order to get a better understanding of the capability of the software and the modeling techniques. All example circuits in this book are designed to be simulated using OrCAD's Capture and PSpice, although other versions of SPICE that are compatible with PSpice may also be used. With a few modifications (described in the next section), almost any SPICE software can be used to run the simulations. In addition, the design and modeling techniques are applicable to many different types of simulators. Some of the circuits, schematics, and SPICE netlists will be emailed to all who make a request of the publisher.

I selected Cadence/OrCAD PSpice for several reasons:

- The PSpice simulator brings state-of-the-art technology to analog and mixed-signal design software.

- It is one of the best SPICE simulators for power electronics and related applications. The libraries included with the simulator have a large number of power semiconductor models, including IGBTs, SCRs, Triacs, Power MOSFETs, Power BJTs, and much more. Many models are in unencrypted ASCII text files, so they can be easily edited.

- A software modeling utility is available as a part of most of the Cadence/OrCAD's offerings. This utility allows you to easily model your own devices from a manufacturer's data sheet parameters.

- All of the power devices use sophisticated subcircuit structures, thus providing very realistic behavior. PSpice's behavioral modeling accommodation is very powerful and extensive.

- Cadence/OrCAD is dedicated to the improvement of their products. They are continually enhancing their software and adding features that increase productivity.

- Cadence/OrCAD maintains a knowledgeable technical support staff and works closely with engineers, in order to make their software as productive as possible.

- PSpice is the most predominant, non-vendor-specific SPICE-based simulator in use today.

PSpice, LTSpice, Tina, SPICE 3, and Other SPICE Extensions

The majority of the models and circuit elements in this book utilize SPICE 2G.6 syntax. Where ever possible generic syntax is used so that the models can be adapted to various simulators. However, some key elements are modeled using PSpice specific and/or Berkeley SPICE 3 syntax extensions. In particular, SPICE 3 has an arbitrary dependent source, or B element, that allows mathematical expressions of voltages, currents, and other quantities to be used. PSpice extends the syntax of the E- and G-controlled source elements even further in order to add many behavioral modeling constructs including mathematical and logical If-Then-Else expressions. Switches with or without hysteresis can be created in both PSpice and SPICE 3 and are also used extensively.

The newer SPICE 3 elements provide greater flexibility and improved performance. Their syntax and behavior are briefly reviewed later, along with several other SPICE "extensions." More information is available in *PSpice A/D Reference Guide*[1]

To emulate the nonlinear large-signal behavior, often found in power devices, such models require arbitrary X-Y transfer functions. The polynomial math features of SPICE 2, while universally accepted, are very limited. Therefore, the more flexible *Behavioral Math Expressions* feature of Berkeley SPICE 3 is used extensively. In addition, there are occasions when a procedural type of behavior is required. To produce this functionality, PSpice uses an *If-Then-Else* syntax. This "syntax extension" has also been added to the Berkeley SPICE 3 B-element in some versions of SPICE, but not all of them. Some SPICE vendors include a table-type function where the transfer function is defined by a series of X-Y data points. The table function is supported in PSpice. However, the advantage of the If-Then-Else capability over the table model is that the transfer function between each X-Y data point can be nonlinear in the If-Then-Else syntax, whereas the Table model only supports linear segments between points.

Nonlinear PWM IC models require basic digital logic functions such as latches and flip-flops. These functions can be efficiently modeled in several ways in PSpice, but are prohibitively complex to model, using SPICE 2 polynomial syntax. Therefore, another PSpice syntax extension, *Boolean Logic Expressions*, was chosen to model the digital functions.

If your simulator has support for the SPICE 3 functions and equivalent support for the PSpice extensions, you can easily translate the syntax used in this book.

PSpice is based on Berkeley SPICE. However, it has been significantly enhanced over the generic Berkeley version in terms of its simulation algorithms, graphical user interface, advanced multi-run analysis, and model support. Shown later is the syntax for the Berkeley SPICE 3 element and PSpice's behavioral extensions, along with some examples on how to translate the syntax extensions to other SPICE simulators.

Nonlinear Dependent Sources (B, E, and G Elements)

Math Expressions

The arbitrary dependent source (B element) allows an instantaneous transfer function to be written as a mathematical expression. This B element is a standard Berkeley SPICE 3 element. The expressions, [*EXPR*], given for V and I may be any function of node voltages, currents through any element, or a variety of traditional math functions. In PSpice, the E- and G-controlled source elements are utilized:

Format: Bname N+ N- [I=EXPR] [V=EXPR]

SPICE 3 Examples:

> B1 0 1 I = sqrt(cos(v(1)/(v(2,3))))
> B4 outp outn V = exp(i(vdd)^2)
> B1 1 0 V=V(2) * abs(I(V1)) + V(3)
> B3 1 2 V=I(R1)
> B2 2 3 I={V(7) * Sin(Time)}^{2}

Format: Ename N+ N- Value={EXPR}
>   Gname N+ N- Value={EXPR}

PSpice Equivalent Examples:

> G1 0 1 value={sqrt(cos(v(1)/(v(2,3))))}
> E4 outp outn value={exp(pwr(I(vdd),2))}
> E1 1 0 value={V(2) * abs(I(V1)) + V(3)}
> E3 1 2 value={I(R1)}
> G2 2 3 value={V(7) * Sin(Time)}

The Berkeley SPICE 3 arbitrary source syntax begins with the letter B. $N+$ and $N-$ are the positive and negative nodes, respectively. The values of the V and I parameters determine the voltages and currents across and through the device, respectively. Unlike PSpice, there is no distinction between current-controlled (G element) and voltage-controlled (E element) sources for the B element. If "I=" is given, then the output is a current source. If "V=" is given, the output is a voltage source. One and only one of these parameters must be given.

---

[2] Some, but not all, SPICE simulators allow the keywords *Time*, *Freq*, or *Temp* in B element expressions.

If-Then-Else Examples in PSpice

The [EXPR] given in the Math Expressions section earlier can also contain a special If-Then-Else logical expression. Many SPICE vendors do not have an equivalent syntax for this capability, as shown later in the PSpice examples, even though it is one of the most used modeling constructs in Power IC modeling.

Format: E*name* N+ N- Value = { IF (*Evaluation*, *Output_Value1* or *Expression*, *Output_Value 2* or *Expression*) }

More Simply: E*name* N+ N- Value = { if (*Evaluation* is true, then V(N+, N-)= *Output_Value 1,* else v(N+, N-)= *Output_Value 2*) }

Evaluation, Output_Value, and *Expression* may consist of any math expression discussed in the Math Expressions section, or Boolean operators. There is virtually no limit to the length or complexity of the expressions that can be used. The *Evaluation* expression can use greater than ">" or less than "<" test. Equal is not allowed.

If-Then-Else Examples

3 Input Nand Gate with User-defined Levels

PSpice: e1 4 0 value={if(v(1) > 1.5, if (v(2) > 1.5, if (v(3) > 1.5, 0.3,3.5), 3.5), 3.5)}

Translation: If v(1) is greater than 1.5, then if v(2) is greater than 1.5, then if v(3) is greater than 1.5, then v(4)=0.3; else v(4)=3.5

3-Region Limiter

PSpice: e1 4 0 value={if (v(1)<.5, v(1)*.5+.25, if (v(1)>1.53, 1.54, v(1)))}

Translation: If v(1) is less than .5, then v(2)=v(1)*.5+2.5; else if v(1) is greater than 1.53, then v(2)=1.54; else v(2)=v(1)

Comparator

PSpice: e1 3 0 value={if(v(1,2) < 0, 5, .2)}

Translation: If voltage difference v(1)-v(2) is less than 0, then v(3)=5; else v(3)=.1

Voltage-Controlled Decision

PSpice: e1 2 0 value={if(v(vctrl) < 0, v(3), v(4))}

Translation: If vctrl is less than 0, then v(2)=v(3); else v(2)=v(4)

Digital Logic Functions

The PSpice If-Then-Else element extension can be used to create models of digital logic functions. This is accomplished by including level tests and Boolean operators in the [EXPR] function. PSpice is a true native mixed-mode simulator, which has a full digital logic simulator included within the program. PSpice also includes digital models of different logic families, and includes exact transistor representations or IBIS (I/O Buffer Interface Specification) representations. The Boolean logic methodology was chosen over these other two digital simulation philosophies because of its efficiency and simplicity.

The E/G element expressions [EXPR] may consist of Boolean operators and any of the functions in the Math Expressions section. There is virtually no limit to the length or complexity of the expressions that can be used. The following operations are defined for the Boolean operations:

& - And | - Or

PSpice Examples:

ENand 5 0 Value = { IF ((V(1)>800mV) & (V(2)>800mV) & (V(3)>800mV), 0, 5) }
EOr 5 0 Value = { IF ((V(1)>800mV) | (V(2)>800mV), 5, 0) }
EInv 3 0 Value = { IF (V(1)>800mV, 0, 5) }

PSpice Example FFLOP Netlist

```
.SUBCKT FFLOP1875 1 2 11 12 5 6
*          CLK D R S QB Q
X1 7 4 2 8 NAND31875_0
X2 8 3 10 9 NAND31875_0
X3 1 8 10 7 NAND31875_1
X4 4 9 1 10 NAND31875_0
X5 4 7 6 5 NAND31875_1
X6 5 10 3 6 NAND31875_0
X7 11 4 INV1875
X8 12 3 INV1875
.ENDS FFLOP1875
*
.SUBCKT NAND31875_0 1 2 3 4
* Nand Gate with 0V initial output voltage, Node 4
E1 5 0 VALUE = { IF ( (V(1)>800mV) & (V(2)>800mV) & (V(3)>800mV), 0, 5 ) }
R1 5 4 40
C1 4 0 50P IC=0
.ENDS NAND31875_0
*
.SUBCKT NAND31875_1 1 2 3 4
* Nand Gate with 5V initial output voltage, Node 4
E1 5 0 VALUE = { IF ( (V(1)>800mV) & (V(2)>800mV) & (V(3)>800mV), 0, 5 ) }
R1 5 4 40
C1 4 0 50P IC=5
.ENDS NAND31875_1
*
.SUBCKT INV1875 1 2
E1 3 0 VALUE = { IF ( V(1)>800mV, 0, 5 ) }
R1 3 2 10
C1 2 0 20P IC=5
.ENDS INV1875
```

PSpice Example Nand Netlist Using Math Equations

```
.SUBCKT X_gate A B out
R1 A B 1meg
E1 3 0 Value={((1+tanh(1000*(1.5-v(A))))*(1+tanh(1000*(1.5-v(B))))) }
R2 3 4 1
C1 4 0 1n
.ENDS
```

Switch Elements (S/W Elements)

Switches are a key part of the most power electronics simulations; they are frequently used to replace a semiconductor model to speed the simulation. PSpice includes three different switches whose characteristics make them suitable for different applications. One of the most frequently used is the switch with hysteresis. If your

15

simulator supports all the standard Berkeley SPICE 3 elements, then this switch can be used without any syntax changes. This type of switch has only recently been included as a primitive element in PSpice.

SPICE 3 Syntax

Format: Sname N+ N- NC+ NC- modelname [ON] [OFF]
Format: Wname N+ N- vname modelname [ON] [OFF]

Example: S1 1 2 3 4 switch1
.Model switch1 SW Ron=0.1 Roff=1G Vt=1 Vh=.5
Example: W1 1 2 Vsense switch1
.Model switch1 CSW H Ron=1m Roff=1G It=1 Ih=.5

The SPICE 3 voltage-controlled switch begins with the letter S. N+ and N- represent the connections to the switch terminals. The nodes NC+ and NC- are the positive- and negative-controlling nodes, respectively. The device's model name (modelname) is mandatory, while the initial conditions are optional. ON or OFF specify the switch state for the DC operating point calculation. The current-controlled switch begins with the letter W, and the statement names a voltage source whose current is used to control the switch. Otherwise the model parameters and operation are the same.

The switch requires a .Model statement in order to describe the switch characteristics. The model type parameter must be SW. Ron is the on resistance, Roff is the off resistance, Vt is the threshold voltage and Vh is the hysteresis voltage.

In PSpice, the type of switch, either with hysteresis or with a smooth transition region, is determined by the model parameters used in the .Model statement. The settings for the PSpice switch with hysteresis are explained below.

PSpice Syntax—Switch with Hysteresis

Format: Sname N+ N- NC+ NC- modelname
Format: Wname N+ N- vname modelname

Example:

S1 1 2 3 4 switch1
.Model switch1 VSWITCH Ron=1m Roff=1G Vt=1 Vh=.5

Example:

W1 1 2 3 4 switch1
.Model switch1 ISWITCH Ron=0.1m Roff=1G It=1 Ih=.5

In older versions of PSpice, the switch with hysteresis is not available. Instead a subcircuit representation can be used to create this function. Passed parameters replace the model parameters.

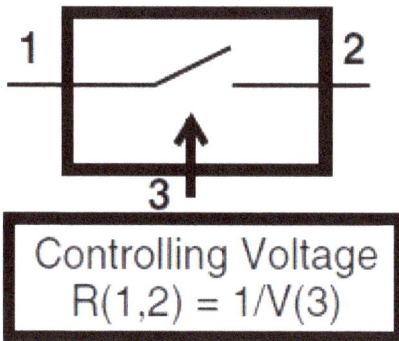

```
Switch Hysterisis Test
* Switch with Hysterisis Test Circuit
VIN 100 0 10V
VCONTROL 102 0 PULSE(0 5V 0 .01 .01 .1 .2)
R100 100 101 10K

X1 0 101 102 0 SWhyste
.TRAN 1nS 1
.PROBE V(101) V(102)

.Subckt SWhyste NodeMinus NodePlus Plus Minus PARAMS: RON=1 ROFF=100MEG VT=1.5 VH=.5
S5 NodePlus NodeMinus 8 0 smoothSW
EBcrtl 8 0 Value = { IF ( V(plus)-V(minus) > V(ref), 1, 0 ) }
EBref ref1 0 Value = { IF ( V(8) > 0.5, {VT-VH}, {VT+VH} ) }
Rdel ref1 ref 70
Cdel ref 0 100p IC={VT+VH}
Rconv1 8 0 10Meg
Rconv2 plus 0 10Meg
Rconv3 minus 0 10Meg
.Model smoothSW VSWITCH (RON={RON} ROFF={ROFF} VON=1 VOFF=0)
.Ends SWhyste
.END
```

Figure 1.1

SWhyste Netlist

Figure 1.2

SWhyste Waveforms

The switch model creates an almost ideal switch in PSpice. The switch is not quite ideal; the resistance cannot change from zero to infinity, but must always have a finite positive value. If the on and off resistances are selected properly, they can be effectively zero and infinity in comparison to other circuit impedances. The switch has hysteresis, which is described by the Vh parameter. For example, the voltage-controlled switch will be in the on state, with a resistance, Ron, at Vt+Vh. The switch will be in the off state, with a resistance, Roff, at Vt-Vh.

The use of an ideal element that is highly nonlinear, such as a switch, can cause large discontinuities to occur in the circuit node voltages. The rapid impedance change, which is associated with a switch that is changing state, can cause numerical roundoff or convergence problems. This leads to erroneous results or timestep difficulties. Consequently, the following steps may be taken to improve the switch behavior:

Set the switch impedances to values that are only high and low enough to be negligible with respect to other elements in the circuit. Using switch impedances that are close to "ideal" under all circumstances will aggravate the discontinuity problem. Of course, when modeling real devices such as MOSFETs, the on resistance should be adjusted to a realistic level, which depends on the size of the device that is being modeled.

If a wide range of on to off resistance must be used (ROFF/RON >1E+12), then the tolerance on errors allowed during the transient analysis should be decreased. This is achieved by specifying the .OPTION TRTOL parameter to be less than the default value of 7.0. When switches are placed around capacitors, the .OPTION CHGTOL parameters should also be reduced. Suggested values for these two options are 1.0 and 1E-16, respectively. These changes inform PSpice to be more careful near the switch points, so no errors are made because of the rapid change in the circuit response.

Smooth Transition Switches

There are two other types of useful switch models. Both have the added advantage of a more controlled and normally smoother transition region between the on and off states.

This can greatly help simulation convergence and are therefore recommended when hysteresis is not required of the switch.

One method uses a subcircuit approach with a dependent source. Another method uses different model parameters in the PSpice S/W elements. Again, these switches do not have hysteresis.

PSpice Syntax—Smooth Transition Switch

Format: Sname N+ N- NC+ NC- modelname
Format: Wname N+ N- vname modelname

Example:

S1 1 2 3 4 switch1

.Model s1 VSWITCH Ron=1m Roff=1G Von=1 Voff=.5

Example:

W1 1 2 3 4 switch1
.Model s1 ISWITCH Ron=0.1m Roff=1G Ion=1 Ioff=.5

Von/Ion is the control quantity that sets the ON state. Voff/Ioff is the control quantity that sets the off state.

The resistance in the transition region is set by the expression:

$$Rs = \exp(Lm + 3 \cdot Lr \cdot (Vc-Vm)/(2 \cdot Vd) - 2 \cdot Lr \cdot (Vc-Vm)^3/Vd^3)$$

Where:

Vc = voltage across control nodes
Lm = log-mean of resistor values = $\ln((RON \cdot ROFF)^{1/2})$
Lr = log-ratio of resistor values = $\ln(RON/ROFF)$
Vm = mean of control voltages = (VON+VOFF)/2
Vd = difference of control voltages = VON-VOFF

Several similar resistance functions and instructions pertaining to their use are given in Yang, P., *Simulation and Modeling*.[2]

Generic Switch Subcircuit

The following SPICE 2-based subcircuit, SSWITCH, is actually a voltage-controlled resistor. Therefore, it can be used as a switch or a potentiometer. It is the simplest way to create a switch function in

SPICE 2. The switch is made with a voltage-controlled current source (G element) tied back onto itself. The netlist is shown in Figure 1.3.

```
SandlerSwitch.CIR

SSwitch Netlist File
* .include C:\Program Files (x86)\LTC\LTspiceIV\lib\sub
VIN 101 0 2.5V
R1 102 0 10K
VPULSE 103 0 PULSE( 0 +5 0 .1MS 0 .1MS 2MS )
X1 101 102 103 SSWITCH

* Open when V(3,0) = 0
* Closed when V(3,0) not 0
* On Resistance is 1/V(3)
* Off Resistance is 1E12
.SUBCKT SSWITCH 1 2 3
R1 1 2 1E12 ; Off Resistance
G1 1 2 POLY(2) 1 2 3 0 0 0 0 0 1
.ENDS

.TRAN .1
.end
```

Figure 1.3

SSWITCH Netlist

The switch is very simple to use. Applying 0 V to the control input (node 3) opens the switch. The open resistance is $1E12\Omega = R1$. It may be changed if desired. Applying any voltage to the switch-control input (node 3) closes the switch, giving it a resistance of $1/V(3)$. For example, applying a voltage pulse from 0 to 1 V to the control input will change the resistance, which is seen from port 1 to port 2 from 1E12 to 1Ω.

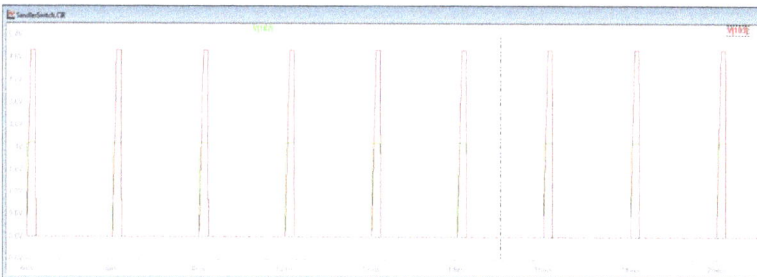

Figure 1.4

SSWITCH Waveforms

Note: Some SPICE programs require a resistor across the voltage-dependent source inputs in order to have a DC path to ground.

Note: In some cases, when the S element switch is used in a model as described in this book, the voltage-controlled resistor, or the smooth transition switch version may be substituted.

Figures 1.5 and 1.6 show a simulation of the three different switches and their transfer functions.

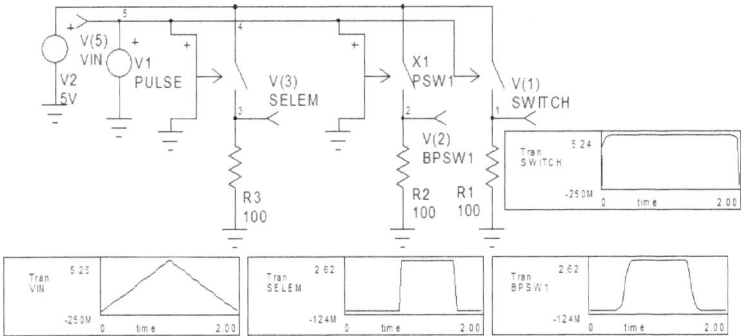

Figure 1.5

Simulation of Three Switches

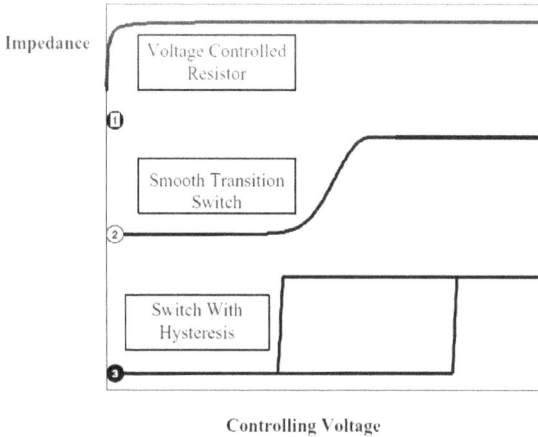

Figure 1.6

The Transfer Function for the PSpice Switch with Hysteresis (selem), Voltage-controlled Resistor (switch) and PSPICE Smooth Transition Switch (PSW1)

The files available for this book contain some of the models, circuits, schematics, and graphs found within the book. The schematics utilize the OrCAD Capture/PSpice format. Capture is a schematic entry program that has been specifically designed for use with the PSpice simulator. Probe is a postprocessor, which is used to analyze SPICE output files by way of waveform graphs and powerful signal processing functions.

An evaluation version of OrCAD/PSpice is available free of charge from OrCAD's web site, www.orcad.com.

SPICE-Based Analyses Types used in this Book

Operating Point Analysis

Operating Point Analysis (OPA) produces the operating point of the circuit, including node voltages and voltage source currents.

The DC analysis determines the quiescent DC operating point

of the circuit with inductors shorted and capacitors opened. A DC analysis, known as the "Initial Transient Solution," is automatically performed prior to a transient analysis in order to determine the transient initial conditions. A DC analysis, known as the "Small Signal Bias Solution," is performed prior to an AC small-signal analysis to determine the linearized, small-signal models for all nonlinear devices. It should be noted that these two operating point calculations can be different, depending on the DC and transient stimulus that is used.

Transfer Function Analysis

Transfer Function Analysis produces a small-signal DC transfer function.

The transfer function analysis calculates the small-signal ratio of the output node to the input source, and also the input and output impedances of a circuit. This analysis may be used to determine the small-signal gain and the input and output impedances of filter circuits. Any nonlinear models, such as diodes or transistors, are first linearized based on the DC bias point, and then the small-signal DC analysis is performed.

Sensitivity Analysis

Sensitivity Analysis produces the DC and AC sensitivities of an output variable with respect to all circuit variables, including model parameters.

The sensitivity function uses the direct approach [35] to support sensitivity calculations for the DC and AC analyses. The DC sensitivity is with respect to the DC operating point. SPICE calculates the difference in an output variable, either a node voltage or a branch current, by perturbing each parameter of each device independently. Because the solution is a function and not a number, the results may be highly non-linear or may demonstrate second-order effects in highly sensitive components, or may fail to show very low, but nonzero sensitivity.

As each variable is perturbed by a small fraction of its value, zero-valued parameters are not analyzed. This analysis is useful when trying to find a worst-case scenario of circuit operation. By finding the most sensitive components and moving their values accordingly, the circuit's performance can then be evaluated.

DC Analysis

DC Analysis produces a series of DC operating points by sweeping one independent source, or two sources in a nested loop.

The DC analysis is used in applications that are dependent upon static variables such as line regulation, load regulation, or the DC modulation gain of a power converter.

The .DC function is a special subset of the DC analysis feature. It is used to perform a series of DC operating points by sweeping voltage and/or current sources and performing a DC operating point at each step value of the source(s). At each step, the DC voltages, currents, and computed device/model parameters can be recorded. The DC statement defines the sources that will be swept, and their corresponding increments.

One or two sources can be involved in the DC sweep. If two sources are involved, the first source will be swept over its range for each value of the second source. This option is useful for obtaining semiconductor device output characteristics or calculating load lines.

AC Analysis

AC Analysis generates a frequency response/Bode plot of the circuit. Magnitude, phase, real, or imaginary data are produced.

The AC analysis is used to evaluate many performance characteristics, many of which are covered in this book. It may be used to determine traits such as circuit stability, impedance, and filter attenuation.

The AC analysis in SPICE computes the small-signal response of the circuit. Output variables are recorded as a function of frequency. Before the AC analysis is performed, SPICE first computes the DC operating point of the circuit. It then determines the linearized small-signal models for all the nonlinear devices in the circuit, based on this operating point. The resultant linear circuit is then analyzed over the specified range of frequencies. It is very important to establish the proper DC circuit biasing in order for the AC analysis to produce useful data. For example, biasing an op-amp in its linear range will give different AC results than if the op-amp is saturated.

Although the AC analysis performs a sinusoidal steady state analysis, it should not be confused with a transient (time domain) analysis using a large-signal SINE wave. The AC analysis is a small-signal analysis in which all nonlinearities are linearized. For instance, if the DC biasing of a transistor gain stage produces a gain of 10, then the gain will remain 10, regardless of the input value. If the input is 1, then the output will be 10. If the input is 100, then the output will be 1000. The gain is linearized. Under nonlinear conditions, however, the gain of the transistor will roll off as the input is increased. The "VName 1 0 SIN..." stimulus is only used for nonlinear time domain analyses, and should not be confused with the "Vname 1 0 AC 1" frequency response stimulus.

Frequency Mixing Note: The AC analysis is a single frequency analysis. Only one frequency is analyzed at a time. Therefore, circuits that perform signal mixing will not benefit from the AC analysis. To see frequency mixing, you will have to run a transient analysis and convert the output waveforms into the frequency domain using a Fourier transform.

Transient Analysis

Transient Analysis runs a nonlinear time domain simulation.

The transient analysis computes the circuit response as a function of time over any time interval. Output data, including node voltages and voltage source currents, can be recorded. During a transient analysis, numerous independent sources may have active time varying stimulus signals.

It is often necessary to start an SMPS simulation with a predefined set of operating conditions. The use initial conditions

(UICs) keyword in the .TRAN statement causes SPICE to skip the initial transient solution (operating point), which is normally performed prior to the transient analysis. If this keyword is included, the values that are specified via "IC =" specifications on the various elements and .IC statements, are used as the sole source for initial conditions. The transient analysis will begin with these values.

Fourier Analysis

Fourier Analysis provides a simple means for evaluating the harmonic content of a time domain waveform. This analysis may be used to determine performance characteristics, such as the conducted emissions performance of a switching power supply or the harmonic content of a sine wave output converter. A Fourier analysis can be performed by SPICE, but is usually performed using a separate data postprocessing program, which operates on the .PRINT transient simulation output data.

Temperature Analysis

SPICE allows the emulated temperature of the circuit, or a particular element, to be varied.

SPICE simulates circuits using a global temperature of 27°C. This can be changed using the .TEMP command. In addition, to set the temperature for an individual device, this feature permits the simulation of a temperature gradient, as well as a "hot" device. Individual device temperatures are set directly on the device call line or in the .Model statement.

Although the Monte Carlo, worst case, and optimization analyses are not inherently part of SPICE 3, most commercial vendors have added them to the list of simulation capabilities. They are an invaluable part of SMPS investigation and design.

Monte Carlo and Worst-Case Analysis

The Monte Carlo tolerance analysis is an ideal application for circuit simulation. The effects of component tolerance variations are difficult to assess by any other means. Imagine sitting in an engineering lab and sorting resistors, capacitors, and other components, in an attempt to find the worst-case tolerance extremes to place in your circuit.

This investigation is usually performed either as a worst-case analysis or as a Monte Carlo analysis. These analyses seem to be used interchangeably, although they are quite different.

A worst-case analysis determines worst-case circuit performance, but does not determine the statistical weighting of performance. As a general rule, the worst-case analysis is preferred if the worst-case values can be easily determined. In many cases, however, it is difficult to know which components must be varied, and in which direction, in order to generate the worst-case result.

A Monte Carlo analysis provides the statistical weighting, but per se does not provide the worst-case result. Monte Carlo analysis is generally used to calculate the mean and standard deviation of a particular performance characteristic. This analysis takes significantly longer to run than the worst-case analysis, because it requires many simulations.

Optimizer Analysis

The optimizer analysis is a powerful PSpice feature that allows a series of simulations and measurements to be automatically performed over a range of component values, based on a design objective specified by the user. Circuit variables may be swept through a specified range of values.

This feature is useful for determining, for example, the damping components of an EMI filter as a design objective.

Chapter 2

SPICE Modeling of Magnetic Components

Introduction

MAGNETIC COMPONENTS ARE a vital part of most power electronic equipment, and, to be useful, the models used in a simulation must faithfully reproduce or predict their behavior. Most of the other electronic components in these circuits have predetermined models that have been derived from standardized components. Magnetic components, however, are rarely standardized and are generally designed for specific applications. In most cases the model, or at least the component values within the model, must be altered for each new circuit simulation.

PSpice has four basic magnetic component models built into it:

- A linear inductor

- An ideal transformer

- A coupled inductor model

- A nonlinear core model

All of these are very useful for simulation but must be used with some care if the correct model is to be obtained.

In some cases, the model may fail dramatically, thereby giving grossly erroneous results, as we shall see later. Most of the time, however, the errors are more subtle. For example, the details of the noise and ringing due to parasitics in the transformer may not be reproduced correctly. Cross-regulation between windings with varying loads, high-frequency winding losses, and the proper distribution of ripple currents in coupled filter inductors are also quantities that are often not modeled accurately. These problems usually arise from shortcomings in the models that are being used and can, for the most part, be corrected.

Basic Transformer Types

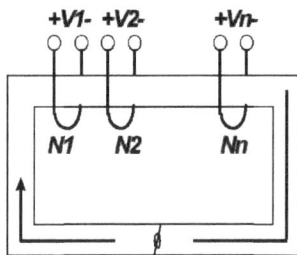

Junction Transformer

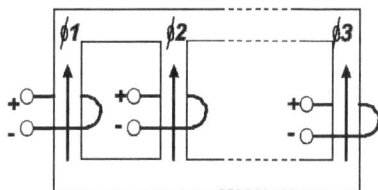

$$\frac{v_1}{n_1} = \frac{v_2}{n_2} = \dots = \frac{v_n}{n_n}$$

$$n_1 i_1 + n_2 i_2 + \dots + n_n i_n = 0$$

Mesh Transformer

$$\frac{v_1}{n_1} + \frac{v_2}{n_2} + \dots + \frac{v_n}{n_n} = 0$$

$$n_1 i_1 = n_2 i_2 = \dots = n_n i_n$$

Junction Transformer

Mesh Transformer

Figure 2.1

Two Basic Transformer Types

A common modeling problem arises because of a failure to realize that there are *two* different basic types of transformers: junction and mesh. Figure 2.1 illustrates these two transformer types, along with the circuit equations that apply to each type.

The junction transformer is widely used in power conversion equipment. It is usually the type used by schematic capture programs and is also used to create ideal transformers having multiple windings.

The mesh transformer is very common for polyphase power applications and also appears in coupled filter inductors and other magnetic control devices. There are also magnetic devices that are combinations of mesh and junction transformers. In a network, these two types of transformers behave very differently. The substitution of one for the other in a simulation will lead to gross errors. Figure 2.2 shows how errors can easily be made.

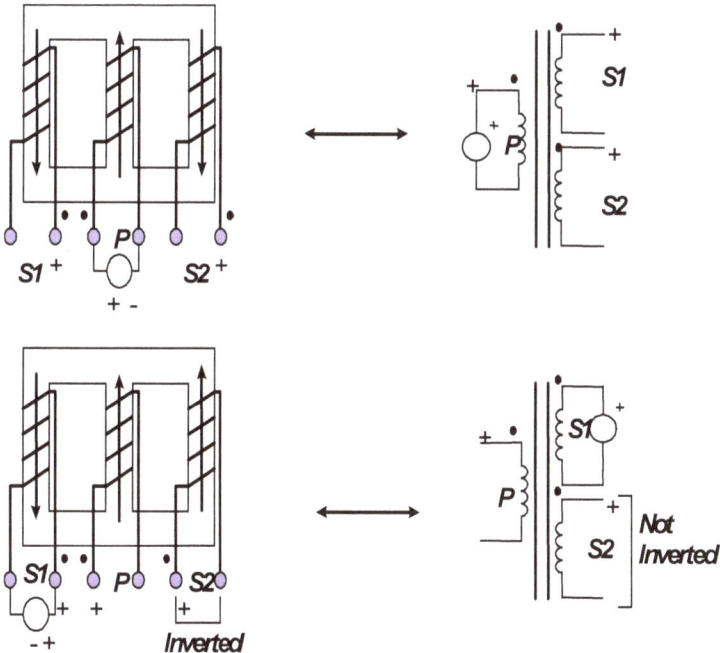

Figure 2.2

Modeling of Mesh Transformers Requires Caution

In Figure 2.2, we show a three-winding, three-leg mesh transformer. If a simple three-winding ideal transformer (the upper right section of Figure 2.2) is selected to simulate this transformer, the output voltage phases will be correct only for some excitations. If, for example, the center winding is excited, then the voltages on the other two windings will be correct. However, if one of the outer leg windings is excited, as shown in the bottom left of Figure 2.2, then the phase of the simulated voltage (bottom right of Figure 2.2) will be incorrect. This represents a gross modeling error and illustrates why the modeling must be performed carefully. The selected model will function correctly as a junction transformer, but it will not function correctly as a mesh transformer.

Most simulation problems can be avoided by using models that are extensions of the basic SPICE models. The most reliable way to create these models is to base them on the actual physical structure of the magnetic component. This is the principle behind the physical models that are derived using reluctance modeling and are described in the Reluctance and Physical Models section. This approach has many advantages beyond the simple generation of a model. Physical models preserve the relationship between the simulation model and the actual component. This means, for example, if the simulation shows excessive voltage ringing due to a parasitic inductance element, this component can be directly related to the structure of the device. This allows the device to be redesigned in order to reduce the problem. This interchange between the simulation and the device design is a powerful tool. The preservation of the intuitive connections between the device and the simulation model also helps to avoid modeling errors and to interpret the simulation results.

Ideal Components in SPICE

Passive Components

The built-in models in SPICE provide reasonable first-order approximations for circuit behavior. Unfortunately, most circuits must be designed to be tolerant of second-order effects, at a minimum, and must occasionally provide compensation in order to achieve a desired performance level. Most frequently, the parasitic and second-order effects are related to changes in frequency.

It may not be clear, especially to novice SPICE users, that when you use a passive component, such as an inductor or a capacitor, you are using an *ideal* element. Parasitics, such as Equivalent Series Resistance (ESR) or parasitic inductance are not included. This is done intentionally to allow you to take advantage of the ideal nature of these elements. However, parasitics can both dominate and plague a circuit design. Therefore, accurate representations are an essential part of a realistic simulation.

Electronic circuits are always modeled over a finite range of the electromagnetic frequency spectrum. There is no need to describe operation of electrical components from DC through the RF, microwave, optical, X-ray, and gamma-ray spectrums. Not only would the model be complex, but it would be inaccurate and would provide unnecessary information.

The nodal equations that SPICE solves are valid only when the circuit elements are small as compared with the wavelength of the highest frequency of interest (high frequencies are limited below the optical band).

Even with this limitation, the useful frequency range runs from millihertz to many gigahertz: over 15 orders of magnitude. The reactance chart of Figure 2.3 shows the expected range of parasitic inductance and capacitance over this range. The darkly shaded region represents the values of impedances that are realistically achieved with common R-L-C components and printed circuit board technology. The lightly shaded region of impedances can be viewed as a transition region where parasitics become increasingly important. The boundary between the lightly shaded region and the unshaded region represents the smallest capacitance or inductance parasitic values, and therefore values in the unshaded area are unrealistic for single discrete components. At the high-frequency end, this suggests the use of smaller-geometry microwave integrated circuits, while the extension of the impedance range at lower frequencies requires larger geometries than are ordinarily found in printed circuit card technology.

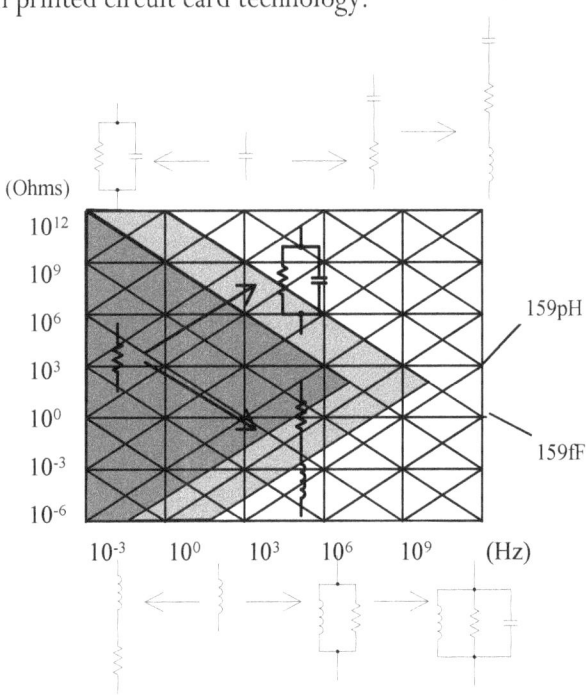

Figure 2.3

Reactance Chart for Modeling R-L-C Components

The modeling additions for various components are shown in the pictorial inlays. First, resistors, which are basically defined at DC, turn into effective capacitors or inductors; their impedance converges to that of free space divided by the square root of the dielectric constant, something in the neighborhood of 125Ω for PC cards. Similarly, capacitor and inductor impedances funnel toward the impedance of the propagating medium at high frequencies and only become properly reactive as the signal frequencies approach DC.

Transformers

The usual method of simulating a transformer using SPICE is via the specification of the open circuit inductance that is seen at each winding, and then the addition of the coupling coefficients to a pair of coupled inductors. This technique tends to lose the physical meaning associated with leakage and magnetizing inductance and does not allow the insertion of a nonlinear core. It does, however, provide a transformer that is simple to create and simulates efficiently. The coupled inductor type of transformer, its related equations, and its relationship to an ideal transformer with added leakage and magnetizing inductance are discussed in the next section.

To make a transformer model that more closely represents the physical processes, it is necessary to construct an ideal transformer and model the magnetizing and leakage inductances separately. The ideal transformer is one that preserves the voltage and current relationships shown in Figure 2.4 and has a unity coupling coefficient and infinite magnetizing inductance. The ideal transformer, unlike a real transformer, will operate at DC. This is a property that is useful for modeling the operation of DC-to-DC converters.

The SPICE subcircuit for the ideal transformer is sometimes called XFMR. The TURNS subcircuit performs a similar function with the exception that the Ratio parameter is equal to $1/\text{NUM}$ (the number of turns).

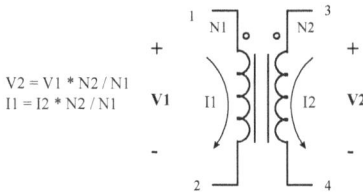

$$V2 = V1 * N2 / N1$$
$$I1 = I2 * N2 / N1$$

Figure 2.4

Ideal Transformer with its Voltage and Current Relationships

The SPICE equivalent circuit is shown in Figure 2.5, and it implements the following equations:

$$V1 * \text{Ratio} = V2$$
$$I1 = I2 * \text{Ratio}$$

```
* XFMR SUBCIRCUIT XFMR.CIR
.SUBCKT XFMR
E 5 4 1 2 {RATIO}
F 1 2 VM {RATIO}
VM 5 6
RP 1 2 1MEG
RS 6 3 1U
.ENDS
```

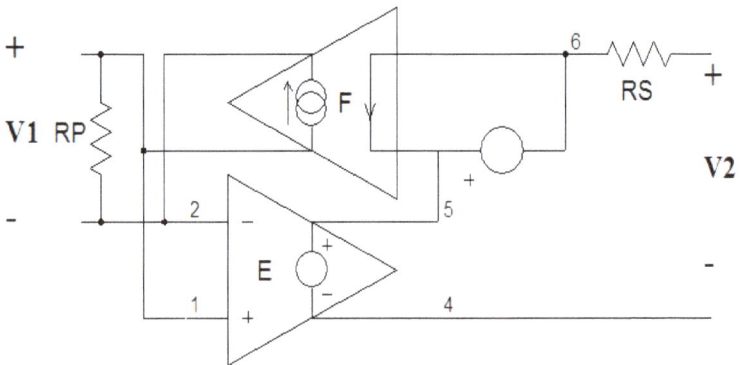

Figure 2.5

The Ideal Transformer (XMFR or TURNS) Model

The ideal transformer (XMFR or TURNS) model allows operation at DC and the addition of magnetizing and leakage inductances, as well as a saturable core, in order to make a complete transformer model.

Parameter passing allows the transformer to simulate any turns ratio.

RP and RS are used to prevent singularities in applications where terminals 1 and 2 are open circuit or terminals 3 and 4 are connected to a voltage source.

RATIO is the turns ratio from winding 1, 2 to winding 3, 4.

The polarity "dots" are on terminals 1 and 3. Multiwinding topologies can be simulated using combinations of this two-port representation [3, 4].

PSpice Coupled Inductor Model

The coupled inductor model is a classical network representation for a transformer.

As shown in Figure 2.6, the model assumes that a transformer can be represented by an inductor for each winding (L_1, L_2, ..., L_n) and a series of mutual inductances between the windings (M_{12}, M_{13}, ..., M_{1n}, ..., M_{nn}).

```
L1  4 5 1uH
L2  6 7 2uH
L3  8 9 3uH
K12 L1 L2 .999
K23 L2 L3 .950
K13 L1 L3 .995
```

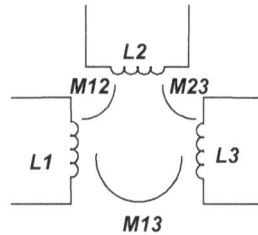

Figure 2.6

SPICE Coupled Inductor Model and Associated Netlist

Note: In PSpice, if all the inductor couplings have the same value the coupling element may also be written as Kall L1 L2 L3 *Couple_value*.

In matrix form, this is expressed as:

$$
\begin{bmatrix} v_1 \\ \cdot \\ \cdot \\ \cdot \\ v_n \end{bmatrix} = \begin{bmatrix} L_{11} & \cdot & M_{ij} & \cdot & M_{1n} \\ & \cdot & L_{22} & \cdot & \cdot & \cdot \\ \cdot & \cdot & \cdot & \cdot & \cdot \\ \cdot & \cdot & \cdot & \cdot & \cdot \\ M_{n1} & \cdot & \cdot & \cdot & L_{nn} \end{bmatrix} \begin{bmatrix} \left(\dfrac{di_1}{dt}\right) \\ \cdot \\ \cdot \\ \cdot \\ \left(\dfrac{di_n}{dt}\right) \end{bmatrix}
$$

Formula 2.1

Inductor Coupling Matrix

Algebraically, the two-winding transformer equations would be:

$$
v_1 = (L_1)\frac{di_1}{dt} + (M_{12})\frac{di_2}{dt}
$$

$$
v_2 = (M_{12})\frac{di_1}{dt} + (L_2)\frac{di_2}{dt}
$$

Formula 2.2

Two-Winding Transformer Equations

Mutual inductance can be expressed in alternative form using coefficients of coupling, k_{ij}. A typical example would be:

$$
k_{12} = \frac{M_{12}}{\sqrt{L_1 L_2}}
$$

Formula 2.3

Mutual Inductance

In a transformer, k_{ij} will normally be very close to 1. A typical PSpice listing for a coupled inductor is shown in Figure 2.6.

This is an abstract model. Most engineers, however, will be thinking in terms of a circuit model that has leakage and magnetizing inductance and a turns ratio.

An example of this type of model is shown in Figure 2.7.

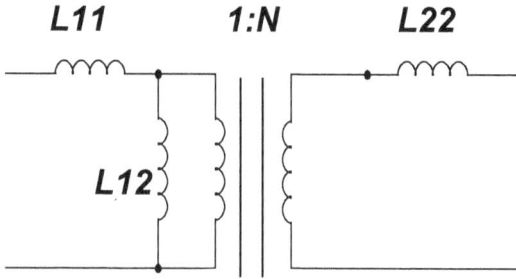

Figure 2.7

Structure of the Pi Model

The circuit equations for this model are:

$$v_1 = (L_{11} + L_{12}) \frac{di_1}{dt} + (n\ L_{12}) \frac{di_2}{dt}$$

$$v_2 = (n\ L_{12}) \frac{di_1}{dt} + \left(L_{22} + n^2 L_{12}\right) \frac{di_2}{dt}$$

Formula 2.4

Pi Model Formulas

The relationships between the two models are:

$$L_1 = L_{11} + L_{12}$$

$$L_2 = L_{22} + n^2 L_{12}$$

$$M_{12} = n\, L_{12}$$

$$k_{12} = \frac{n L_{12}}{\sqrt{(L_{11} + L_{12})(L_{22} + n^2 L_{12})}}$$

Formula 2.5

Relationship between Coupled-Inductor and Pi Formulas

To use the coupled inductor model, it is necessary to first determine the values in the Pi model and then convert them to the values for the coupled inductor model.

For two- or three-winding transformers, this is a straightforward process, but when four or more windings are used, the conversion relationships become quite complex.

In these cases, it is better to stay with the physical model and implement it using the ideal components that are available in PSpice.

There may be another problem with the coupled inductor model. In a typical transformer, the magnetizing inductance (L_{12}) might be 5mH. The leakage inductances may be only 0.5μH.

The value for k must be specified with enough accuracy to recreate this difference accurately; that is, a difference of 10^4.

For n = 1, k_{12} = 0.99990 for the preceding values. Inversion of Eq. (2.5) illustrates the problem:

$$L_{11} = L_1 - \frac{k_{12}}{n}\sqrt{L_1 L_2}$$

$$L_{22} = L_2 - nk_{12}\sqrt{L_1 L_2}$$

$$L_{12} = \frac{k_{12}}{n}\sqrt{L_1 L_2}$$

Formula 2.6

Inversion of the Coupled-Inductor and Pi Formulas

L_{11} and L_{22} are the small difference between two large numbers. In general, you should compute k_{ij} to four decimal places.

Reluctance and Physical Models

The basic problem when simulating a magnetic component is to translate the physical structure of the device into an equivalent electric circuit.

PSpice will use the equivalent circuit to simulate the device.

Reluctance modeling, combined with a duality transformation, provides a means to accomplish this task. Reluctance modeling creates a magnetic circuit model that can then be converted into an electric circuit model.

Table 2.1 shows a number of analogous quantities between electric and magnetic circuits. By comparing the form of the equations in each column, the following analogous quantities can be identified:

- EMF (V) and MMF (F)

- Electric field (E) and magnetic field (H) intensities

- Current density (J) and flux density (B)

- Current (I) and flux (ϕ)

- Resistance (R) and reluctance (R)

- Conductivity (σ) and permeability (μ)

Reluctance is computed in the same manner as resistance, that is, from the dimensions of the magnetic path and the magnetic conductivity (μ). For a constant cross-sectional area (A_m), the reluctance is:

$$R' = \frac{l_m}{\mu A_m}$$

Formula 2.7

Reluctance Formula

In Table 2.1, $\mu = \mu_o \mu_r$ and μ_r = relative permeability.

The inductance of a magnetic circuit is directly related to R and N (the number of winding turns):

$$L = \frac{N^2}{R} = N^2 P$$

$$M_{12} = \frac{N_1 N_2}{N_{12}} = N_1 N_2 P_{12}$$

Formula 2.8

Inductance of a Magnetic Circuit

In Formula 2.8, P = permeance = $1/R$.

Electric	Magnetic
$V \equiv$ electric circuit voltage (Electromotive force)	$F \equiv NI =$ magnetic circuit voltage (magnetomotive force)
$E \equiv$ electric field intensity	$H \equiv$ magnetic field intensity
$V = -\int E \bullet d\overline{l}_c = El_c$	$F = \oint \overline{H} \bullet d\overline{l}_m = Hl_m$
$E = \dfrac{V}{l_c}$	$H = \dfrac{F}{l_m} = \dfrac{NI}{l_m}$
$J \equiv$ current density	$B \equiv$ magnetic flux density
$J = \sigma E$	$B = \mu H$
$\sigma =$ conductivity	$\mu =$ permeability
	$\mu_0 = 4\pi \times 10^{-7}$ H/m
$I \equiv$ electric current	$\phi \equiv$ magnetic flux
$I = -\int_s \overline{J} \bullet d\overline{s} = JA_c$	$\phi = \int_s \overline{B} \bullet d\overline{s} = BA_m$
$R =$ resistance	$R' =$ reluctance
$R = \dfrac{V}{I} = \dfrac{l_c}{\sigma A_c}$	$R' = \dfrac{F}{\phi} = \dfrac{l_m}{\mu A_m} = \dfrac{N^2}{L}$
$G = 1/R =$ conductance	$P = 1/R' =$ permeance

Table 2.1

Electric and Magnetic Circuit Analogous Quantities

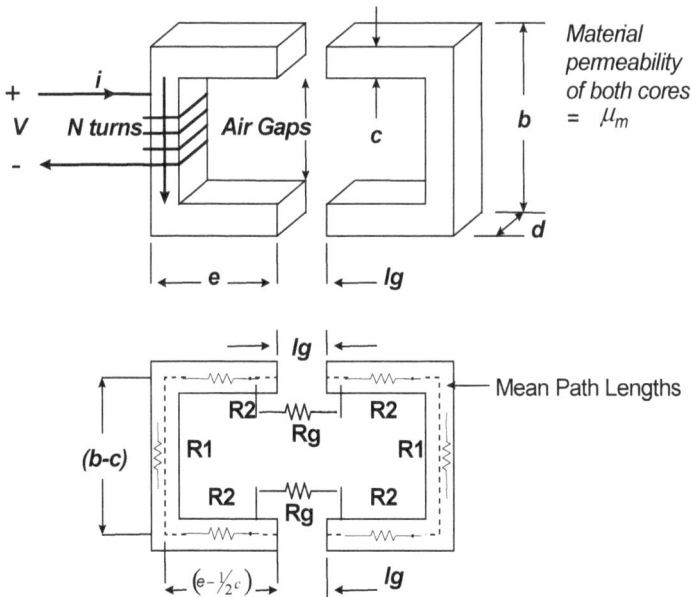

Figure 2.8

The Development of the Reluctance Model for a Simple Inductor with an Air Gap

The example shown in Figure 2.8 illustrates the development of the reluctance model for a simple inductor with an air gap in the core. The model develops as follows:

- Divide the core, including the air gaps, into sections and assign a reluctance to each as shown in the Figure 2.8 schematic.

- Compute the reluctance for each section.

- Assign a magnetic voltage source to the winding with F = NI.

- Draw the equivalent network as shown in Figure 2.9.

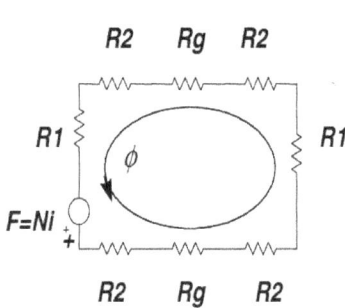

$$R_1 = \frac{(b-c)}{\mu_m \mu_0 A_c}$$

$$R_2 = \left[\frac{e - \frac{1}{2}c}{\mu_m \mu_0 A_c} \right]$$

$$R_g = \frac{l_g}{\mu_0 A_c}$$

$$4\pi \times 10^{-7} \, Henry\Big/_{meter}$$

μ_0 = Permeability of free space

μ_m = Core Material Relative Permeability

Figure 2.9

Reluctance Model for the Inductor of Figure 2.8

Figure 2.9 shows the reluctance model that represents the magnetic structure at the top of Figure 2.8.

Now we need to convert this reluctance model to an equivalent electric circuit model.

But, before we can do that, it will help to briefly review the duality transformation. We can then proceed to convert the reluctance model.

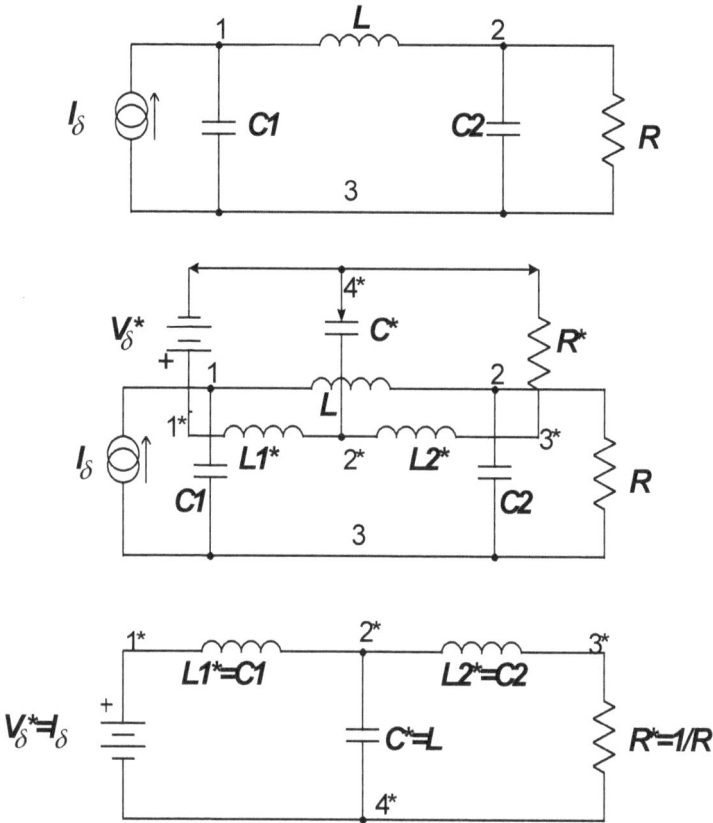

Figure 2.10

Review of the Duality Transform Process

An example of a duality transformation is given in Figure 2.10.

A node is placed within each mesh, including the outer mesh. Branches, which intersect each of the branches in the original network, are connected between each node. In each of the intersecting branches, current and voltage are interchanged.

The result is a new network that is the topological and electrical dual of the original network. A listing of dual quantities is given in Table 2.2.

Quantity	Dual element
V	I^*
I	V^*
q	ϕ^*
ϕ	q^*
R	$R^*= G =1/R$
G	$G^*= R =1/G$
C	L^*
L	C^*
Open circuit	Short circuit
Short circuit	Open circuit
D	$D^*=1-D$
Voltage generator	Current generator
Current generator	Voltage generator
Mesh	Node
Node	Mesh

Table 2.2

Duality Relationships

The conversion from a reluctance model to a circuit model requires the following steps:

- Draw the reluctance (R) model from the device structure and an estimate of the flux paths.

- Using duality, convert the R model to a permeance (P) model.

- Scale the P model for the winding turns by multiplying P by N.

- Scale this model for the winding voltage by multiplying again by N.

- Replace the scaled permeances with inductors.

- For multiple windings, use ideal transformers in order to provide the correct voltages.

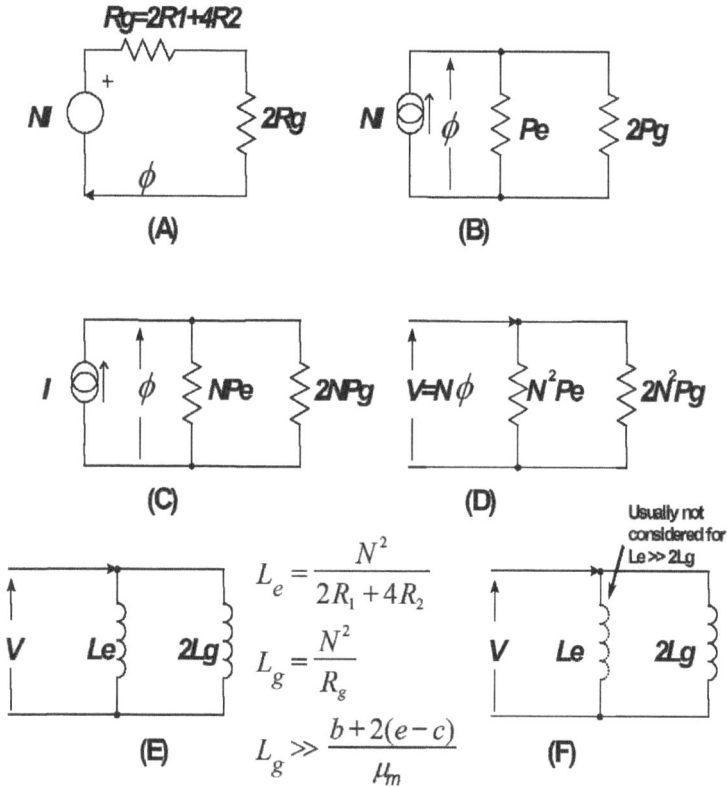

Figure 2.11

Reluctance Modeling Example

A simple example shows how this process works. Keep in mind that the objective is to convert the physical model, which is in terms of magnetic quantities associated with the actual structure, to an electrical model, which is in terms of lumped inductances, ideal transformers, and winding voltages and currents. This is the model we want to use in the simulation. In Figure 2.11A, the reluctance network has been simplified by combining the material reluctances into one element and the air gap reluctances into another.

Figure 2.11B shows the dual network in which reluctances have become permeances, the magnetic current (ϕ) has become a

47

magnetic voltage, the magnetic voltage source has become a magnetic current source, and series branches have become parallel branches.

The next step, Figure 2.11C, is to scale the network in order to remove N from the current source, thereby leaving only the winding current, I. ϕ must be kept constant; the multiplication of the current source by $1/N$ implies that each of the permeances must be multiplied by N.

The winding voltages are introduced by invoking Faraday's law, $V = N\dot{\phi}$. Each element in the network is now multiplied by N, as shown in Figure 2.11D. The resulting network is now in terms of the winding voltage and the permeances scaled by N^2. From Equation (2.8), we know that $L = N^2P$, so that the scaled permeances can be replaced by inductances (as shown in Figure 2.11E and F).

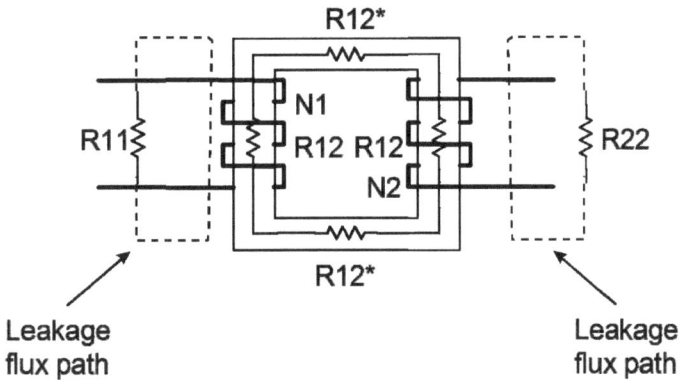

Figure 2.12

A Two-Winding Transformer

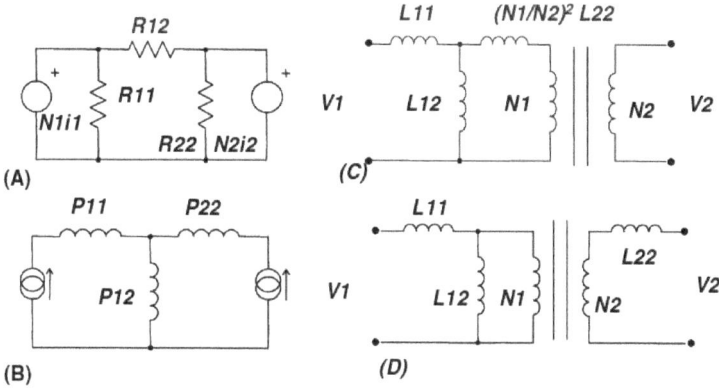

Figure 2.13

Reluctance Model for a Two-Winding Transformer

We can now apply this process to a two-winding transformer like that shown in Figure 2.12. The reluctance model, which is shown in Figure 2.13, includes a voltage source for each winding (N_1 and N_2), a reluctance for the common flux path (R_{12}), and reluctances for the leakage flux associated with each winding (R_{11} and R_{22}). The reluctance model is transformed into a permeance model in Figure 2.13B. This model is then scaled using N_1 as the reference winding, and inductances are inserted as shown in Figure 2.13C. The transformer turns ratio is maintained via the use of an ideal transformer. This is the well-known Pi model. As shown in Figure 2.13D, L_{22} can be moved to the secondary by scaling by the square of the turns ratio ($N2^2/N1^2$).

The transformer shown in Figure 2.12 is easy to understand but reflects a physical structure that is rarely used. A much more common transformer structure takes the form of multiple layers on a common bobbin, on the center leg of an E-E core.

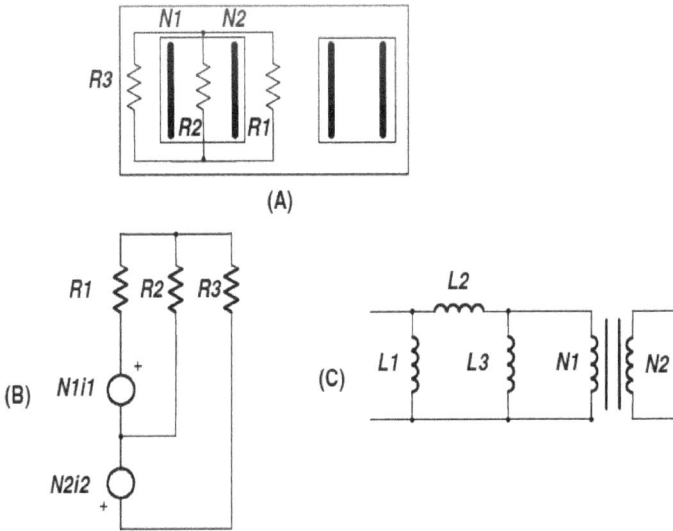

Figure 2.14

A Realistic Transformer Model with Multiple Layers on the Center Leg of an E-E Core

A cross section of such a transformer is shown in Figure 2.14A, along with reluctances that represent the core (R_1 and R_3) and the leakage flux between the windings (R_2). The corresponding reluctance model and the final circuit model are shown in Figure 2.14B and C. Note that this model is different from the previous one (Figure 2.13C). In the case of two windings, the two models can be shown to be equivalent using a delta-wye transform. When four or more windings are present, however, the model does not typically reduce to the Pi model. In fact, the Pi model is not valid for transformers with more than three windings.

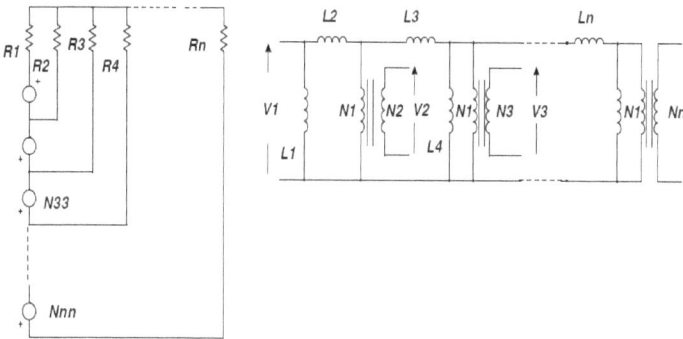

Figure 2.15

Extension of the Reluctance Generated Circuit Model to an n-Layer Transformer

The extension of Figure 2.14 to an n-layer transformer is shown in Figure 2.15. In the typical case, where the magnetizing inductances are large compared with the leakage inductances, the numerous shunt magnetizing inductors can be replaced with a single shunt inductance, as shown in Figure 2.16.

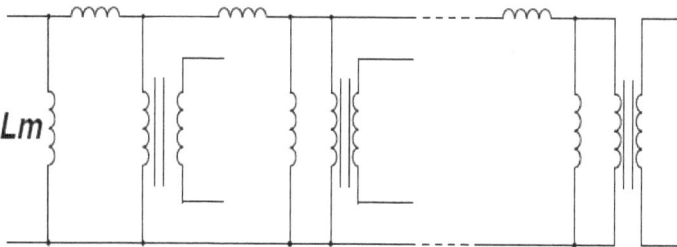

Figure 2.16

Eliminating Multiple Magnetizing Inductance Elements

In most cases, the multiple magnetizing inductors in an n-winding transformer can be reduced to a single equivalent without any great error.

An exception would be the case where there is an air gap on an outer leg or a magnetic shunt is present.

Note: This model performs equally well for transformers with interleaved winding layers. The layers that represent each winding are simply connected in series in order to make the final model.

Even though this model is more complex than the simple Pi model, it has the major advantage of correctly placing the leakage impedances with respect to the windings. This helps to make the simulation of cross-regulation, under varying winding loads, much more accurate in a multiple-winding transformer.

Using this modeling process, more and more details from the physical structure can be added to the model.

The problem, however, is that the model may become very complex. This makes it more difficult to use. In general, the simplest possible model that gives acceptable results should be used, and complex models should be avoided whenever possible. The need for a complex model depends entirely upon how accurately the small details of the device performance need to be modeled and how willing you are to develop the necessary model.

The following examples show more complex applications of reluctance modeling.

Figure 2.17 shows an example of a four-winding mesh transformer that might be used in a polyphase power system. The reluctance modeling proceeds as shown previously and results in the model given in Figure 2.17C.

Note how different this model is from an equivalent four-winding junction transformer. Instead of cascaded parallel windings, the windings are in series. This is because mesh and junction transformers are topological duals.

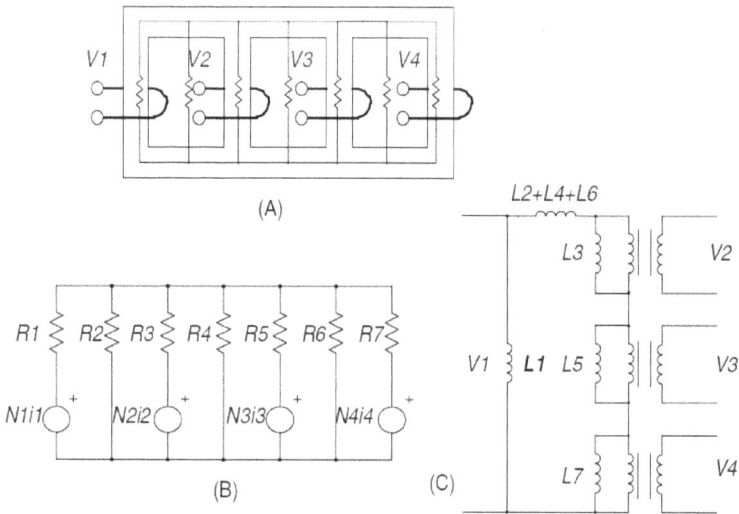

Figure 2.17

A Four-Winding Mesh Transformer (A), along with its Reluctance Model (B), and the Resulting Equivalent Circuit (C)

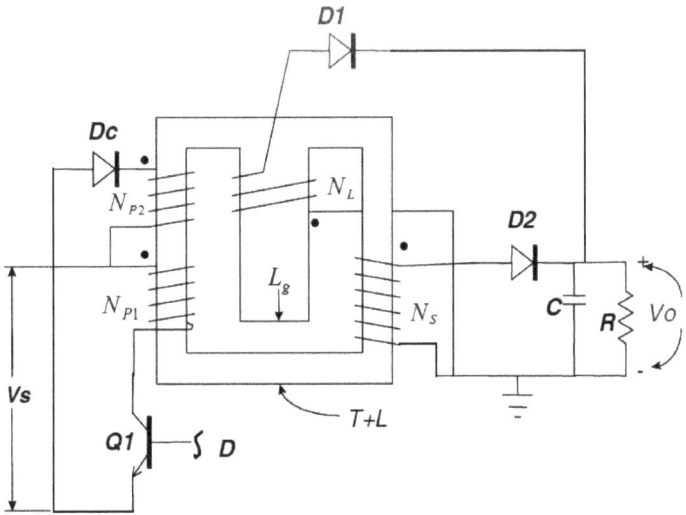

Figure 2.18A

An Integrated Magnetic Forward Converter Circuit

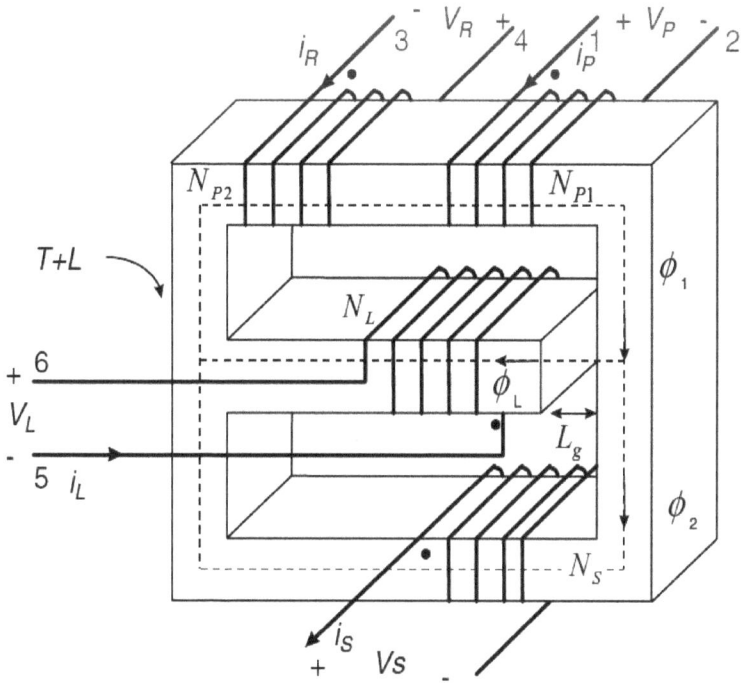

Figure 2.18B

The Magnetic Structure used in the Integrated Forward Converter

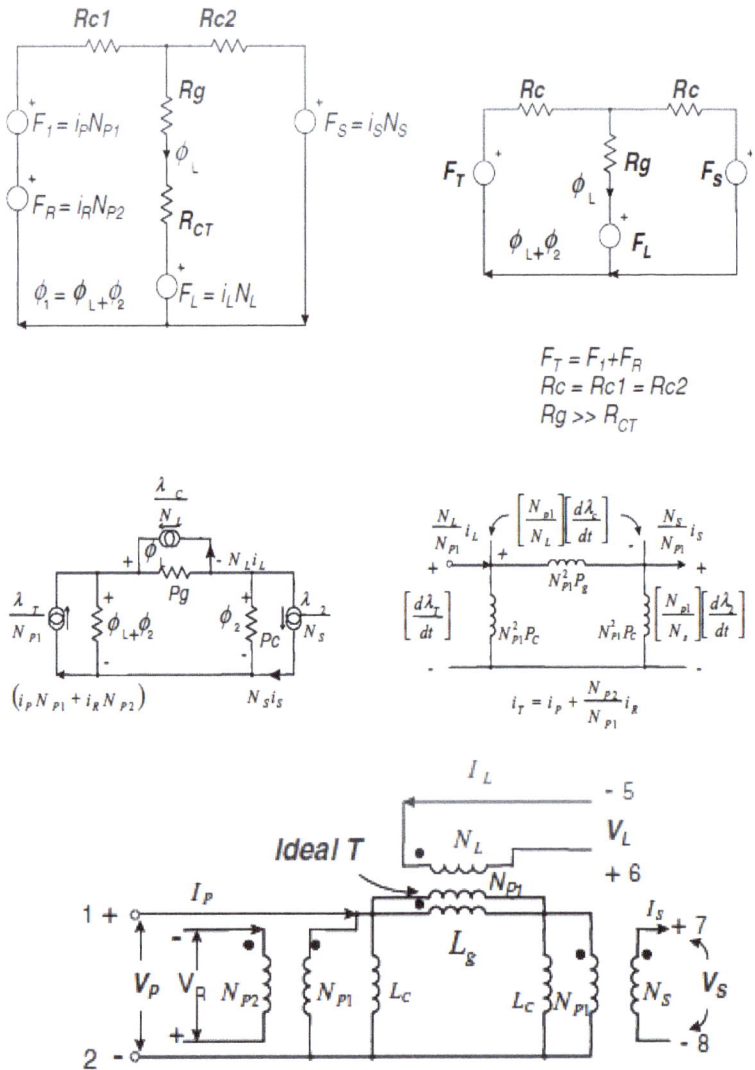

Figure 2.19

The Reluctance Modeling Procedure for the Transformer used in the Forward Converter

Integrated magnetic structures that incorporate transformers and inductors into a common structure are becoming more common. An example of an integrated magnetic forward converter is given in Figure 2.18A. A sketch of the magnetic structure is given in Figure 2.18B. The reluctance model and the series of steps required to convert it to a circuit model are shown in Figure 2.19.

Again, the process is exactly as shown earlier; however, it is more complex now. The completed model, which has been inserted back into the circuit simulation, is shown in Figure 2.20.

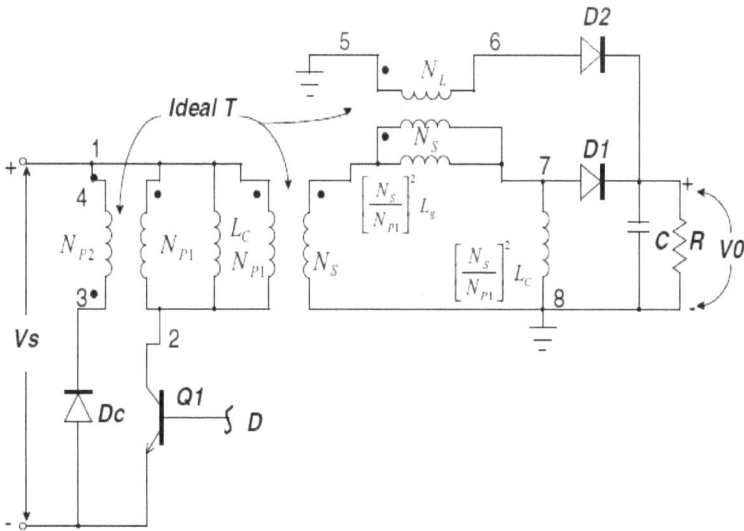

Figure 2.20

The Completed Forward Converter shows how the Reluctance Derived Transformer is Integrated into the Circuit

Using the reluctance modeling procedure, the derivation of an appropriate model is straightforward, although a bit tedious.

Without this process, the appropriate model is far from obvious.

Saturable Core Modeling

It would be difficult to accurately model power circuits without the ability to model magnetics. This section details the SPICE 2 and SPICE 3 methods that are used to simulate various types of magnetic cores including molypermalloy powder (MPP) and ferrite.

The presented techniques can be extended to many other types of cores, such as tape wound, amorphous metal, etc.

SPICE 2 Compatible Core Model

A saturable reactor is a magnetic circuit element consisting of a single coil wound around a magnetic core. The presence of a magnetic core drastically alters the behavior of the coil by increasing the magnetic flux and confining most of the flux to the core. The magnetic flux density, B, is a function of the applied MMF, which is proportional to ampere turns.

The core consists of a many tiny magnetic domains that are made up of magnetic dipoles. These domains set up a magnetic flux that adds to or subtracts from the flux that is set up by the magnetizing current. After overcoming initial friction, the domains rotate like small DC motors and become aligned with the applied field. As the MMF is increased, the domains rotate until they are all in alignment and the core saturates. Eddy currents are induced as the flux changes, thereby causing added loss.

A saturable core model that utilizes the PSpice subcircuit feature is available from Meares and Hymowitz.[3] The saturable core subcircuit is capable of simulating nonlinear transformer behavior including saturation, hysteresis, and eddy current losses.

To make the model even more useful, it has been parameterized. This is a technique that allows the characteristics of the core to be determined via the specification of a few key parameters. At the time of the simulation, the specified parameters are passed into the subcircuit.

The equations in the subcircuit (inside the curly braces) are then evaluated and replaced with a value that makes the equation-based subcircuit compatible with PSpice.

The parameters that must be passed to the subcircuit include the following:

- Flux capacity in volt-seconds (VSEC)

- Initial flux capacity in volt-seconds (IVSEC)

- Magnetizing inductance in henries (LMAG)

- Saturation inductance in henries (LSAT)

- Eddy current critical frequency in hertz (FEDDY)

The saturable core may be added to a model of an ideal transformer to create a complete transformer model. To use the model, just place the core across the transformer's input terminals and specify the parameters.

A special subcircuit test point has been provided to allow the monitoring of the core flux (node 3). Because there are two connections in the subcircuit, no connection is required at the top subcircuit level other than the dummy node number.

A sample PSpice call to the saturable core subcircuit looks similar to the following:

```
SaturableReactor
X1  2  0  3  CORE Params: USEC=50U IUSEC=-25U LMAG=10MHY LSAT=20UHY FEDDY=20KHZ
```

The generic saturable core model is listed in Figure 2.21.

```
SaturableReactor

.SUBCKT CORE 1 2 3
F1 1 2 VM1 1
G2 2 3 1 2 1
E1 4 2 3 2 1
VM1 4 5
RX 3 2 1E12
CB 3 2 {USEC/500} IC={IUSEC/USEC*500}
RB 5 2 {LMAG*500/USEC}
RS 5 6 {LSAT*500/USEC}
UP 7 2 250
D1 6 7 DCLAMP
UN 2 8 250
D2 8 6 DCLAMP
.MODEL DCLAMP D(CJO={3*USEC/(6.28*FEDDY*500*LMAG)} + UJ=25)
.ENDS
```

Figure 2.21

**A Netlist for a Nonlinear Magnetic Core using SPICE 2
Primitive Elements**

How the Core Model Works

Modeling the physical process performed by a saturable core is most easily accomplished by developing an analog of the magnetic flux. This is done by integrating the voltage across the core and then shaping the flux analog with nonlinear elements to cause a current flow that is proportional to the desired function. This gives good results when there is no hysteresis, as illustrated in Figure 2.22.

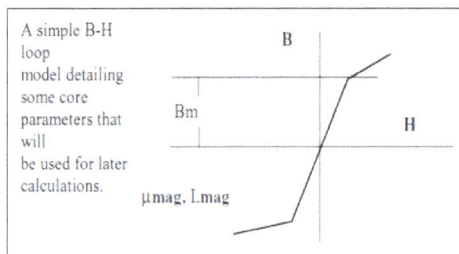

Figure 2.22

**A Simple B-H Loop Model Detailing some Core
Parameters that will be used for Later Calculations**

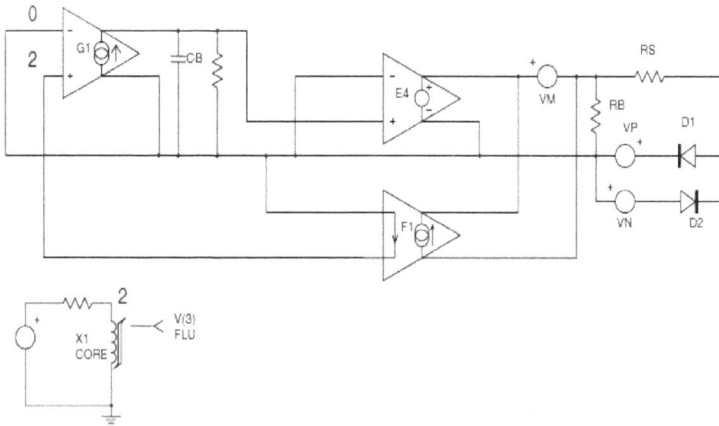

Figure 2.23

The Saturable Reactor Model

Note: In Figure 2.23, the symbol below the schematic reveals the core's connectivity and subcircuit flux-density test point.

The input voltage is integrated using the voltage-controlled current source G and the capacitor CB. An initial condition across the capacitor allows the core to have an initial flux. The output current from F is shaped as a function of flux using voltage sources VN and VP and diodes D1 and D2. The inductance in the high-permeability region is proportional to RB, while the inductance in the saturated region is proportional to RS. Voltages VP and VN represent the saturation flux. Core losses can be simulated by adding resistance across the input terminals; however, another equivalent method is to add capacitance across resistor RB in the simulation.

Current in this capacitive element is differentiated in the model to produce the effect of resistance at the terminals. The capacitance can be made a nonlinear function of voltage, which results in a loss term that is a function of flux. A simple but effective way of adding the nonlinear capacitance is to specify a value for the diode parameter CJO. The other option is to use a nonlinear capacitor across nodes 2 and 6; however, the capacitor's polynomial coefficients are a function of saturation flux, thereby causing their recomputation if VP and VN are changed.

Core losses will increase linearly with frequency. A noticeable increase in MMF occurs when the core exits saturation, an effect that is more pronounced for square-wave excitation than for sinusoidal excitation, as shown in Figure 2.25.

These model properties agree closely with observed behavior [5]. The model is set up for orthonol and steel core materials that have a sharp transition from the saturated to the unsaturated region. The transition out of saturation is less pronounced for permalloy cores.

To account for the different response, the capacitance value in the diode model (CJO in DCLAMP), which affects core losses, should be reduced. Also, reducing the levels of voltage sources VN and VP will soften the transition.

The DC B-H loop hysteresis, which is usually unnecessary for most applications, is not modeled because of the additional model complexity. This causes a prediction of lower loss at low frequencies. The hysteresis, however, does appear as a frequency-dependent function, as seen previously, and provides reasonable results for most applications, including magnetic amplifiers.

The model in Figure 2.23 simulates the core characteristics and takes into account the high-frequency losses associated with eddy currents and transient widening of the B-H loop, which is caused by magnetic domain angular momentum.

The saturable core model is capable of being used with both sine wave (Figure 2-24) and square wave (Figure 2.25) excitation. The circuit in Figure 2.27 was used to generate the graphs.

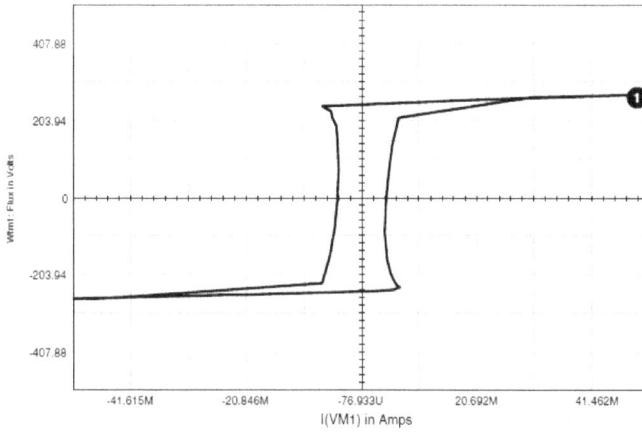

Figure 2.24

SPICE 2 Syntax Saturable Core Model under Square Wave Excitation

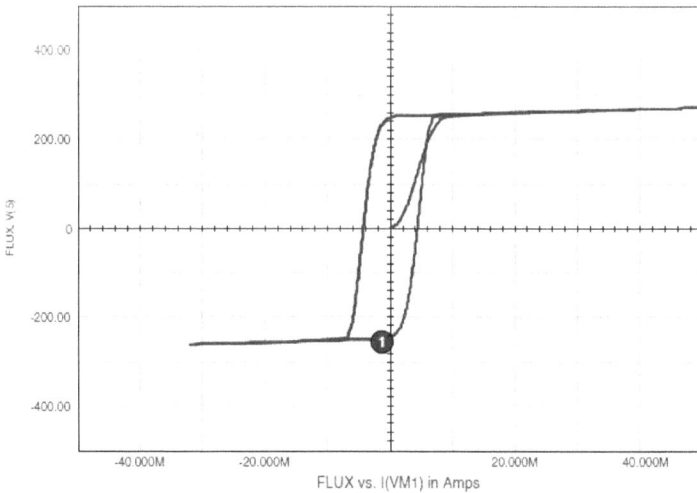

Figure 2.25

SPICE 2 Syntax Saturable Core Model under Sine Wave Excitation

Calculating Core Parameters

The saturable core model is defined in electrical terms, thus allowing the engineer to design the circuitry without knowledge of the core's physical composition. After the design is completed, the final electrical parameters can be used to calculate the necessary core magnetic/size values. The core model may be altered so that it accepts magnetic and size parameters. The core could then be described in terms of N, Ac, Ml, μ, and Bm and would be more useful for studying previously designed circuits. But the electrical model is better suited to the natural design process. The saturable core model's behavior is defined by the set of electrical parameters below The core's magnetic/size values can be easily calculated from the following equations that use CGS units.

Parameters Passed to Model

VSEC	Core capacity in volt-seconds
IVSEC	Initial condition in volt-seconds
LMAG	Magnetizing inductance in henries
LSAT	Saturation inductance in henries
FEDDY	Frequency when LMAG
	Reactance $=$ Loss resistance in hertz

Equation Variables

Bm	Maximum flux density in gauss
H	Magnetic field strength in oersted
Ac	Area of the core in cm^2
N	Number of turns
Ml	Magnetic path length in cm
m	Permeability

Faraday's law, which defines the relationship between flux and voltage, is given by Formula 2.9.

$$E = N\frac{d\varphi}{dt}*10^{-8}$$

Formula 2.9

Relationship between Flux and Voltage

…where E is the desired voltage, N is the number of turns, and φ is the flux of the core in Maxwell's equation.

The total flux may also be written as:

$$\varphi_T = 2 * Bm * Ac$$

Formula 2.10

Total Flux Calculation

Then, from Eqs. (2.9) and (2.10):

$$E = 4.44 * Bm * Ac * F * N * 10^{-8}$$

Formula 2.11

And…

$$E = 4.0 * Bm * Ac * F * N * 10^{-8}$$

Formula 2.12

E-Field Calculation

…where Bm is the flux density of the material in gauss, Ac is the effective core cross-sectional area in cm^2, and F is the design frequency.

Formula 2.11 is for sinusoidal conditions, while Formula 2.12 is for a square-wave input.

The parameter VSEC can then be determined by integrating the input voltage, resulting in:

$$\int edt = N\varphi_T = N * 2 * Bm * Ac * 10^{-8} = VSEC$$

Formula 2.13

Secondary Voltage Calculation

Also from E = L di/dt, we have:

$$\int edt = Li$$

Formula 2.14

Secondary E-Field Calculation

The initial flux in the core is described by the parameter IVSEC. To use the IVSEC option, you must put the UIC keyword in the ".TRAN" statement. The relationship between the magnetizing force and current is defined by Ampere's law as:

$$H = 0.4 * \pi * N * \frac{i}{Ml}$$

Formula 2.15

H-Field Calculation

Where H is the magnetizing force in oersteds, i is the current through N turns, and Ml is the magnetic path length in centimeters.

From Eqs. (2.13), (2.14), and (2.15) we have:

$$L = N^2 * Bm * Ac * \frac{\left(0.4 * \pi * 10^{-8}\right)}{H * Ml}$$

Formula 2.16

Inductance Calculation

With $\mu = B/H$, we have:

$$L(mag, sat) = \mu \left(mag, sat\right) * N^2 * 0.4 * \pi * 10^{-8} * \frac{Ac}{Ml}$$

Formula 2.17

Inductance Calculation (expanded)

The values for LMAG and LSAT can be determined by using the proper value of μ in Equation (2.17).

The values of permeability can be found by looking at the B-H curve and choosing two values for the magnetic flux: one in the linear region where the permeability will be maximum and one in the saturated region. Then, from a curve of permeability versus magnetic flux, the proper values of m may be chosen.

The value of μ in the saturated region will have to be an average value over the range of interest. The value of FEDDY, the eddy current critical frequency, can be determined from a graph of permeability versus frequency, as shown in Figure 2.26.

If we choose the approximate 3 dB point for μ, we can determine the corresponding frequency.

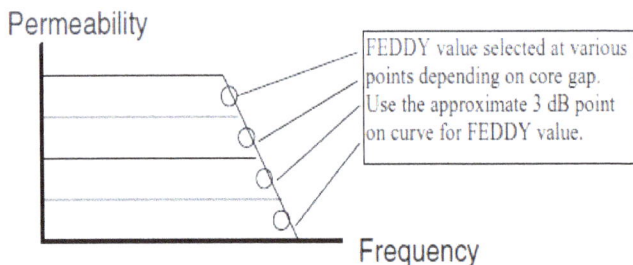

Figure 2.26

The Permeability versus Frequency Graph is used to Determine the Value for FEDDY

It should be noted that a similar core model can be constructed using generic physical parameters as opposed to generic electrical design parameters.

For example, see the following COREX subcircuit...

```
CoreX
.SUBCKT COREX 1 2 3 PARAMS: BI=0 N=1
RX 3 2 1E12
CB 3 2 {N*2*BR*ACORE*1E-8/500} IC={BI/BR*500}
F1 1 2 VM1 1
G2 2 3 1 2 1
E1 4 2 3 2 1
VM1 4 5
RB 5 2 {.625*N*UMAG/(LPATH * BR)*500}
RS 5 6 {.625*N*USAT/(LPATH * BR)*500}
VP 7 2 250
D1 6 7 DCLAMP
VN 2 8 250
D2 8 6 DCLAMP
* MULTIPLIER 3 AND VJ=25 GO TOGETHER
.MODEL DCLAMP D(CJO={3*LPATH * BR/(6.28*FEDDY*500*.625*N*UMAG)} VJ=25)
.ENDS
```

Where the passed physical parameters are as follows:

ACORE   Magnetic cross-sectional area in cm^2
LPATH   Magnetic path length in cm
FEDDY   Frequency when Lmag reactance $=$ loss resistance
UMAX   Maximum permeability, dB/dH

USAT   Saturation permeability, dB/dH
BR   Flux density in gauss at H = 0 for saturated B-H loop
BI   Initial flux density, default = 0
N   Number of turns

Using and Testing the Saturable Core

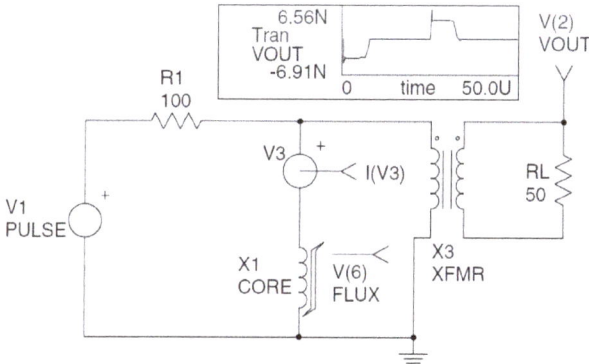

Figure 2.27

Saturable Core Test Circuit Schematic I(V3) = I(VM1)

Saturable Core Test Circuit

```
SaturableCoreTest
.TRAN .1US 50US 0 .1US
.PROBE
.PRINT TRAN V(3) V(6) I(VM1) V(4)
R1 4 3 100
RL 2 0 50
X1 1 0 6 CORE Params: VSEC=25U IVSEC=-25U LMAG=10MHY LSAT=20UHY FEDDY=25KHZ
X3 3 0 2 0 XFMR  Params: RATIO=.3
VM1 3 1
V2 4 0 PULSE -5 5 0US 0NS 0NS 25US
*Use the above statement for Square wave excitation
*V2 4 0 SIN 0 5 40K
*Use the above statement for Sin wave excitation
*Adjust Voltage levels to insure core saturation
.END
```

The test circuit shown in Figure 2.27 can be used to evaluate a saturable core model.

Specify the core parameters in the curly braces and adjust the voltage levels in the "V2 4 0 PULSE" or "V2 4 0 SIN" statements to ensure that the core will saturate.

You can use Eqs. (2.11) and (2.12) to get an idea of the voltage levels that are required in order to saturate the core. The .TRAN statement may also need adjustment, depending on the frequency that is specified by the V2 source. The core parameters must remain reasonable, or the simulation may fail.

When the simulation is finished, you can plot V(5) versus I(VM1) (flux versus current through the core) to obtain a B-H plot.

An improved version of this model, adding low-frequency hysteresis [102, 103], is shown below.

SVSEC and IVSEC are based on peak flux values. LMAG: For an ungapped core, $L = L_M$ (total path around core); for a gapped core, $\mu_R = 1$, L = gap length, A_E = core area (m^2). LSAT: Use core dimensions but with $\mu_R = 1$. REDDY: Equals LMAG reactance when permeability versus frequency is 3 dB down.

Magnetizing current associated with low-frequency hysteresis is provided by current sinks IH1/IH2.

With no voltage across terminals 1 and 2, these currents circulate through their respective diodes, and the net terminal current is zero. When voltage is applied, the appropriate diode starts to block and its current sink becomes active.

```
SaturableCoreTestImproved
.SUBCKT CORE 1 2 3
DH1  1 9 DHYST
DH2  2 9 DHYST
IH1  9 1 {IHYST}
IH2  9 2 {IHYST}
F1   1 2 UM 1
G1   2 3 1 2 1
E1   4 2 3 2 1
UM   4 5
C1   3 2 {SVSEC/250} IC={IVSEC/SVSEC*250}
RB   5 2 {LMAG*250/SVSEC}
RS   5 6 {LSAT*250/SVSEC}
UP   7 2 250
D1   6 7 DCLAMP
UN   2 8 250
D2   8 6 DCLAMP
E2   10 0 3 2 {SVSEC/250}
.MODEL DHYST D
.MODEL DCLAMP D(CJO={3*SVSEC/(250*REDDY)} VJ=25)
.ENDS
```

Where:

SVSEC	Volt-sec at saturation = $B_{SAT} \cdot A_E \cdot N$
IVSEC	Volt-sec initial condition = $B \cdot A_E \cdot N$
LMAG	Unsaturated inductance = $\mu_O \, \mu_R \cdot N^2 \cdot A_E \, / \, L_M$
LSAT	Saturated inductance = $\mu_O \cdot N^2 \cdot AE \, / \, L_M$
IHYST	Magnetizing I @ 0 flux = $H \cdot L_M \, / \, N$
REDDY	Eddy current loss resistance

SPICE 3 Compatible Core Model

A magnetic core model has three major elements: permeability, hysteresis, and core loss. Unfortunately, both the permeability and the core loss are nonlinear functions. The models in this chapter properly represent the nonlinear permeability and the hysteresis. The core loss has not been modeled in this SPICE 3 version.

The model is based upon the premise that a magnetic element is represented by an inductance. The inductance is related to the permeability and geometrical properties of the core. The current through the inductor can then be simply stated as:

$$I = \frac{1}{L} \int V dt$$

This function can be modeled as a simple integrator. To properly represent the B-H loop characteristics, the nonlinearities of the inductance need to be defined.

Fortunately, graphical data are available that provide the percentage of initial permeability versus DC bias for several core types. Using curve-fitting techniques, the nonlinear permeability can be approximated in closed-loop form.

The nonlinear permeability can then be used to modify the slope of the integrator. The resulting equation, which we will model, is:

$$I = \frac{1}{L * \%U} \int V dt$$

The results have shown that the B-H characteristics properly represent the hysteresis and remenance effects of the core. Core loss must be represented at a single operating condition, or may be entered outside of the model.

This can be accomplished via the use of parameter passing. In this case, the 3 dB point on the permeability versus frequency graph was used. The configuration of the model is shown in Figure 2.28.

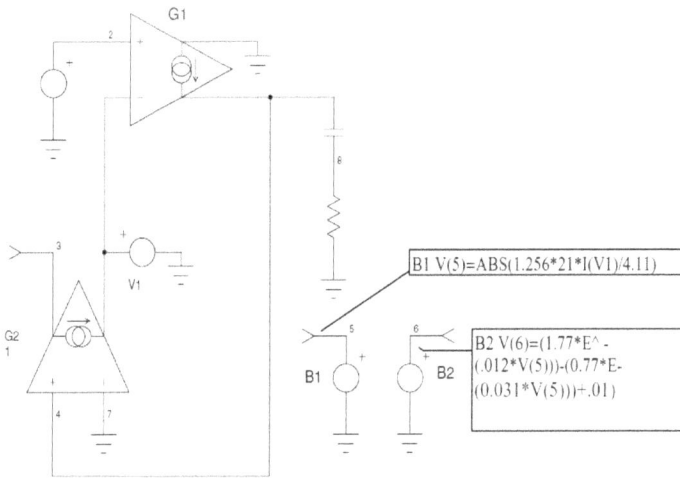

Figure 2.28

Schematic of the SPICE 3 Core Model

Where V(6) = % Permeability and V(5) = H.

In PSpice, the SPICE 3 B-elements are replaced by voltage-controlled voltage or current source equivalents (E or G elements). B1 calculates the magnetizing force in the inductor using the relationship:

$$H = \left| \frac{.4\pi \, NI}{l_m} \right|$$

Where N is the number of turns, I is the current through the element (measured by V1), and l_m is the magnetic path length of the core. Because H is a real value, its absolute value is used. B2 calculates the percent permeability using the equation defined above. B3 calculates the voltage across the element, divided by the percent permeability.

G1 integrates the value of BS3 and presents it to G2, which forces a current flow through the element. With the values of G1 and G2 both established as 1, the current through the element is:

$$I = \frac{1}{C * \%U} \int V dt$$

Because this is in the desired form, we can solve for all of the variables.

Example 1—MPP Core

Using the permeability versus DC bias data provided by Magnetics®, multiple iterations and curve-fitting techniques, a closed form solution for the 60u material was found to be approximated by:

$$\%U_i = 1.77e^{-.021H} - 0.77e^{-.031H}$$

where U_i is the initial inductance of the core and H is the magnetizing force in Oersteds.

$$C = L = \left(\frac{N}{1000}\right)^2 A_L$$

where A_L is the inductance reference of the core.

$$B1 = \left|\frac{0.4\mu NI(VI)}{l_m}\right|$$

$$B2 = 1.77e^{-.012V(B1)} - 0.77e^{-.031V(B1)} + .02$$

$$B3 = \frac{V(3,4)}{V(B2)}$$

$$R2 = \frac{1}{2\pi f_{eddy}C}$$

The following circuit uses the above derivation to model a Magnetics® 55121 MPP core with 21 turns. The constants given in the data book for the 55121 core provide the following values: A_L = 35 mH, l_m = 4.11 cm, core weight=.015 lb, f_{eddy}=7 MHz, and U_i.=60. We can calculate the components of the model as:

$$C = \left(\frac{21}{1000}\right)^2 *35mH = 15.4\mu F$$

$$B1 = \left|\frac{0.4\pi\,(21)\,I\,(V1)}{4.11}\right|$$

$$R1 = \frac{1}{2\pi\,(7\,MHz)(15.4\mu F)} = 0.0015$$

The SPICE netlist is provided later (Figure 2.29). Note that R1 represents the winding's DC resistance. The test circuit sweeps the current through the "core" while the percent permeability and magnetizing force are monitored and displayed in (Figure 2.30). Actual data points are plotted as dots, while the calculated results are plotted using line style. An AC impedance plot is also performed (Figure 2.31). Calculating the inductance from the impedance curve yields 15.6µH, which agrees with the expected 15.4µH.

$$L = \frac{1}{2\pi\,(10.19kHz)} = 15.6\mu H$$

```
MPP55121 Core
MPP: MODELING A MAGNETICS® 55121 MPP CORE
* PSpice version
.DC I1 .1 100 .10
.AC DEC 20 100HZ 10MEGHZ
.PROBE
.PRINT AC  V(4)  VP(4)
* Node 4 Impedance
.PRINT DC  V(6)  V(5)
* Node 6 = H, Node 5 = % Permeability
G2 3 1 9 0 1
V1 1 0
G1 0 9 2 1 1
C1 9 8 15.4U
R2 8 0 1.5M
E1 5 0 Value ={ ABS(1.256*21*I(V1)/4.11) }
E2 6 0 Value ={(1.77*Exp(-(.012*V(5))))-(.77*Exp(-(.031*V(5))))+.01 }
E3 2 0 Value ={ V(3,1)/V(6) }
I1 0 4 AC 1
R1 4 3 .04
RT4 4 0 1G
RT3 3 0 1G
RT9 9 0 1G
.END
```

Figure 2.29

Netlist for a 55121 MPP Core

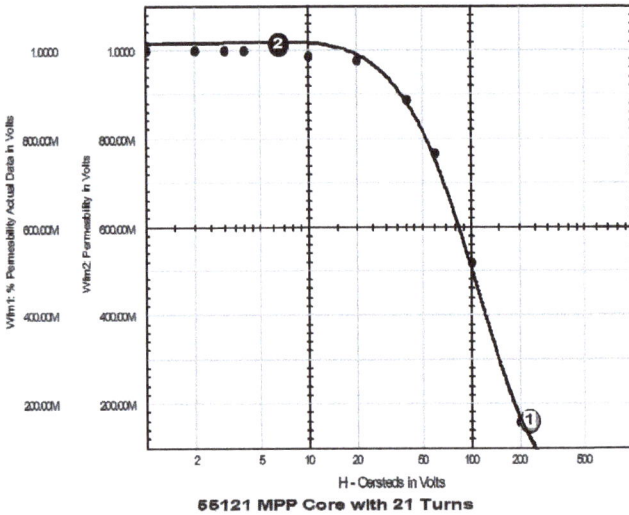

55121 MPP Core with 21 Turns

Figure 2.30

Permeability versus Magnetizing Force

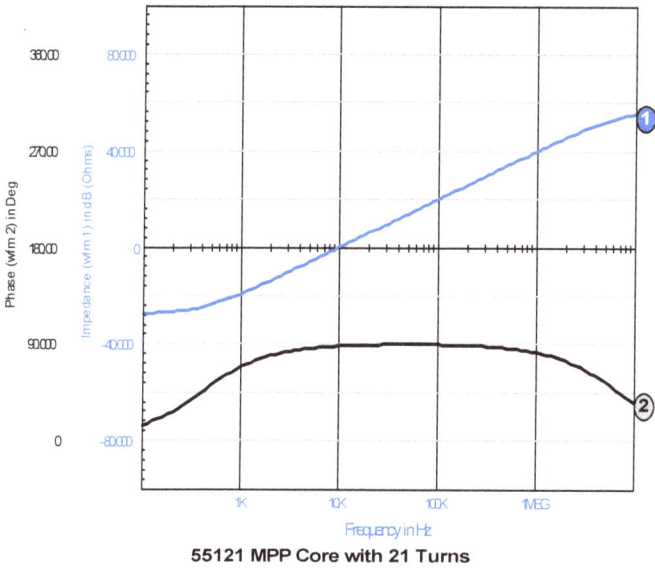

55121 MPP Core with 21 Turns

Figure 2.31

Impedance for the 55121 Core

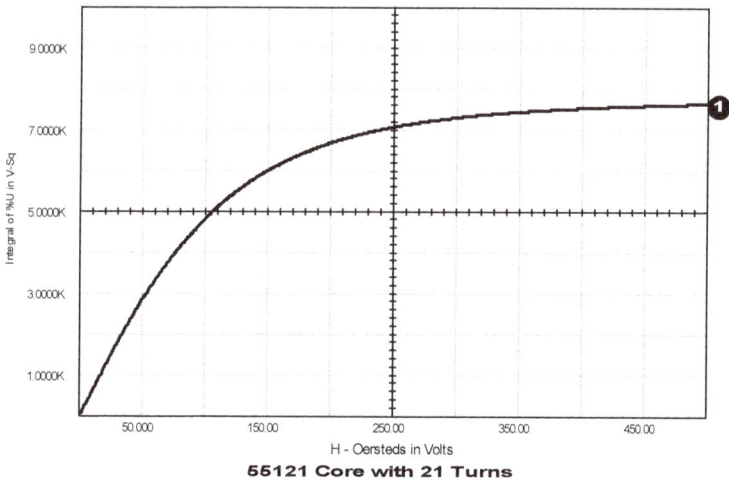

55121 Core with 21 Turns

Figure 2.32

DC B-H Curve

The percent permeability versus magnetizing force curve was integrated and multiplied by the initial permeability per Ben-Yaakov and Adar.[4]

The resulting graph is the DC B-H curve shown in Figure 2.32. The curve shows a maximum flux density of approximately 7500 G, which agrees with the specified value of 7000 G.

Ferrite Cores

The same principles apply to ferrite cores as well as MPP cores.

In this example, a model is generated for ferrite "F" material. Again, trial-and-error and curve-fitting techniques may be used in order to obtain a closed-form expression of percent permeability versus magnetizing force. Graphical data are provided in the Magnetics Ferrite Data Book.

Although the MPP model is represented using exponential functions, the ferrite model is much more accurately represented via a power function. The resulting expression for ferrite "F" material is:

$$\%U = \frac{1.149 * 1.09\,H^{-1.1376}}{1.05 + 1.094\,H^{-1.1376}}$$

The result of the %U calculation was multiplied by the initial permeability (3000) in order to obtain the same terms as those contained in the Ferrite Data Book.

Figure 2.33 shows the actual permeability versus magnetizing force. Actual data points are plotted as dots, while the calculated results are plotted using line style.

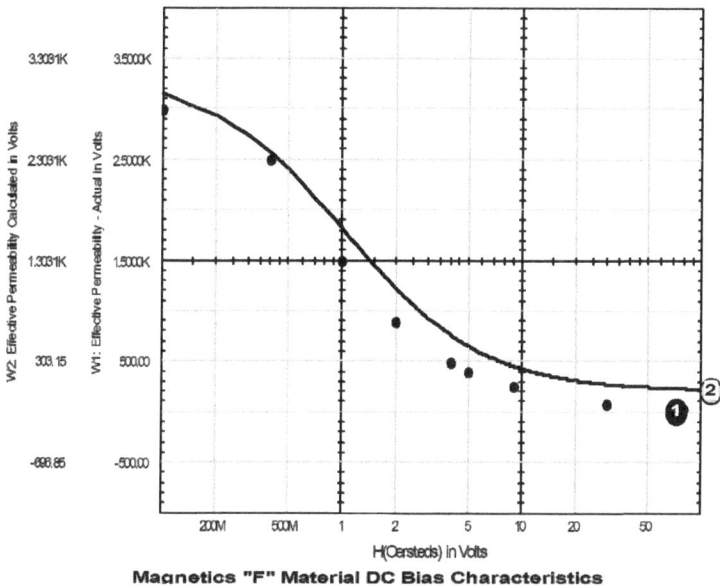

Magnetics "F" Material DC Bias Characteristics

Figure 2.33

Permeability versus Magnetizing Force

Example 2—Ferrite Core

As an example, a model was created for an F2213 pot core with 1 turn.

The data sheet parameters for the F2213 pot core defines the values as follows: A_L=4900 mH, l_m=3.12 cm, U_i= 3000, and f_{eddy}=1 MHz. The schematic in Figure 2.34 shows the circuit model for the core.

The basic structure of the model is very similar to that of the MPP core model. The major differences lie in the definition of the nonlinear element B2 and the fact that the core loss is shown as a parallel resistor rather than a series resistor.

Also, note that a resistor is not added to represent DC resistance (DCR), because it would be a property of the winding.

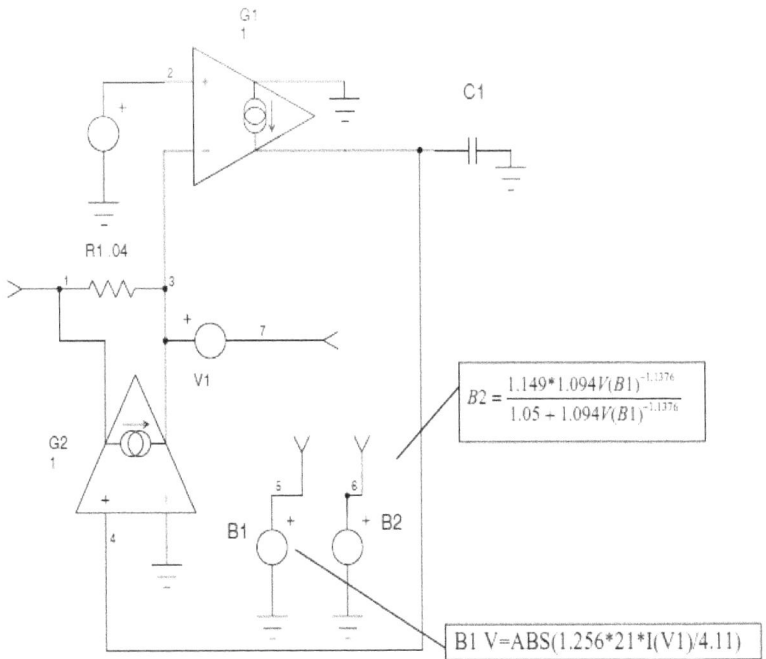

Figure 2.34

Schematic for the F2213 Pot Core

Where $V(6) = \%$ Permeability, $V(5) = H$

$$B1 = \left| \frac{0.4\pi\,(1)\,I\,(V1)}{3.12} \right| = 0.4026I\,(V1)$$

$$C1 = \left(\frac{1}{1000} \right)^2 * 4900mH = 4.9\mu F$$

$$B3 = \frac{V(3,4)}{V(B2)}$$

$$B2 = \frac{1.149 * 1.094V(B1)^{-1.1376}}{1.05 + 1.094V(B1)^{-1.1376}}$$

$$R1 = 2\pi\, f_{eddy} C1 = 30.77 Ohm$$

A test circuit is required in order to generate the B-H loop curve. A pulse source is used to excite the core through a limiting resistor. The flux level and magnetizing force, H, must be measured. To measure the flux level, we can use the following form of Maxwell's equation:

$$Flux = \frac{Vt * 10^8}{A_c N}$$

...where A_c is the core area in cm^2 and N is the number of turns.

If we use a voltage-controlled current source with a gain of 1, we can charge a 1F capacitor and scale the capacitor voltage by a factor of:

$$\frac{10^8}{A_c N}.$$

The core area is given in the data sheet as 0.635 cm^2, which calculates to a scaling factor of 157.5 × 10^6. We could use the magnetizing force that was calculated by B1, but we took its absolute value. We will use a current-controlled voltage source to measure the excitation current because we can define the scaling factor as $\frac{0.4\pi}{3.12} I = 0.403 I$. The completed model, including the test circuit, is shown in Figure 2.35.

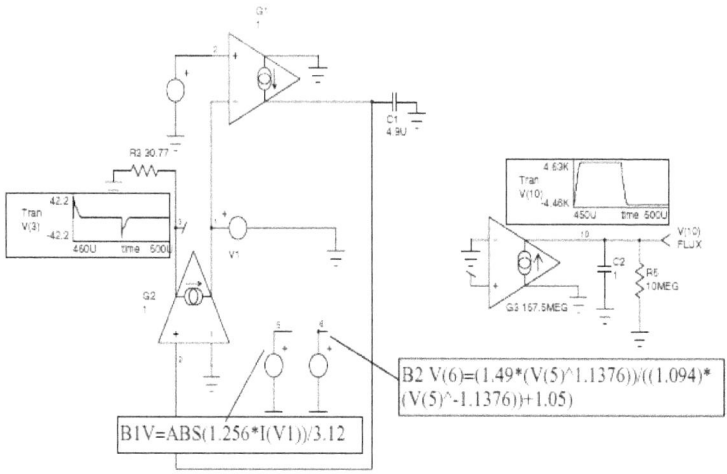

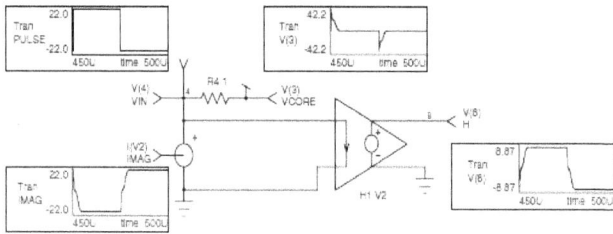

B2 V(6)=(1.49*(V(5)^1.1376))/((1.094)*(V(5)^-1.1376))+1.05)

B1V=ABS(1.256*I(V1))/3.12

```
📄 MAGF
 MAGF: Test Circuit to Generate the B-H Loop Curve
 * PSpice version
 .TRAN .1U 500U 450U .1U UIC
 .PROBE
 * I(U2)=IMAG
 * U(10)=FLUX
 * U(8)=H
 * U(3)=UCORE
 * U(4)=PULSE
 .PRINT TRAN U(4) I(U2) U(10) U(8)
 U1 1 0
 G1 0 9 2 1 1
 C1 9 0 4.9U IC=0
 E1 5 0 Value = { ABS(1.256*I(U1))/3.12 }
 E2 6 0 Value = { (1.149*(U(5)^-1.1376))/((1.094*(U(5)^-1.1376))+1.05) }
 E3 2 0 Value = { U(3,1)/(U(6)+.001) }
 Uin 4 0 PULSE -20 20 10N 10N 10N 25U 50U
 R3 3 0 30.77
 R4 4 3 1
 G3 0 10 3 0 157.5MEG
 C2 10 0 1 IC=0
 R5 10 0 10MEG
 H1 8 0 U2 -.403
 G2 3 1 9 0 1
 RT9 9 0 1G
 .END
```

Figure 2.35

Test Circuit Schematic and Netlist for the F2213 Pot Core

The circuit was simulated and an X-Y plot was created. The results are shown in Figure 2.36. The curve agrees with the Magnetics B-H loop data.

The pulse voltage waveform and the core voltage waveform are also shown.

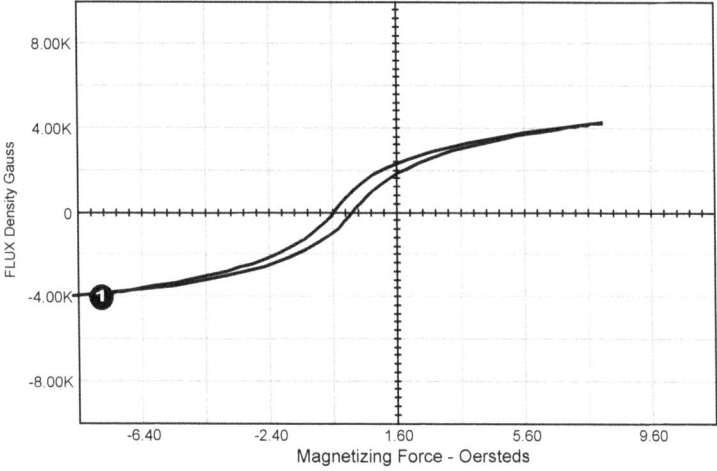

Magnetics "F" Ferrite B-H Loop

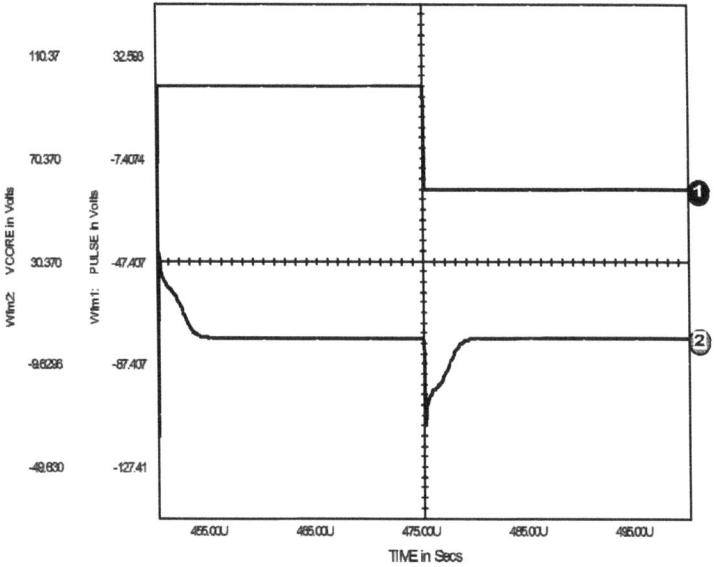

Magnetics "F" Material

Figure 2.36

B-H Loop for the F2213 Pot Core (top) and Pulse Waveform Response (bottom)

Constructing a Transformer

As a final exercise in this chapter, we will combine the core model which we just completed, along with the turns subcircuit, and model a two-winding transformer.

To make a transformer model that more closely represents the physical processes, it is necessary to construct an ideal transformer and model the magnetizing and leakage inductances separately.

The ideal transformer was discussed previously in this chapter. It has a unity coupling coefficient and infinite magnetizing inductance. The ideal transformer, unlike a real transformer, will operate at DC, a property useful for modeling the operation of DC-to-DC converters.

The magnetizing inductance is added by placing the saturable reactor model (suitably scaled) across any one of the windings. Coupling coefficients are inserted in the model by adding the series leakage inductance for each winding as shown in Figure 2.37.

The leakage inductances are measured by finding the short-circuit input inductance at each winding and then solving for the individual inductance.

These leakage inductances are independent of the core characteristics, as shown in reference [104]. The final model, incorporating the saturable core model and an ideal transformer subcircuit, along with the leakage inductance and winding resistance, is shown in Figure 2.37.

PSpice models cannot represent all possible behavior because of the limits of computer memory and run time. This model, as most simulations, does not represent all cases.

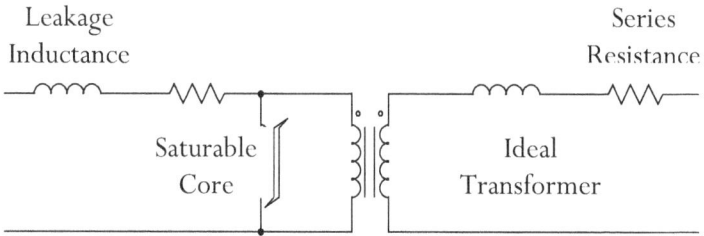

Figure 2.37

A Complete Transformer Model

Note: The saturable core may be combined with the ideal transformer, XFMR, and some leakage inductance and series resistance to create a complete model of a transformer.

Modeling the core as a single element referred to one of the windings works in most cases; however, some applications may experience saturation in a small region of the core, causing some windings to be decoupled faster than others, invalidating the model.

Another limitation of this model is for topologies with magnetic shunts or multiple cores. Applications like this can frequently be solved by replacing the single magnetic structure with an equivalent structure using several transformers, each using the model presented here.

Another example is shown in Figure 2.38. The SPICE 3 core model remains unchanged.

We have simply added two transformer (turns) subcircuits. The primary winding has 10 turns, and the secondary has 20 turns. The secondary of the turns subcircuit is always 1 turn, which is the reason that we developed the core with 1 turn. The circuit was stimulated with a 10V peak 20kHz square-wave voltage applied through a 1Ω series resistor, and also with a 50V peak 25kHz square-wave voltage.

The input and output voltage of the transformer are shown in Figure 2.39. Note that the output voltage agrees with the turns ratio, for it is twice the level of the input voltage.

The second plot illustrates the core saturation characteristics, which are represented by the B-H loop.

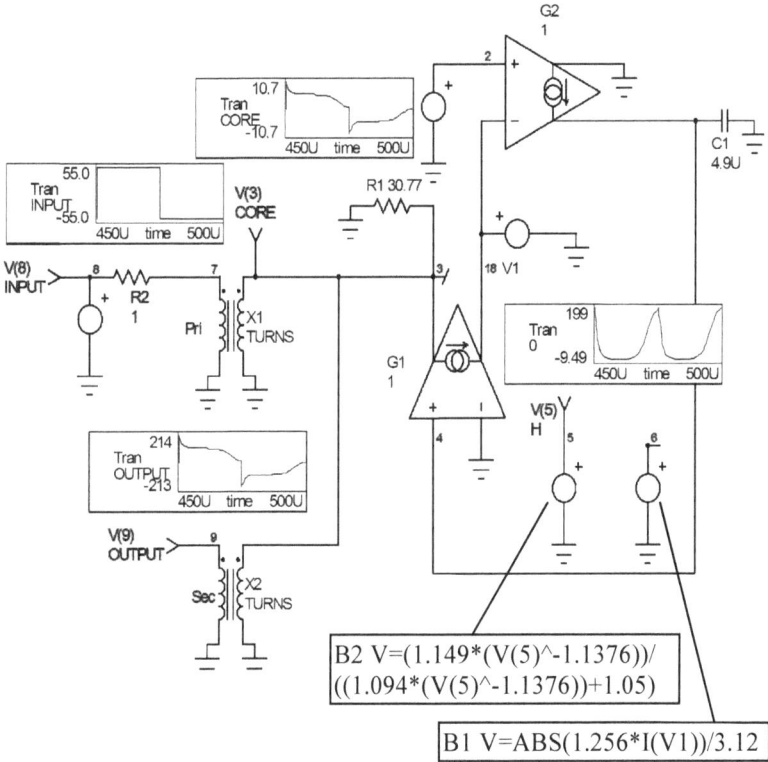

B2 $V=(1.149*(V(5)^\wedge-1.1376))/((1.094*(V(5)^\wedge-1.1376))+1.05)$

B1 $V=ABS(1.256*I(V1))/3.12$

```
Two-Winding Transformer
EX5: Model for a Two-Winding Transformer
* PSpice version
.AC DEC 20 100HZ 10MEGHZ
.TRAN .1U 500U 450U UIC
* V(9)=OUTPUT
* V(3)=CORE
* V(8)=INPUT
* V(5)=H
.PRINT AC  V(9)  VP(9)  V(3)  VP(3)
.PRINT AC  V(8)  VP(8)
.PRINT TRAN  V(9)  V(3)  V(8)  V(5)
V1 1 0
G2 0 4 2 1 1
C1 4 0 4.9U IC=0
E1 5 0 Value ={ ABS(1.256*I(V1))/3.12 }
E2 6 0 Value = { (1.149*(V(5)^-1.1376))/((1.094*(V(5)^-1.1376))+1.05) }
E3 2 0 Value = { V(3,1)/(V(6)+.001) }
R1 3 0 30.7700
X1 7 0 3 0 TURNS Params: NUM=10
X2 9 0 3 0 TURNS Params: NUM=20
* Turns is similar to XFMR except Ratio = 1/Num
V2 8 0 AC 1 PULSE -50 50 1N 1N 1N 25U 50U
R2 8 7 1
G1 3 1 4 0 1
RT4 4 0 1G
.END
```

Figure 2.38

Schematic and Netlist for the Two-Winding Transformer Test Circuit

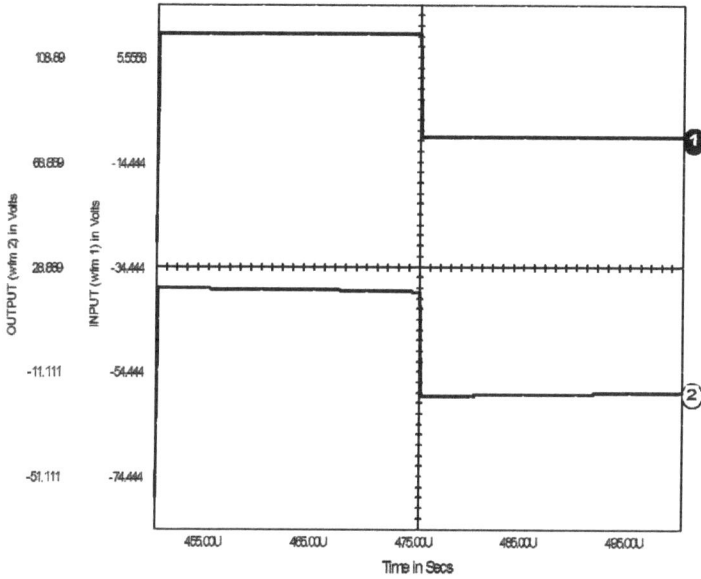

F42213 Ferrite Core Transformer Np=10 Ns=20

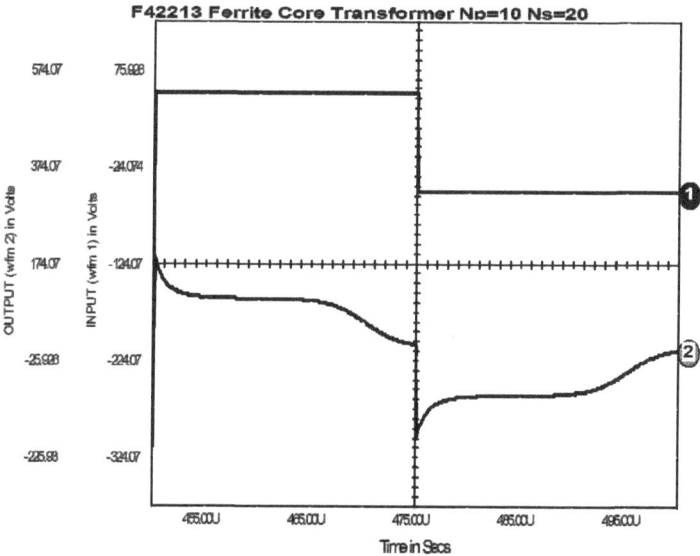

F42213 Ferrite Core Transformer Np=10 Ns=20

Figure 2.39

Input and Output Voltages for the Complete Transformer
Circuit (top) and Transient Core Saturation
Characteristics (bottom)

High-Frequency Winding Effects

Winding resistance can be modeled by adding a series resistance to each winding as shown in Figure 2.40. At low frequencies R_w is simply the DC resistance of the winding. At the higher frequencies more common in power conversion, however, the winding resistance is more complex because of the presence of skin and proximity effects within the windings.

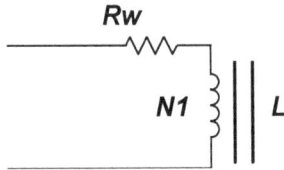

Figure 2.40

Winding Resistance Model

There are several reasons for wanting to correctly model the winding resistance:

• Reproduce the winding loss.

• Reproduce the effect of winding resistance on voltage drop within and cross-regulation between windings.

• Reproduce the damping effect that the winding resistance will have on parasitic ringing.

To achieve these goals, it is necessary to determine the effective resistance, including the high-frequency effects.

Procedures for estimating winding resistance are well known and can be used to establish model parameters. A typical graph of winding resistance versus frequency for windings with different numbers of layers is given in Figure 2.41. The graph is normalized for a 1Ω DC resistance and a frequency where the layer thickness is 1 skin depth (δ):

$$\delta_{CU} = \frac{.661}{\sqrt{\pi \mu \sigma f_s}} \; meter$$

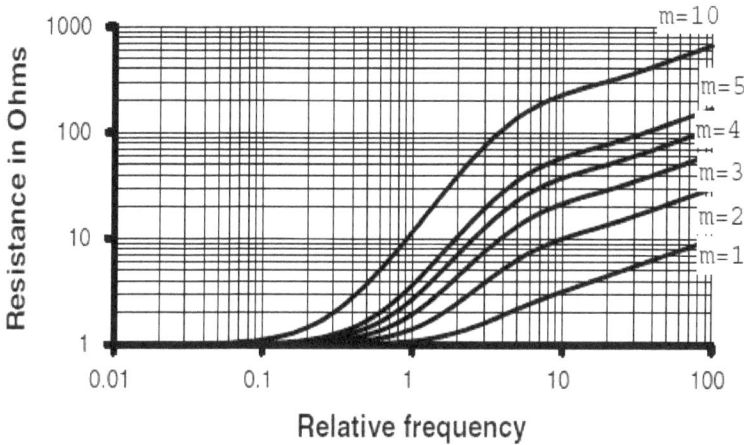

Figure 2.41

HF Winding Resistance, Normalized to 1 Ω (Rdc) at the Frequency where the Layer is 1 Skin Depth Thick

The current waveform in the winding is assumed to be a sine wave. The key feature of the graph is the rapid increase in resistance above a corner frequency that is determined by the number of layers. The winding resistance is frequency dependent and the change in resistance can be quite large.

The winding resistance is also dependent upon the shape of the current waveform. Figure 2.42 is an example of a three-layer winding with a symmetrical bipolar PWM current waveform. Note that the winding resistance is everywhere greater than it would be for a sine wave, which is also plotted for comparison. This is due to the harmonic content of the waveform. Notice also that as the duty cycle (D) is varied from a square wave (D=0.5) to a smaller duty cycle, the winding resistance first decreases and then increases as it becomes quite large at low duty cycle values. This seemingly bizarre behavior is due to the changing harmonic spectrum as the duty cycle is modulated.

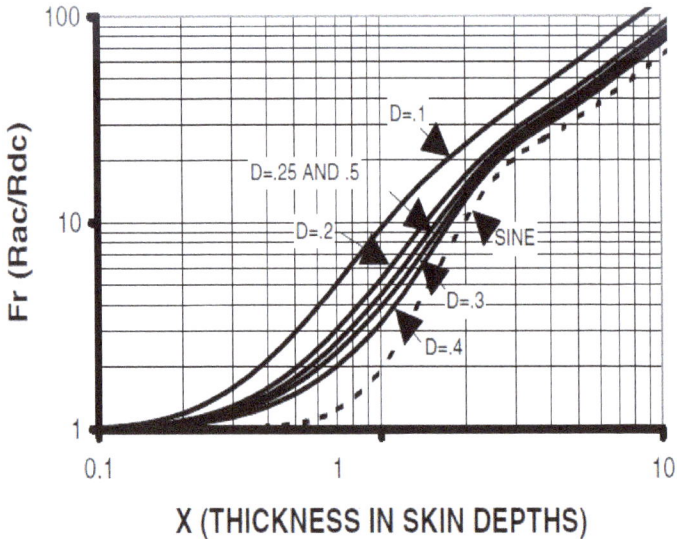

Figure 2.42

Fr for a Bipolar PWM Current (m=3)

In a typical high-frequency power converter, the winding resistances will vary as a function of frequency, modulation, load distribution between the windings, and temperature.

In general, it is not practical or necessary to model all of these effects, but there are some useful approximations.

If winding loss is the most important concern, then the winding resistance can be represented by a simple series resistor in each winding, the values of which are chosen to represent the effective AC resistance at the highest loss condition of load, duty cycle, and temperature.

This choice will overstate the loss at other conditions, but it is usually preferable to understatement under the worst-case conditions.

It is possible to approximate a frequency variable resistor with a network of linear components, as shown in Figure 2.43. At low frequencies, the inductor is essentially a short circuit and R $=R_1$.

At high frequencies, the inductor is an open circuit and R $= R_1$ + R_2. The change in resistance follows the single-pole asymptotic approximation, which is shown in the graph in Figure 2.43. The equations for the real and imaginary components of the network driving point impedance (z) are also given.

$$\text{Im}[z] = R_1\left[\frac{fn(k-1)/k}{fn^2/k^2+1}\right]$$

$$\text{Re}[z] = R_1\left[\frac{fn^2/k+1}{fn^2/k^2+1}\right]$$

$$k = \frac{R_1+R_2}{R_1} = \frac{R_{hf}}{R_{if}}$$

$$fn = \frac{f}{f_0}$$

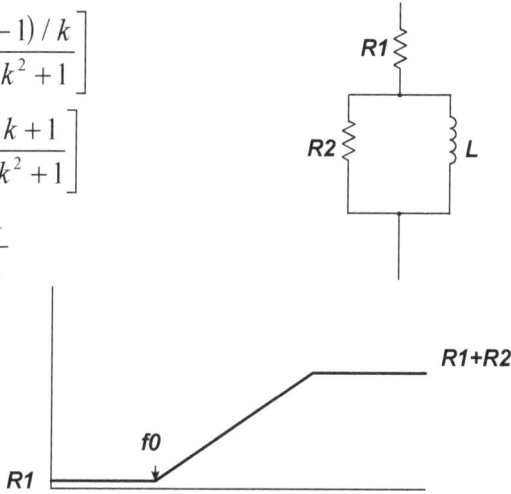

Figure 2.43

A Resistance that Varies with Frequency can be Simulated with a Network of Linear Components

A graph of the real part of z is given in Figure 2.44 for different resistance ratios.

For a suitable choice of f_0 and k, the change of resistance can be modeled over a substantial frequency range.

93

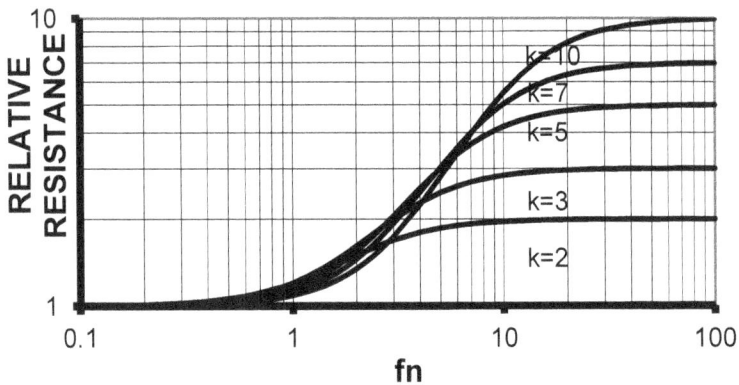

Figure 2.44

Graph of Re[z] for Different Resistance Ratios

There is, however, an important limitation associated with this network. The ratio of the real/imaginary parts of z are plotted in Figure 2.45.

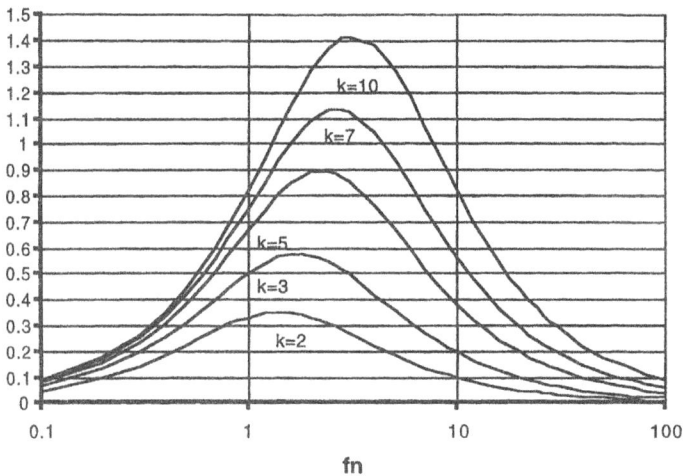

Figure 2.45

Graph of Im[z]/Re[z] for Different Resistance Ratios

Because of the presence of the inductor in the network, there will be some inductive reactance.

As shown by the graph, this peaks between the upper and lower resistive break points. For small resistance ratios, the inductive reactance is relatively small, but as the ratio gets larger, the inductance becomes significant and this simple network is no longer just a variable frequency resistor but is also a variable frequency inductor.

This may not be a problem if a series inductor is being used to simulate the leakage inductance of the winding. If the leakage inductance is large enough, it may mask the network inductance sufficiently so that its effect can be ignored.

Where it is necessary to model a frequency-dependent resistor, but the inductance must be kept small, it is possible to use a multi-element network as shown in Figure 2.46. If each resistance step is kept small, then the resistance is approximated accurately over a wide range of frequencies—while still introducing only a small inductive reactance.

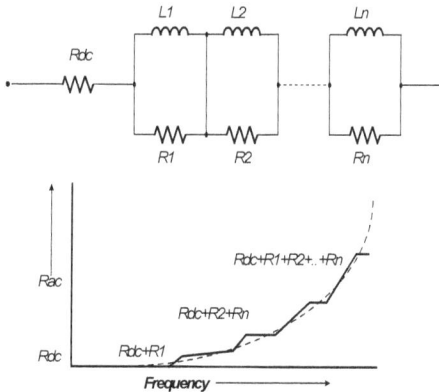

Figure 2.46

High-Frequency Resistance Model using a Multi-Element Network

Chapter 3

EMI Filter Design

NEARLY ALL POWER circuits contain an input electromagnetic interference (EMI) filter. The main purpose of the EMI filter is to limit the interference that is conducted or radiated from the power circuit. Excessive conducted or radiated interference can cause erratic behavior in other systems that are in close proximity of, or that share an input source with, the power circuit. If this interference affects the power circuit, it can cause erratic operation, excessive ripple, or degraded regulation, which can lead to system level problems.

Input EMI filters may also be used to limit inrush current, reduce conducted susceptibility, and suppress spikes. The specifications for the allowable interference are generally driven by the power circuit specification. The most common specifications include MIL-STD-461 for military applications and FCC for commercial applications. Many other EMI specifications also exist.

This chapter will deal with the design and analysis of EMI filters that will reduce conducted interference and conducted susceptibility and limit inrush current. The design of the input filter is slightly more critical when the power circuit is a regulated switching circuit, rather than a linear circuit, because a negative input resistance is created by the regulated switching circuit.

Although it is possible to simulate the radiated interference of a power circuit, it is beyond the scope of this book.

Basic Requirements

The design of an input EMI filter begins with the definition of two basic requirements:

- The filter must provide the power converter with lower output impedance than the negative input resistance of the power circuit.

- The input filter attenuation must be sufficient to limit the resulting interference to a level that is below the imposed specification.

The following flowchart provides a step-by-step approach that may be used to design an input filter.

EMI Filter Design Flowchart

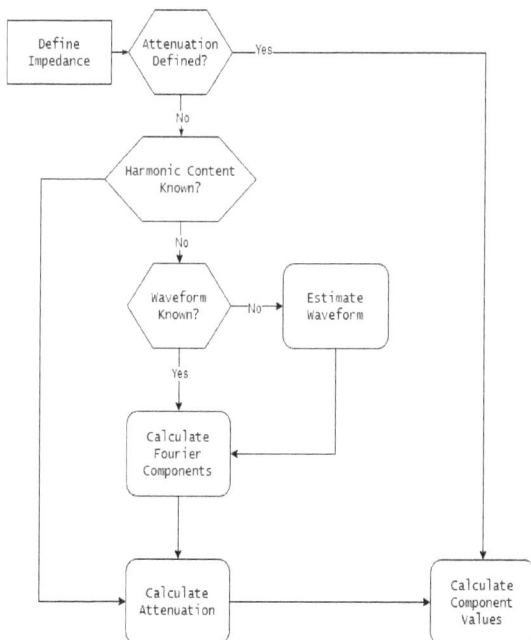

Defining the Negative Resistance

The negative resistance of the power circuit can be defined by looking at the following conditions:

$$P_{in} = \frac{P_{out}}{efficiency}$$

$$I_{in} = \frac{P_{in}}{V_{in}}$$

$$R_{in} = \frac{V_{in}}{I_{in}} = \frac{V_{in}^2}{P_{in}} = \frac{V_{in}^2 * efficiency}{P_{out}}$$

The input resistance is negative because as the input voltage increases, the input current decreases. As a simple example, we can use PSpice to analyze the input resistance of the power circuit. PSpice can analyze the input resistance in a number of ways.

The simplest method is the transfer function (.TF) analysis, which calculates the DC gain and the small signal input and output impedance. The following example uses the PSpice.TF analysis to measure the input resistance of a switching power circuit.

Example 1—Input Resistance Analysis

Input File

```
RIN: INPUT RESISTANCE
.TF V(5) V1
V1 5 0 20
G1 5 0 Value = { 100/V(5) }
.END
```

Output File

```
D:\SPICE\CIRCUITS\RIN
.TF V(5) V1
V1 5 0 20
B1 5 0 I=100/V(5)
.END


.END
```

Circuit : D:\SPICE\CIRCUITS\RIN
Date: Wed Feb 8 10:40:36 1995

**** SMALL SIGNAL DC TRANSFER FUNCTION

Output_impedance_at_V(5)	0.000000e+000
v1#Input_impedance	-4.00000e+000
Transfer_function	1.000000e+000
Total run time:	0.333 seconds
Memory used: = 1223 Kbytes	

The B1 source simulates a power circuit with an input power of 100W. V1 applies 20VDC to the power circuit, and the .TF measures the input impedance at node 5 and the output impedance at V1. The results are placed in the output file. Note that PSpice calculated the input impedance as a negative resistance of 4Ω, in agreement with the above derivation.

Defining the Harmonic Content

The next step in designing an input EMI filter is to determine the harmonic content of the power circuit input current. If the input current waveform is known, a Fourier analysis can be performed in order to establish the harmonic content of the waveform; however, even if the exact waveform is not known, we can estimate the waveform with reasonable accuracy. The design can be optimized later, if necessary.

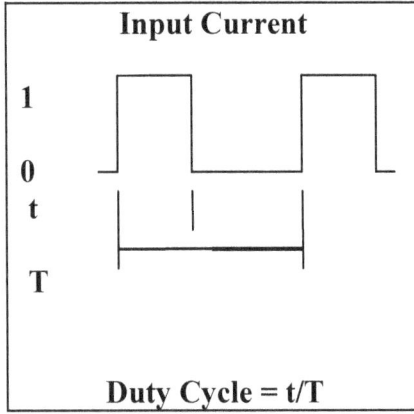

Figure 3.1

Pulsating Waveform used in the Fourier Series Computation

Consider the pulsating waveform in Figure 3.1. With a peak amplitude of one and a base amplitude of zero, we can compute the Fourier series of harmonic *n* as follows:

$$A_n = \frac{2}{T} \int_0^t \sin(nt)$$

$$B_n = \frac{2}{T} \int_0^t \cos(nt)$$

$$C_n = \sqrt{A_n^2 + B_n^2}$$

If we assume that the input ripple current is pulsating and if we know the duty cycle, we can proceed to the Fourier analysis. If the duty cycle is not known, we will assume a value of 50%. This assumption is the worst case, because the Fourier analysis of a pulsed waveform has a maxima at a value of 50%. In the next example, we will use SPICE to calculate the Fourier coefficients of a 50% duty cycle pulse.

Example 2—.FOUR Analysis

The following example demonstrates the use of the .FOUR analysis. V1 is a pulsed voltage source, which has a 50% duty cycle and a 100kHz frequency. The .FOUR statement calculates the magnitude and phase of the DC value and the first nine harmonics. The result is placed in the output file as shown below.

```
EX2: DEMONSTRATING THE USE OF THE .FOUR ANALYSIS
.OPTIONS NUMDGT=3
.TRAN .01U 20U
.FOUR 100KHZ U(1)
U1 1 0 PULSE 0 1 0 0 0 5U 10U
.END
```

FOURIER COMPONENTS OF TRANSIENT RESPONSE V(1)

DC COMPONENT = 5.010000E-01

HARMONIC NO	FREQUENCY (Hz)	FOURIER COMPONENT	NORMALIZED COMPONENT	PHASE (DEG)	NORMALIZED PHASE(DEG)
1	1.000E+05	6.366E-01	1.000E+00	-3.600E-01	0.000E+00
2	2.000E+05	2.000E-03	3.142E-03	8.928E+01	9.000E+01
3	3.000E+05	2.122E-01	3.333E-01	-1.080E+00	4.088E-09
4	4.000E+05	2.000E-03	3.142E-03	8.856E+01	9.000E+01
5	5.000E+05	1.273E-01	2.000E-01	-1.800E+00	2.044E-08
6	6.000E+05	2.000E-03	3.142E-03	8.784E+01	9.000E+01
7	7.000E+05	9.093E-02	1.428E-01	-2.520E+00	5.723E-08
8	8.000E+05	2.000E-03	3.142E-03	8.712E+01	9.000E+01
9	9.000E+05	7.072E-02	1.111E-01	-3.240E+00	1.226E-07

TOTAL HARMONIC DISTORTION = 4.288115E+01 PERCENT

As you can see from the output file, the fundamental harmonic has a peak value that is 63.6% of the peak pulse amplitude. Although this provides the required information, it is far from elegant.

A better solution is to calculate the harmonics in Probe.

The resulting plot is shown in Figure 3.2, which shows the worst case for a pulsed waveform and could be conservatively used for the design of the input filter.

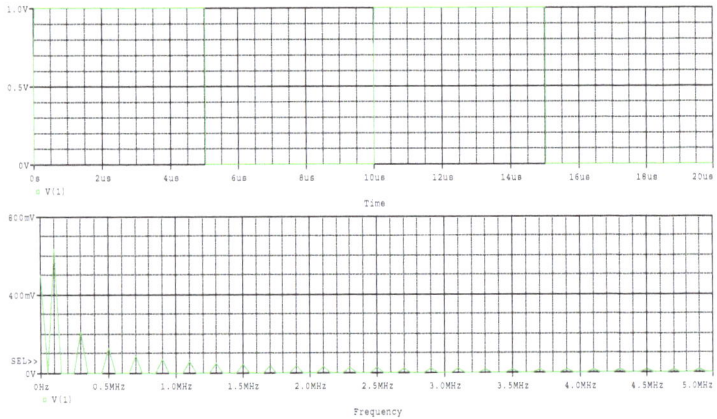

Figure 3.2

The FFT Feature of the Probe Graphical Waveform Post Processor is Used to Calculate the Harmonics of a Square Wave

Example 3—.STEP Command Calculates Harmonics

The next example uses the PSpice .STEP command to sweep the duty cycle from 5% to 95% and look at the fundamental amplitude of the resulting square wave. As in the previous example, V1 is a pulsed voltage source. In this case, the pulse has an initial amplitude of 1V and switches to 0V after delay "TON." "TON" is swept from 0.5 to 9.5μs in 0.5-μs steps.

When the simulation is finished, you can use Probe to display the X-Y data, or you may view the output file in a text editor. You will have a graph of the fundamental harmonic versus "TON." This confirms the previous statement that the 50% duty cycle was the maxima and provides a reference you may find helpful in the future.

```
EX3: .STEP ANALYSIS
.PROBE
.PARAM TON=0.5u
.STEP PARAM TON 0.5u 9.5u 0.5u
.TRAN .1U 10U
.PRINT TRAN V(1)
V1 1 0 PULSE 1 0 {TON}
.END
```

The FFT results of the .STEP analysis are shown in Figures 3.3 and 3.4.

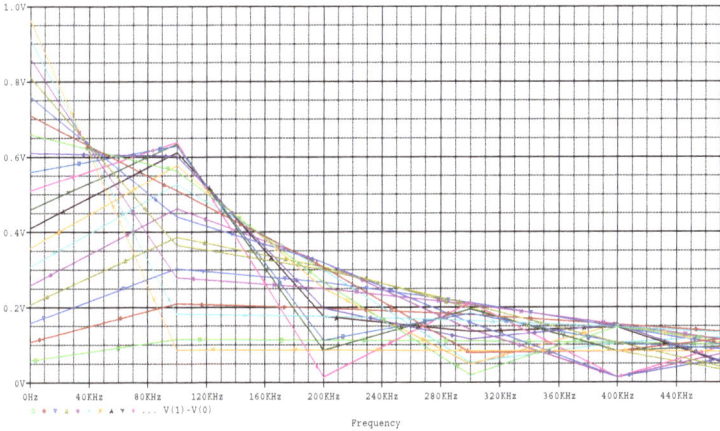

Figure 3.3

FFT of the .STEP Analysis

Note: The waveform with the largest amplitude at 100kHz corresponds to the 50% duty cycle (TON= 5μs).

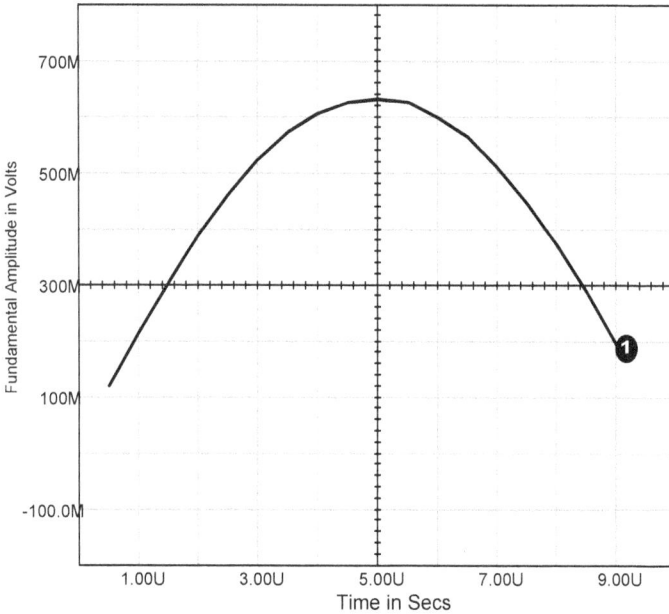

Fundamental Harmonic vs Ton for 10uSec Pulse Tra

Figure 3.4

.STEP Analysis Result shows the 50% Duty Cycle as the Maxima

Example 4—EMI Filter Design

In order to design the EMI filter, we need to define a converter that will operate with it. For the purpose of this example, let us assume that we have a power converter that will operate with an input voltage of 18 to 32 VDC. The converter output power will be 75W and will have an operating efficiency of 75%. The converter will have a switching frequency of 100kHz. The conducted emissions requirement allows the 1mA peak to be reflected back to the input lines. A second-order filter will be used.

Let us follow the procedures that were defined in the EMI design flowchart. Step 1 is to calculate the input impedance.

Calculating the Input Impedance

The input impedance was defined earlier in this chapter as:

$$\frac{V_{in}^2 * efficiency}{P_{out}}$$

It is obvious that the lowest impedance will occur at the minimum input voltage. This value can be calculated as:

$$\frac{18^2 \times 0.75}{75} = 3.24\Omega$$

Calculating the Harmonic Content

Because no detail is provided regarding the pulse current waveforms, we will assume that the duty cycle is 50%. The average input current is:

$$I_{avg} = \frac{P_{out}}{V_{in} * efficiency} = \frac{75}{18 \times 0.75} = 5.56A$$

At a duty cycle of 50%, the peak amplitude will be 11.12A. In the previous harmonic analysis, we defined the fundamental harmonic to be $0.636I_{pk} = 7.08A$.

Calculating the Required Attenuation

With a maximum reflected ripple current of 1mA peak, we can define the attenuation required as:

$$Attenuation = \frac{7.08}{0.001} = 7080 = 77 \text{ dB}$$

Calculating the Component Values

The attenuation for a second-order filter can be defined as:

$$\text{Attenuation} = \left(\frac{f_{\text{switch}}}{f_{\text{filter}}}\right)^2$$

We can compute the filter frequency as:

$$\frac{100\text{ kHz}}{\sqrt{\text{Attenuation}}} = \frac{100\text{ kHz}}{84.14} = 1188\text{ Hz.}$$

The values of L and C can be defined by setting their impedances to the input converter input impedance at the filter resonant frequency, as defined above.

$$C = \frac{1}{2\pi(1188)(3.24)} = 41.35\ \mu\text{F}$$

$$L = \frac{3.24}{2\pi(1188)}434\ \mu\text{H}$$

Note that the characteristic impedance of the filter is defined by:

$$Z_o = \sqrt{\frac{L}{C}} = \sqrt{\frac{434\ \mu\text{H}}{41.35\ \mu\text{F}}} = 3.24\ \Omega$$

…which is equal to the converter input impedance. In an actual design, it is a good practice to provide a 6dB margin for these characteristics.

Damping Elements

While this filter provides the proper impedance matching and the required attenuation, the impedance will be quite high at the resonant frequency of the filter. The only damping elements in the circuit are the DC resistance (DCR) of the inductor and the equivalent series resistance (ESR) of the capacitor (which we have not defined). It is normally necessary to provide damping of the L-

C filter in order to restrict the impedance of the filter at the resonant frequency. A shunt series R-C network is used for this purpose. The value of the damping capacitor is generally 3 to 5 times greater than that of the filter capacitor, and the value of the damping resistor is generally close to the characteristic impedance of the filter. The PSpice .Step command is ideal for defining these elements.

The following circuit is designed to measure the impedance of the filter, while sweeping the damping capacitor from 120 to 200μF in 40-μF increments. For each value of the damping capacitor, the damping resistor will be swept from 0.5 to 2 times the characteristic impedance (1.6 to 6.4Ω) in 0.6-Ω increments. The test results, PSpice listing and schematic of the test circuit (Figure 3.5) are shown below.

```
EX4: TO MEASURE THE IMPEDANCE OF A FILTER
.AC DEC 10 100HZ 1MEGHZ
.PARAM CDAMP=120u
.PARAM RDAMP=1.6
*.STEP PARAM CDAMP 120U 200U 40U
.STEP PARAM RDAMP 1.6 6.4 .6
.PROBE
C1 1 0 41.35U
C2 1 2 {CDAMP}
R1 2 0 {RDAMP}
I1 0 1 AC 1
L1 0 1 434U
.END
```

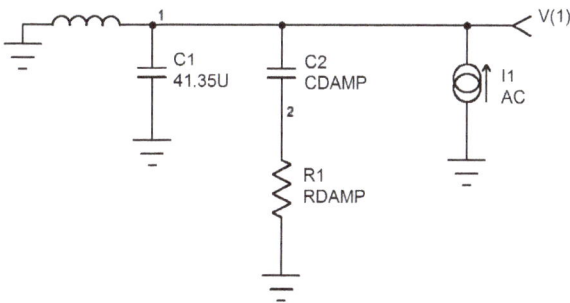

107

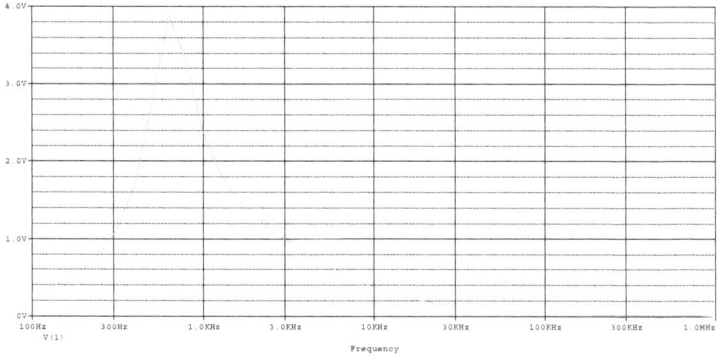

Figure 3.5

Schematic and Frequency Plot of the Test Circuit used to Measure the Impedance of the Filter

Note: The waveform V(1) is equivalent to the impedance because the input is a current (I1 1 0 AC 1). The case for CDAMP = 120μF and RDAMP = 1.6Ω is shown.

The results are provided in the output file and are shown below.

Sweep Analysis of EX4.ckt

Count	CDAMP	RDAMP	Maximum
1	1.20000e-004	1.60000e+000	3.891
2	1.20000e-004	2.20000e+000	3.440
3	1.20000e-004	2.80000e+000	3.557
4	1.20000e-004	3.40000e+000	3.916
5	1.20000e-004	4.00000e+000	4.395
6	1.20000e-004	4.60000e+000	4.840
7	1.20000e-004	5.20000e+000	5.248
8	1.20000e-004	5.80000e+000	5.619
9	1.20000e-004	6.40000e+000	6.104
10	1.60000e-004	1.60000e+000	2.994
11	1.60000e-004	2.20000e+000	2.869
12	1.60000e-004	2.80000e+000	3.153

13	1.60000e-004	3.40000e+000	3.672
14	1.60000e-004	4.00000e+000	4.161
15	1.60000e-004	4.60000e+000	4.614
16	1.60000e-004	5.20000e+000	5.033
17	1.60000e-004	5.80000e+000	5.580
18	1.60000e-004	6.40000e+000	6.121
19	2.00000e-004	1.60000e+000	2.489
20	2.00000e-004	2.20000e+000	2.593
21	2.00000e-004	2.80000e+000	3.024
22	2.00000e-004	3.40000e+000	3.547
23	2.00000e-004	4.00000e+000	4.038
24	2.00000e-004	4.60000e+000	4.494
25	2.00000e-004	5.20000e+000	5.040
26	2.00000e-004	5.80000e+000	5.591
27	2.00000e-004	6.40000e+000	6.137

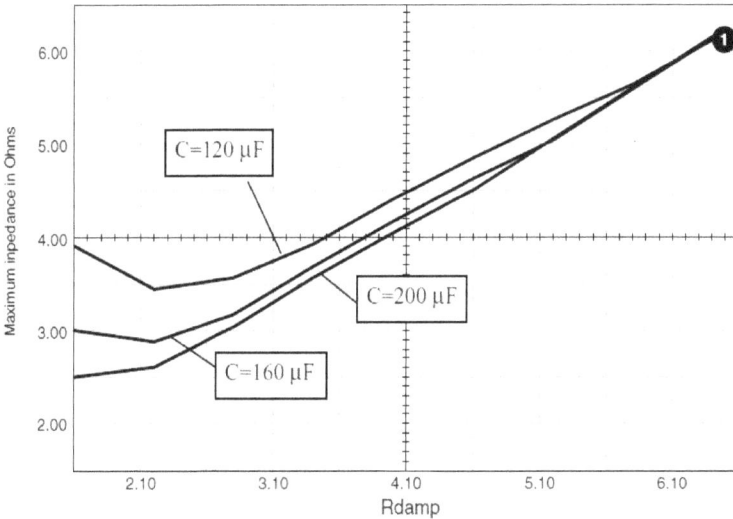

Figure 3.6

Family of Curves showing the Maximum Impedance versus the Damping Resistor Value

Note: Each curve represents a different capacitor value.

The impedance was exceeded with the 120µF damping capacitor (see Figure 3.6). If we use a 160µF capacitor, the impedance will be minimized with a 2.2Ω damping resistor. A lower impedance could be achieved with a 200µF damping capacitor and a 1.6Ω damping resistor. We will select the 160µF capacitor and the 2.2Ω resistor.

The following simulation shows the impedance characteristics and the reflected ripple of the filter (see also Figures 3.7 and 3.8).

```
EMI2: TO SHOW THE REFLECTED RIPPLE OF THE FILTER
.AC DEC 10 100HZ 100KHZ
.TRAN 1U 10M 9980U .1u UIC
.PROBE
C1 2 0 41.35U
C2 2 1 160U
R1 1 0 2.2
I1 0 2 AC 1 PULSE 0 11 0.1U   0.1U   0.1U 5U 10U
L1 0 2 434U IC=-5.5
.END
```

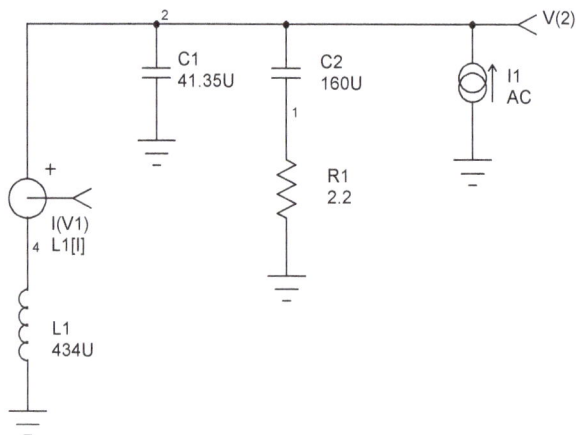

Figure 3.7

Circuit used to show the Impedance and the Reflected Ripple of the Filter

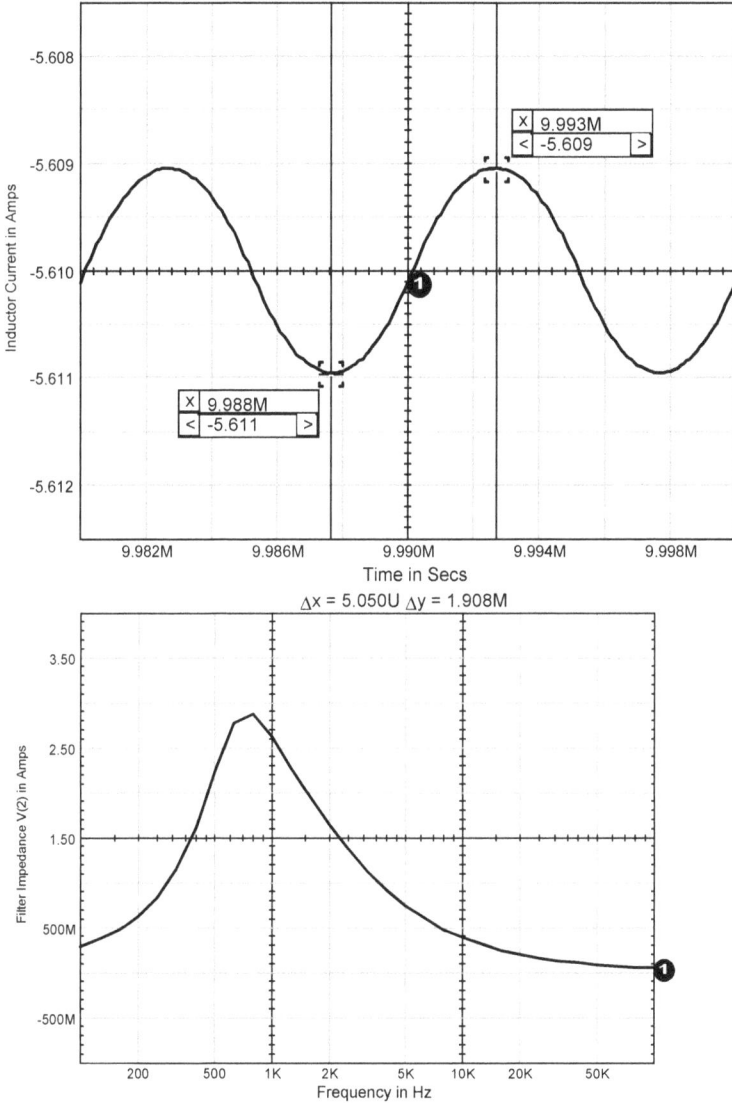

Figure 3.8

Current in the Inductor (top) due to a Current Pulse Input, and Impedance Characteristics over Frequency (bottom) for the Filter Circuit of Figure 3.7

Fourth-Order Filters

Because the physical size of power converters is continually shrinking, higher order filters are being used more often than not. The filter is designed in much the same way as the second-order filter. The following example demonstrates the design of a fourth-order filter using the same design parameters as those that we used for the previous filter.

The "octave" rule basically states that resonances should be at least an octave apart. In an effort to be conservative, let us use a factor of 2.5. The attenuation of the filter can be defined as:

$$\text{Attenuation} = \left(\frac{f_{\text{switch}}}{f_1}\right)^2 * \left(\frac{f_{\text{switch}}}{2.5f_1}\right)^2 = \frac{f_{\text{switch}}^4}{6.25f_1^4}$$

If we set the attenuation at 7080, as in the previous example, and solve for f_1 we obtain f_1=6.895 kHz. The second pole is then at $2.5f_1$=17.237 kHz.

The impedance of each section should be designed to be lower than the impedance of the converter, which we had determined to be 3.24 Ω in the previous example. The filter is loaded by the negative resistance of the converter and produces a combined impedance of:

$$Z_{\text{loaded}} = \frac{Z_{\text{in}} * Z_{\text{o}}}{Z_{\text{in}} + Z_{\text{o}}}$$

The loaded filter Q is defined as:

$$Q = \frac{Z_{\text{loaded}}}{Z_{\text{o}}}$$

…where Z_{O} is the filter characteristic impedance defined by:

$$Z_{\text{o}} = \sqrt{\frac{L}{C}}$$

If we combine the above equations, we have:

$$Q = \frac{Z_{in} * Z_o}{(Z_{in} + Z_o) Z_o}$$

$$Z_o = -\left(\frac{Q-1}{Q}\right) Z_{in}$$

The filter Q is generally maintained below a value of 2. If we set $Q=2$ and solve for Z_O we obtain:

$$Z_o = -\left(\frac{2-1}{2}\right)(-3.24) = 1.62 \ \Omega$$

If we use this impedance and the calculated resonant frequencies, we can define both inductors and both capacitors.

$$L_1 = \frac{1.62}{2\pi(6895)} = 37 \ \mu H$$

$$C_1 = \frac{1}{2\pi(6895)(1.62)} = 14 \ \mu F$$

$$L_2 = \frac{1.62}{2\pi(17,237)} = 15 \ \mu H$$

$$C_2 = \frac{1}{2\pi(17,237)(1.62)} = 5.7 \ \mu F$$

As shown in the previous example, we can use the .Step command to sweep the values of the damping capacitor and the damping resistor. If we use a range of 3 to 5 times the value of the real capacitor, we will sweep the damper capacitor from 42 to 70μF in steps of 14μF. We will sweep the damper resistor from one-half to twice the Z_O of the filter, i.e. from 0.8 to 3.2Ω in 0.2-Ω steps.

The schematic for the fourth-order filter and its impedance response are shown in Figure 3.9.

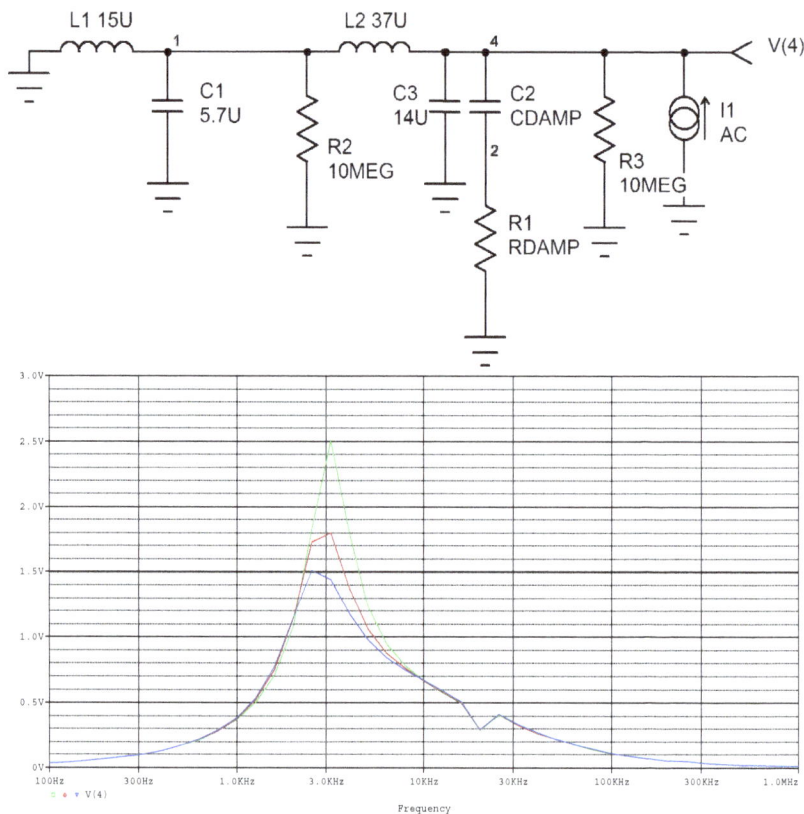

Figure 3.9

Fourth-Order Filter Schematic and Impedance Response

Note: Two 10MΩ resistors have been added. To aid circuit convergence, the resistors were added to the nodes that are purely reactive. The circuit listing and output file are shown below.

A sweep of the maximum impedance as a function of the damping resistor and the damping capacitor was also performed. The results of the sweep are shown in Figure 3.10. Each curve is for a different value of damping capacitor.

```
4THORD: A 4TH ORDER FILTER
.AC DEC 10 100HZ 1MEGHZ
.PROBE
.PARAM CDAMP=42u
.PARAM RDAMP=0.8
.STEP PARAM CDAMP 42U 70U 14U
*.STEP PARAMRDAMP .8 3.2 .2
.PRINT AC V(4) VP(4)
C1  1 0 5.7U
C2 4 2 {CDAMP}
R1 2 0 {RDAMP}
I1 0 4 AC 1
L2 1 4 37U
C3 4 0 14U
R2 1 0 10MEG
R3 4 0 10MEG
L1 0 1 15U
.END
```

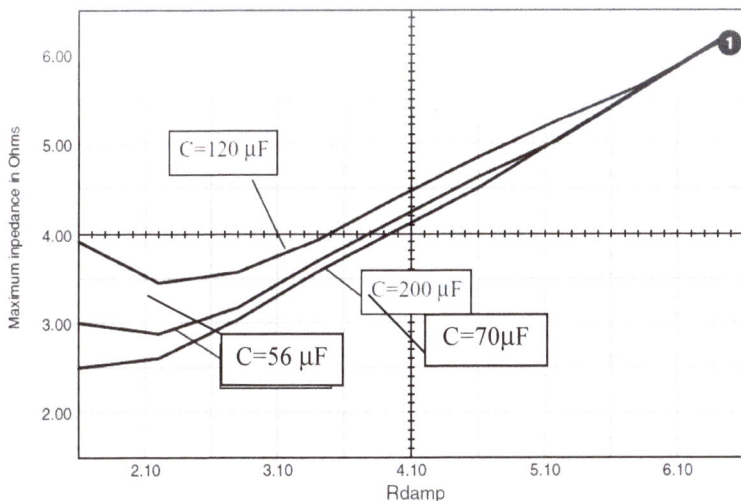

Figure 3.10

Family of Curves showing the Maximum Impedance of the Fourth-Order Filter

115

Count	CDAMP	RD	AMP Maximum
1	4.20000e-005	8.00000e-001	2.507
2	4.20000e-005	1.00000e+000	2.215
3	4.20000e-005	1.20000e+000	2.027
4	4.20000e-005	1.40000e+000	2.024
5	4.20000e-005	1.60000e+000	2.083
6	4.20000e-005	1.80000e+000	2.133
7	4.20000e-005	2.00000e+000	2.285
8	4.20000e-005	2.20000e+000	2.458
9	4.20000e-005	2.40000e+000	2.627
10	4.20000e-005	2.60000e+000	2.791
11	4.20000e-005	2.80000e+000	2.950
12	4.20000e-005	3.00000e+000	3.103
13	5.60000e-005	8.00000e-001	1.799
14	5.60000e-005	1.00000e+000	1.716
15	5.60000e-005	1.20000e+000	1.659
16	5.60000e-005	1.40000e+000	1.727
17	5.60000e-005	1.60000e+000	1.820
18	5.60000e-005	1.80000e+000	1.979
19	5.60000e-005	2.00000e+000	2.158
20	5.60000e-005	2.20000e+000	2.334
21	5.60000e-005	2.40000e+000	2.505
22	5.60000e-005	2.60000e+000	2.670
23	5.60000e-005	2.80000e+000	2.830
24	5.60000e-005	3.00000e+000	2.985
25	7.00000e-005	8.00000e-001	1.512
26	7.00000e-005	1.00000e+000	1.448
27	7.00000e-005	1.20000e+000	1.461
28	7.00000e-005	1.40000e+000	1.582
29	7.00000e-005	1.60000e+000	1.728
30	7.00000e-005	1.80000e+000	1.913
31	7.00000e-005	2.00000e+000	2.093
32	7.00000e-005	2.20000e+000	2.269
33	7.00000e-005	2.40000e+000	2.440
34	7.00000e-005	2.60000e+000	2.606
35	7.00000e-005	2.80000e+000	2.767
36	7.00000e-005	3.00000e+000	2.922

As evident from the data, we could "squeak by" with the 56μF damper or conservatively use the 70μF value. We will use 68μF, which is the nearest standard value to 70μF. The damper resistance is optimum at 1Ω.

Note: The 1Ω value includes the ESR of the capacitor, so select the resistor value less than the ESR value of the capacitor.

The results of our new filter simulation are shown in Figure 3.11.

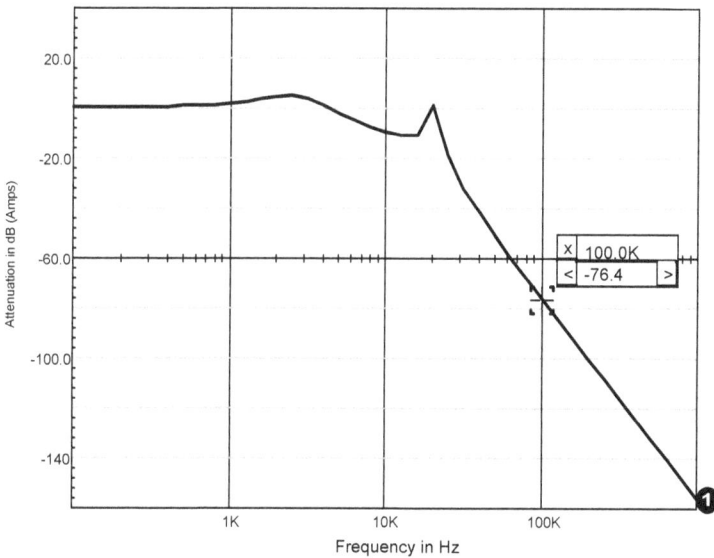

Figure 3.11

Filter Attenuation with Optimized Damper Section Values

The attenuation is very close to the desired 77dB limit, and the impedance is well below the 3.24Ω stability requirement. Notice the peaking of the undamped first stage of the filter. The .STEP analysis may be used to determine optimum values for the damper section also, if desired. We will use the same capacitor ratio as we had determined for the second stage. This yields a damper capacitor value of approximately 33μF, and we will use the same 1Ω value for the damper resistor. While we are at it, let us change the 5.7μF capacitor to 6.8μF in order to obtain a standard value and to slightly improve the attenuation. Notice that the peaking of the first stage has nearly been eliminated, and the attenuation has been improved to meet the requirement of 77dB (see Figure 3.12).

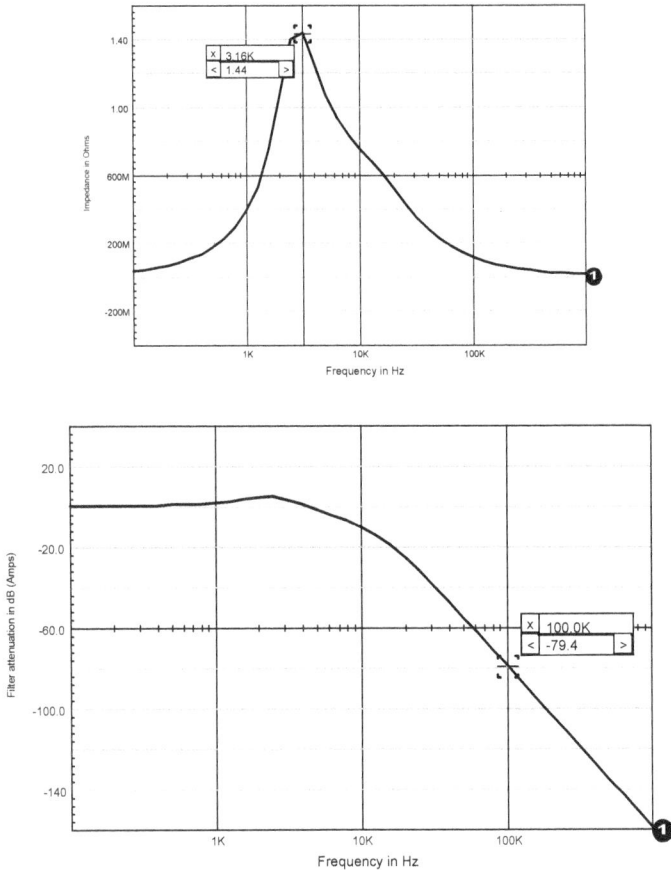

Figure 3.12

The Filter Attenuation Graph shows the Elimination of the Peaking in the First Stage after Changes in the Damper Section

Inrush Current

In many applications, the input voltage is applied as a step. This may be the result of a switch or relay closure. The current that is drawn by the filter during this application of power is referred to as the inrush current. The inrush current may be of concern, because of stress or fuse ratings. We can evaluate the inrush characteristics of our filter by applying a step input from 0 V to the maximum input voltage (32V in our design) while monitoring the current that is drawn by our filter.

Note: We can use the same model for both the AC and transient analyses.

The results of the inrush current simulation are shown in Figure 3.13. The inrush current has a peak value of 34A. The output voltage of the filter is also displayed. When a 32V step voltage was applied, the filter output overshot to almost 48V. This is an important consideration for selecting and derating the components that are used in the switching converter that follows the filter.

```
4THORD2.cir
.AC DEC 10 100 1meg
.TRAN 1u 500u
.PROBE
C2 1 2 68U
C3 1 0 14U
R1 2 0 1
R2 3 0 10MEG
R3 1 0 10MEG
L1 4 3 15U
L2 3 1 37U
I1 0 1 AC=1
V1 4 0 PULSE 0 32
C1 3 0 6.8U
C4 3 5 33U
R4 5 0 1
.END
```

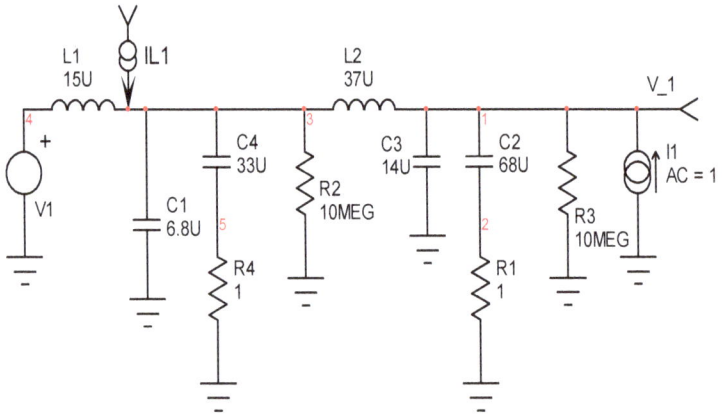

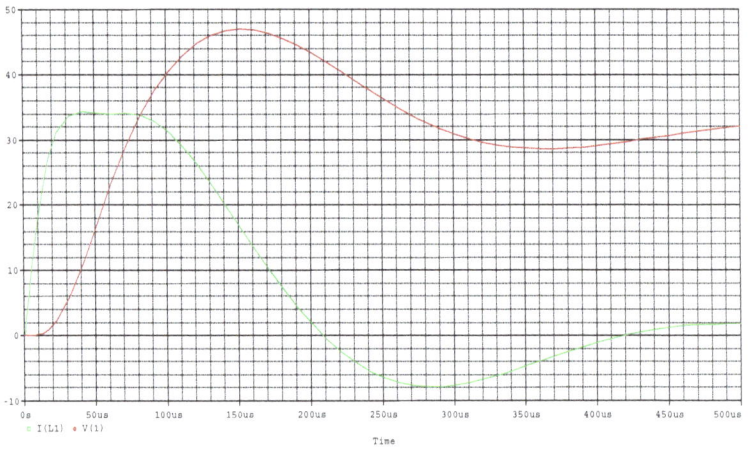

Figure 3.13

Schematic, Netlist, and Simulation Results for the Inrush Current Simulation

MPP Inductors

The previous example utilized ideal inductors. In real applications, however, the inductors generally do not provide a constant inductance. Rather, they tend to saturate as current is passed through them. One of the more popular cores used in these applications is Magnetics[®] MPP style.

Using MPP cores for our EMI filter provides a more realistic model than the ideal inductor model. The following simulations use a Magnetics 55131 core with 29 turns for the 15μH inductor and a Magnetics 55121 core with 36 turns for the 37μH inductor (see Figure 3.14). DC resistances are 0.035Ω and 0.025Ω, respectively. Note the third terminal on the inductor symbol. The extra terminal is used to monitor the instantaneous inductance value.

```
4THINRS3.cir
.PROBE
.AC DEC 10 100 1meg
.TRAN .1u 500u 0 .5u
C2 2 3 68U
C3 2 0 14U
R1 3 0 1
C4 1 7 33U
R2 1 0 10MEG
R3 2 0 10MEG
R4 7 0 1
I1 0 2 AC=1 ; DC=-4.5 used for Figure 3.16
X1 6 1 8 MP55131 Params: N=29 DCR=.035 IC=0
X2 1 2 9 MP55121 Params: N=36 DCR=.035 IC=0
V1 4 0 PULSE 0 32
V2 4 6
C1 1 0 6.8U
.END
```

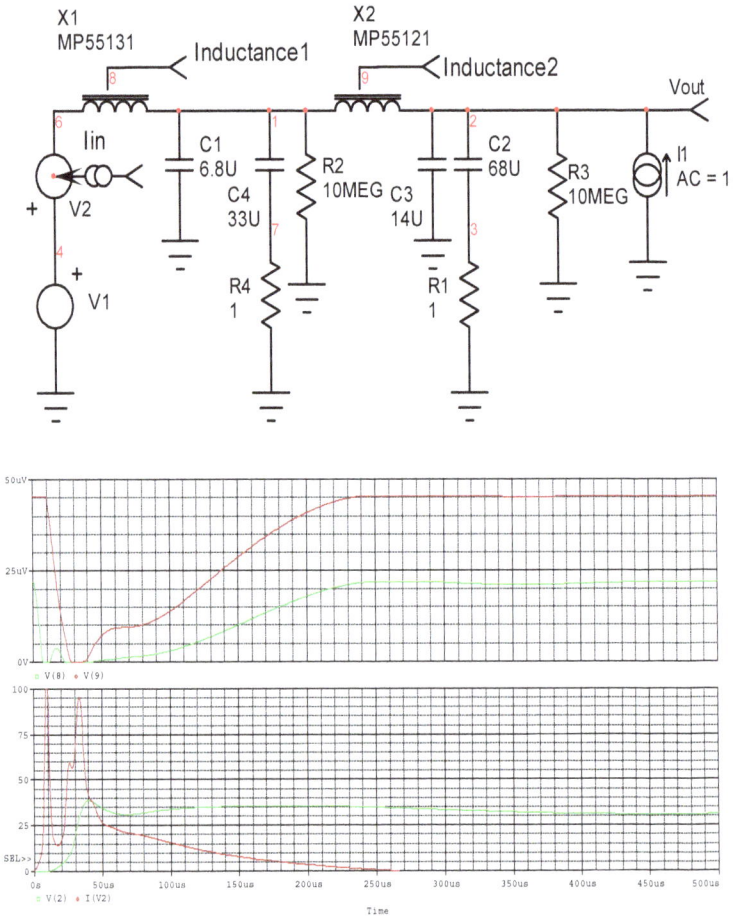

Figure 3.14

A More Realistic Simulation using MPP Cores for EMI filter Design

Note: The instantaneous inductance is shown for both MPP cores (top graph) and for the input current and output voltage.

This simulation also calculates the attenuation and impedance of the filter without DC current using the AC analysis (see Figure 3.15).

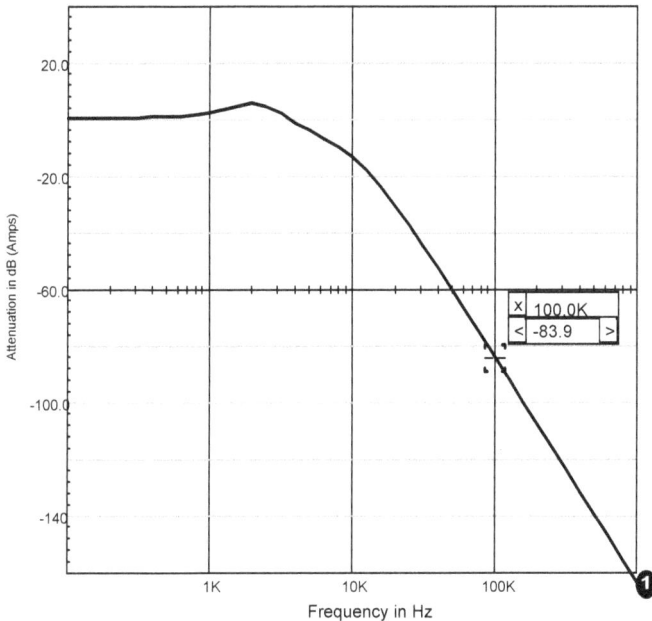

Figure 3.15

Simulation Result of the Attenuation without a DC Current

If we add a DC current value of 4.5A (100W/22V), we will see the data for the filter as it operates under full load conditions. The inductance of each MPP core can be monitored using markers as the simulation progresses. The schematic will provide the values at the steady state condition. If we view the inductance, we will see the value of inductance during the inrush current.

The first simulation in Figure 3.14 showed the results of the simulation without DC current.

As you can see, the inrush current is considerably higher than the value we expected in the first simulation. This is due to the saturation of the inductors. The waveforms in Figure 3.14 show the inductance during the inrush current.

The input inductor is almost completely saturated by the inrush current. The inductance value in the schematic is somewhat higher than the design value.

The second simulation in Figures 3.16 and 3.17 shows the results of the simulation with a DC value of 4.5A added to the current source I1.

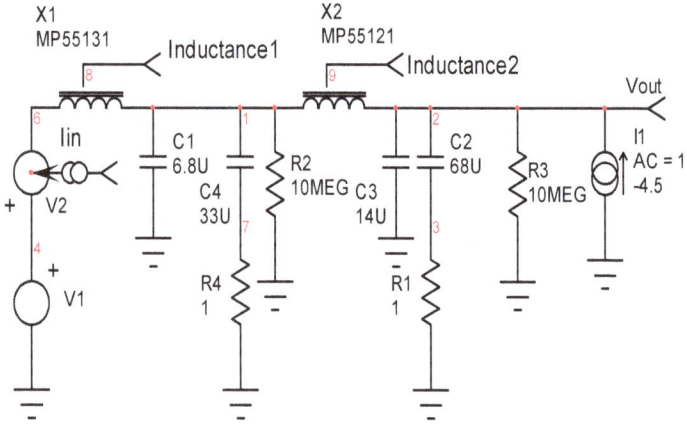

Figure 3.16

A Realistic Model using MPP Cores with a 4.5A Steady State Current

The current is negative because of the direction of the current source. The inductor values are almost identical to the design values.

The inrush current analysis has not been performed, because it is unrealistic to have the 4.5A current flowing when the converter is turned on. The attenuation analysis was performed, and the results are shown in Figure 3.17.

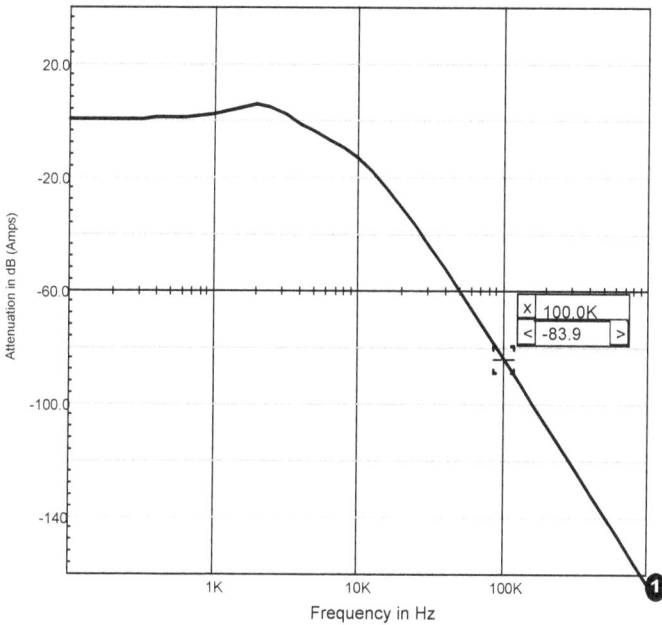

Figure 3.17

Effect of the DC Current on the Attenuation Analysis

The attenuation has been degraded by approximately 4dB as a result of the DC current; however, it is still sufficient to meet the 77dB requirement.

The inrush current simulation is one of the most difficult simulations to correlate with real hardware. This is generally due to the effects of the source impedance of the test setup. Keep in mind that the power supplies and cables have resistance and inductance. The SPICE model must account for these elements, or they must absolutely be minimized. With this in mind, it is certainly feasible to get good correlation with a little care.

The example circuit in Figure 3.18 was constructed for the purpose of determining the accuracy of the model. The 28.8μH input inductor is constructed as 24 turns on a 58271 core, and the two 25.1μH inductors are constructed as 28 turns on two stacked

58291 cores. The results are shown in Figures 3.19 and 3.20. The inductance of these two inductors is shown in Figure 3.18. Note that the input inductor drops by more than 60% as a result of the inrush current.

```
emi inrush correlation.cir
.PROBE
.TRAN 10n 250u 0 50n
C2 10 11 3U
C3 9 2 1U
R1 11 0 4.99
R2 2 0 4.99
C4 9 0 1U
X1 9 7 3 MP58291 Params: N=28 DCR=.13 IC=0
X2 7 10 6 MP58291 Params: N=28 DCR=.13 IC=0
X3 1 9 8 MP58271 Params: N=24 DCR=.1 IC=0
V1 4 1 DC=0
V2 4 0 PULSE 0 28 50u .1U .1U 100M 200M
C1 10 0 1U
.END
```

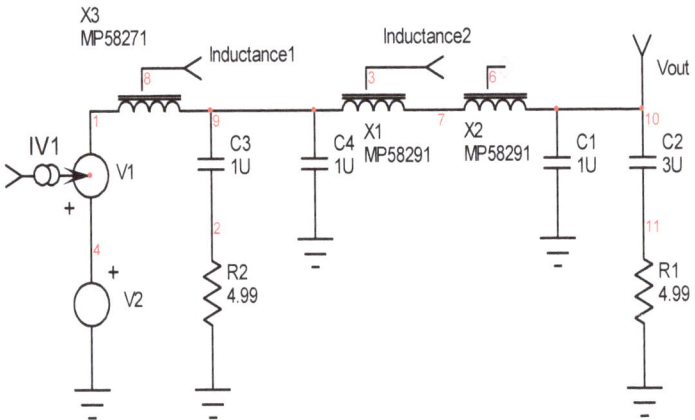

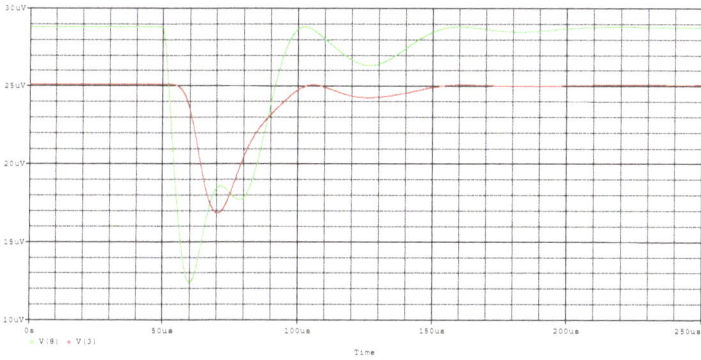

Figure 3.18

EMI Filter Constructed for Inrush Correlation

Note: The inductance of the cores is shown over time.

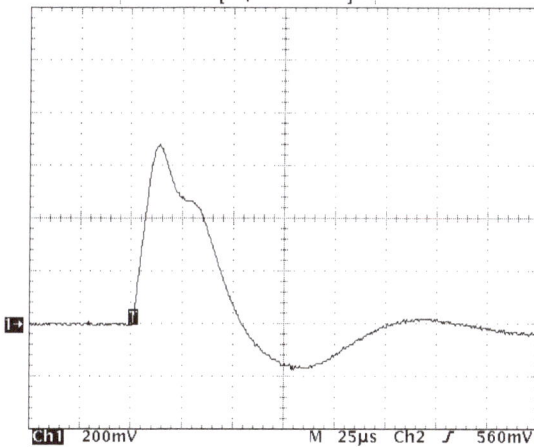

Figure 3.19

Inrush Measured Result

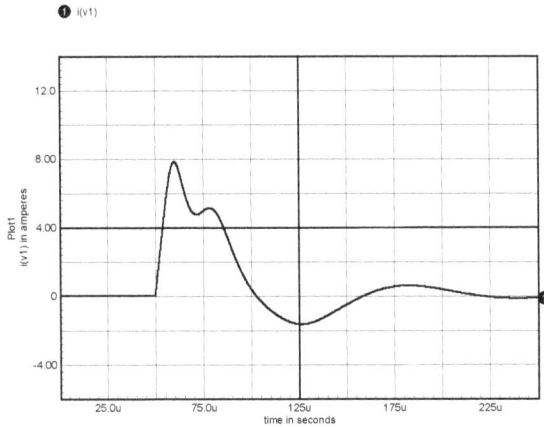

Figure 3.20

Inrush Simulated Result

The correlation results are excellent despite the saturation of the input inductor.

Inrush Current Limiting

Some circuits are sensitive to the level of inrush current. In order to limit this current, two basic possibilities exist: the input inductors can be oversized in order to prevent saturation, or an inrush limiting scheme can be used.

Many schemes have been used as effective inrush current limiters. Some of the more popular schemes are as follows:

- Add a relay or SCR across a current-limiting resistor. This allows the filter capacitors to charge through a limiting resistor and then shorts the resistor after the input capacitors are charged.

- Solid-state devices such as MOSFETs can be used to limit the input filter's dv/dt in order to limit the current.

- Use resistors with a negative temperature coefficient. These devices are commercially available and provide a limiting resistance at turn-on. Once they are loaded, the resistors heat up and drastically reduce in value.

As a final example, let us simulate an inrush current limiting scheme. The following schematic shows the addition of a MOSFET inrush limiter. The zener diode limits the gate voltage to 15V, which is well below the 20V rating. If the zener were not present, the gate voltage would charge to the input voltage and damage the MOSFET.

```
INRSHLMT.cir
.PROBE
.TRAN 1u 500u 0 .5u
C2 2 3 68U
C3 2 0 14U
R1 3 0 1
C4 1 7 33U
R2 1 0 10MEG
R3 2 0 10MEG
C6 5 10 .01U
R4 7 0 1
R6 6 5 100K
I1 0 2 AC=1
X1 6 1 8 MP55131 Params: N=29 DCR=.035 IC=0
X2 1 2 9 MP55121 Params: N=36 DCR=.035 IC=0
V1 4 10 PULSE 0 32
D1 10 5 DN965
V2 4 6
C1 1 0 6.8U
.END
```

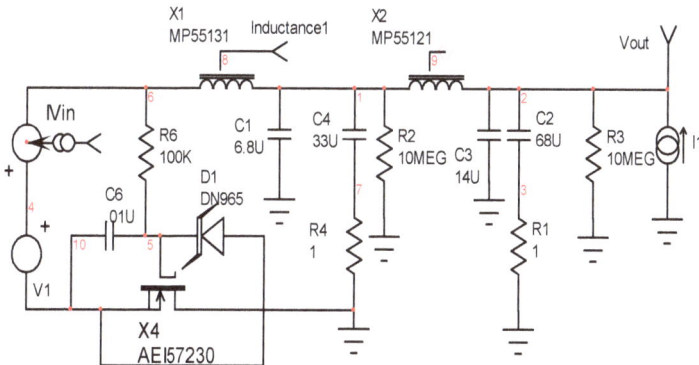

129

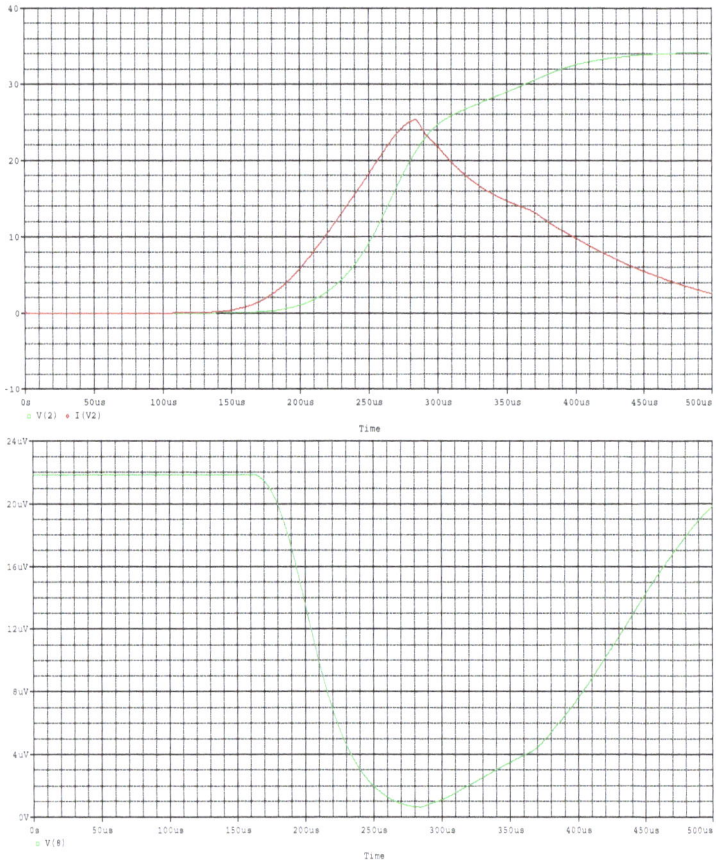

Figure 3.21

A Filter Design using a MOSFET Inrush Current Limiter Scheme

The waveforms show the inrush current with the addition of the MOSFET limiter. Different values of R6 and C6 will produce different results; however, this is adequate in order to demonstrate the concept. The selected MOSFET has an conduction-resistance (R_{DSON}) that limits the power dissipation to an acceptable value.

Other implementations of inrush current limiting use negative temperature coefficient (NTC) thermistors designed specifically for this application. Resistor inrush limiters, which are bypassed using an SCR or a relay after the initial inrush, are also fairly common. In this case it is important to assure that the load on the filter is not applied until *after* the bypass device is enabled; otherwise the input filter may not fully charge, resulting in a second inrush when the bypass device is enabled.

Chapter 4

Buck Topology Converters

MANY POWER CONVERTERS in use today are based on buck topologies. The buck topology includes all converters that produce an output voltage which is proportional to a controlled duty cycle. The switched voltage is averaged by an L-C filter, which results in a DC voltage. Examples of buck topologies include buck regulators, forward converters, and push-pull converters.

Hysteretic Switching Regulator

The circuit shown in Figure 4.1 is the simplest form of a buck regulator. The circuit was popular in the 1970s because of its simplicity and extremely low parts count. The 723 regulator IC operates as a comparator that has a driver and a voltage reference. The circuit has many drawbacks, such as variable frequency and poor dynamic control, because it is basically an uncompensated oscillator. The advent of high-technology pulse width modulator control ICs has almost replaced this form of regulator. Circuits such as this can still be found in many linear data books and low-cost commercial products. The circuit does, however, demonstrate the principles of switching regulators.

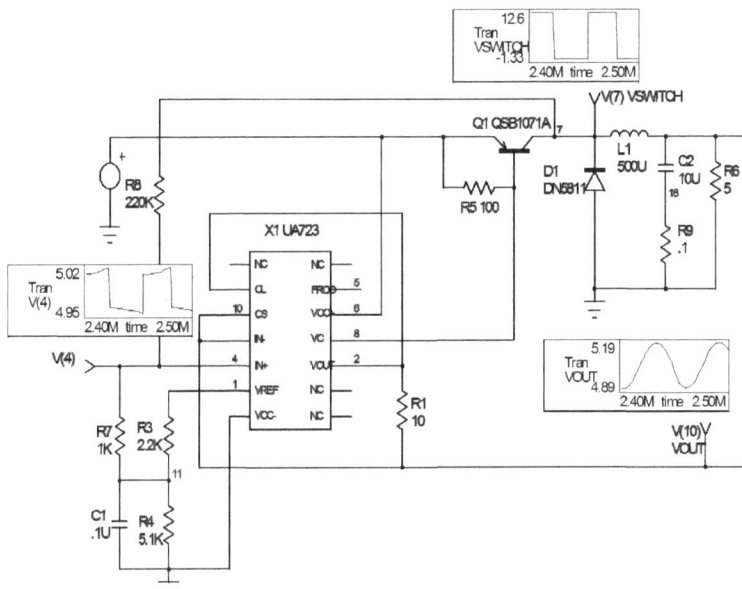

Figure 4.1

The Simplest Form of a Buck Regulator Circuit

The input voltage is switched by Q1. The switched voltage is averaged by L1 and C2.

During the switch-off time, a current circulates through D1. The averaged output is fed to the load resistor R6. Resistor R8 introduces the hysteresis (positive feedback) and causes the circuit to oscillate. The switch voltage and output voltage waveforms are shown in the graphs in Figure 4.1.

```
HYSTREG: BUCK REGULATOR
.TRAN .1U 2500U 2400U UIC
.PROBE
* V(10)=VOUT
* V(7)=VSWITCH
R1 2 10 10
R3 1 11 2.2K
R4 11 0 5.1K
C1 11 0 .1U IC=5
Q1 7 8 6 QSB1071A
R5 6 8 100
U1 6 0 PULSE 0 12
D1 0 7 DN5811
L1 7 10 500U IC=1
C2 10 16 10U IC=5
R6 10 0 5
R7 4 11 1K
R8 7 4 220K
R9 16 0 .1
X1 10 10 4 1 0 2 8 6 5 2 UA723
.END
```

Average (State Space) versus Switching Level Transient Models

Switching circuit models typically fall into two major categories: average models and nonlinear transient switching models. Average models, also known as state space models, represent the operation of switching circuits via linear techniques, as opposed to switching techniques. All linear circuits fall into the category of average models. There are a number of citations in the References section that discuss the usage of average models in detail.

Transient models represent switching circuits in the time domain, in a manner as close to actual functionality as possible. It may seem desirable to simulate all circuits using transient models; however, transient models simulate much more slowly than their averaged model counterparts. Many characteristics, such as open-loop gain, are difficult to simulate using transient models.

Both types of models are included in this book and both may be used in the transient analyses for different purposes. You will quickly learn to determine which modeling technique you should apply to a specific problem.

The previous example uses transient simulation, which simulates the actual time-dependent functions of the circuit, such as the turn-on and turn-off of the semiconductor switch. There are many benefits of using this modeling approach. The model is very accurate; it displays phenomena such as switching spikes, propagation delays, and ripple and sampling effects; and it allows testing of different control ICs.

There are also disadvantages of the nonlinear approach. Simulations tend to take much longer, although with the ever-increasing computer power available on the desktop, simulations that were impractical only a few years ago can now be run in a matter of minutes.

There are some techniques that are available to speed up the simulation. They are listed in Chapter 9. More importantly, however, AC analysis is not possible because switching devices are either in their on or off state. To simulate such a circuit, the switching action must be averaged so that a small signal model can be generated.

Average modeling is reasonably accurate and extremely fast and supports AC as well as some transient analyses. The average models are therefore useful for simulations such as conducted susceptibility, open-loop phase gain, output impedance, and input impedance. The major drawback is that time domain information, such as ripple, spikes, gate charge, and instantaneous switching loss, is not available.

The generalized solution is to use the correct model depending on the behavior you want to investigate. Table 4.1 provides some assistance. Both models may be used during the development of a product and the ensuing worst-case tolerance analysis.

Examples of both methods are shown in this chapter.

Type of Analysis	Strategy
Power stage semiconductor stress analysis at startup	Transient Models - Accelerate startup by reducing soft-start time constant, if applicable. Use average model transient results as a road map.
Power stage semiconductor stress analysis at steady state	Transient Models - Initialize close to steady state average DC results. Only initialize largest time constants like output filter L and C, or compensation capacitors.
Power stage stress analysis with short circuited output	Transient Models - Initialize circuit then dynamically short output with voltage controlled switch.
Line or load transient response	Average Models - Disable UVLO for correct Dc results. Do not initialize circuit. Allow natural DC solution, then run transient analysis using source or switch to cause line or load transient.
Magnetic saturation, short circuit condition	Transient Models - Initialize circuit for steady state, then short output with a switch.
AC loop stability analysis	Average Models - Allow natural DC solution. Do not use initial conditions. Split feedback loop using a large inductor (blocks AC) then couple AC source signal to input side with a large capacitor.
Input noise filter design - ripple current measurement	Average or Transient Models - Drive the power stage using a voltage source with a fixed duty cycle. Controller with feedback is not necessary.

Table 4.1

Simulation Strategies for Typical Power Supply Analysis[5]

Average Modeling Example

As an example of average modeling, let us consider a simple buck regulator circuit. In order to keep the example simple, we will assume that we are using voltage mode control.

Voltage mode control was popular when pulse width modulator ICs, such as the SG1524, were first introduced. Most of the newer pulse width modulators utilize current mode control (which we will cover later in this chapter). The pulse width modulator compares the output of an error amplifier (V_C) to a fixed sawtooth waveform that has a lower voltage (V_L) and has an upper voltage (V_H). The output of the IC is a duty cycle, which is used to turn the semiconductor switch on and off. The duty cycle can be calculated as:

$$D = \frac{V_C - V_L}{V_H - V_L}$$

The output of the converter is the average of the switch duty cycle. The converter output is then defined as:

$$V_o = V_{in} D$$

Combining these two equations, we can obtain the modulator transfer function as:

$$V_o = \frac{V_{in}(V_C - V_L)}{V_H - V_L}$$

Similarly, the input current can be modeled as:

$$I_{in} = I_o D$$

Figure 4.2*a* demonstrates the basic structure and operation of the state averaging "PWM switch" subcircuit [5,66]. This model replaces the pulse width modulator switches. In Figure 4.2*b*, a DC analysis is performed, in which we sweep V2 from 0 to 1. This terminal is the duty cycle control, so we are sweeping the duty cycle from 0% to 100%.

As we monitor the output voltage and the input current, we can see that the output voltage is equal to $V_1 D$, and the input current is equal to $I_1 * D$, which agrees with our simplified derivation above.

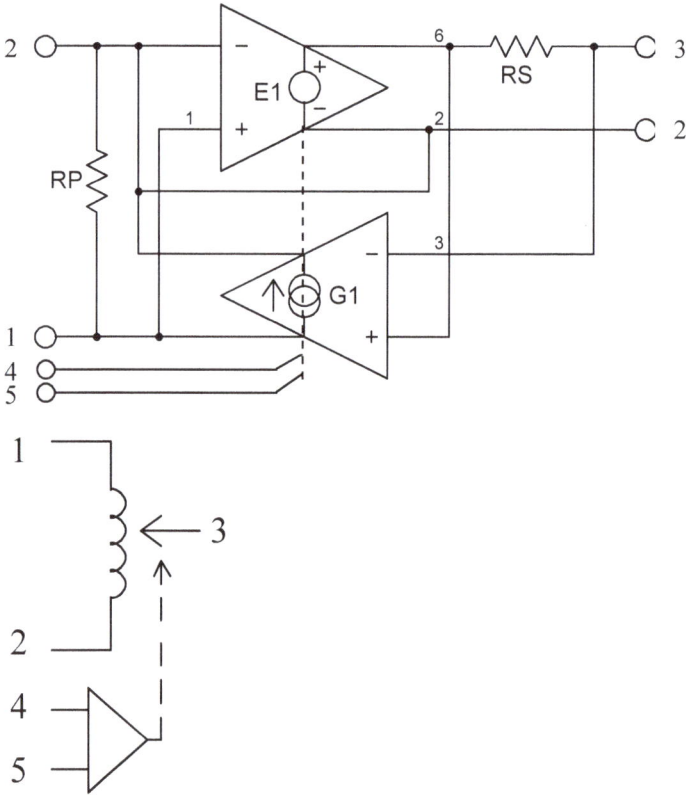

```
*Pulse Width Modulator
.SUBCKT PWM 1 2 3 4 5
E1 6 2 POLY(2) 1 2 4 5 0 0 0 0 1
G1 1 2 POLY(2) 6 3 4 5 0 0 0 0 1K
RP 1 2 1MEG
RS 3 6 1M
.ENDS
```

Figure 4.2

Pulse Width Modulator (PWM) Equivalent Circuit

Note: The dashed line indicates that the voltage $V_{(4,5)}$ controls the dependent sources G1 and E1. The PWM subcircuit sweeps the duty cycle from 0% to 100%.

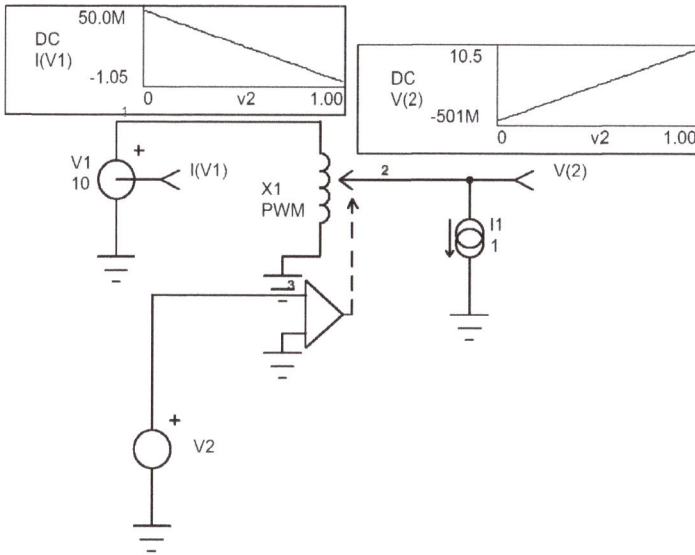

```
PWM: TO SIMULATE A VOLTAGE MODE CONVERTER
.DC V2 0 1 .01
.PROBE
.PRINT DC V(2) I(V1)
X1 1 0 2 3 0 PWM
V2 3 0
I1 2 0 1
V1 1 0 10
.END
```

SG1524A Buck Regulator

The PWM switch can easily be combined with a PWM IC model, such as the SG1524 pulse width modulator subcircuit, to simulate a complete voltage mode converter. The PWM switch represents the $V_o = V_{in}D$ function, while the SG1524 subcircuit correctly models the modulator gain.

The next example combines the SG1524A subcircuit with the PWM switch to model a voltage mode buck regulator (Figure 4.3). The SG1524 model is parameterized, which makes it more flexible. The parameters passed to the SG1524A subcircuit are:

T=10μs   Switching period

TO=1μs   Dead time

TS=0.25μs Transistor storage time

EP=3.5V   Peak sawtooth voltage

EO=0.5V   Minimum sawtooth voltage

You can view the SMPS_Book.LIB file to see how the parameters are utilized in the SG1524 subcircuit.

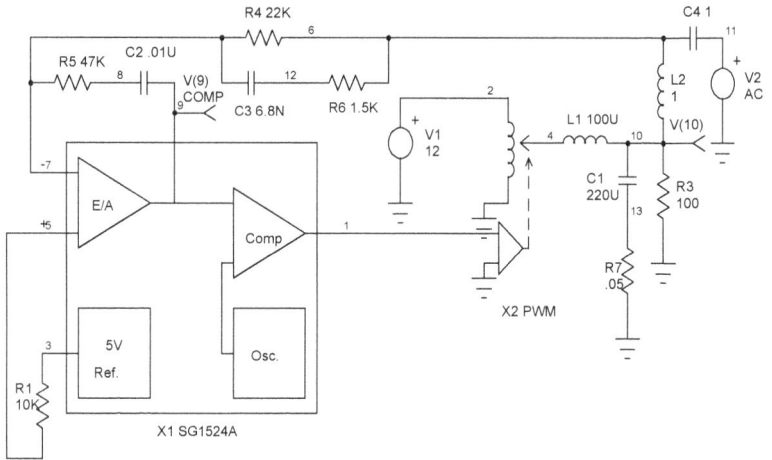

```
1524BUCK:  TO MODEL A VOLTAGE MODE BUCK REGULATOR
.OP
.AC DEC 25 100HZ 1000KHZ
.PROBE
* V(9)=COMP
.PRINT AC  V(10)  VP(10)  V(9)  VP(9)
X2 2 0 4 1 0 PWM
V1 2 0 12
R1 3 5 10K
L1 4 10 100U
C1 10 13 220U
R3 10 0 100
R4 7 6 22K
R5 7 8 47K
C2 8 9 .01U
C3 7 12 6.8N
L2 10 6 1
C4 6 11 1
V2 11 0 AC 1
R6 12 6 1.5K
R7 13 0 .05
X1 7 5 9 1 3 SG1524A Params: T=10U TO=1U TS=.25U EP=3.5 EO=.5
.END
```

Figure 4.3

Schematic and Top-Level Netlist of a Complete Voltage Mode Converter using the PWM Switch and SG1524

The regulator model is extremely simple. The SG1524A subcircuit contains the error amplifier, reference, and comparator sections. The comparator compares the output of the error amplifier with a sawtooth and generates a resultant duty cycle. The duty cycle is modified by the storage time and dead time parameters, which are passed to the subcircuit.

The output filter causes a double pole at:

$$F = \frac{1}{2\pi \sqrt{L_1 C_1}} = 1073 \, \text{Hz}$$

One of these two poles is canceled by R4 and C3, which has a corner frequency of:

$$F = \frac{1}{2\pi\, R_4 C_3} = 1064\ \text{Hz}$$

A third pole is caused by capacitor C2, which is used to provide maximum DC gain for regulation purposes. R5 provides a zero with C2 at a frequency of:

$$F = \frac{1}{2\pi\, R_5 C_2} = 338\ \text{Hz}$$

The zero is below the frequency of the output filter pole in order to improve phase margin. If the output filter has a lower Q (it normally does not), then the zero could be at a frequency that is closer to the output filter pole. An additional zero exists, because of the output filter capacitor ESR at:

$$F = \frac{1}{2\pi\, R_1 C_7} = 14,475\ \text{Hz}$$

This zero is canceled by R6 and C3, which has a corner frequency of:

$$F = \frac{1}{2\pi\, R_6 C_3} = 15,611\ \text{Hz}$$

The DC gain of the modulator is approximated by:

$$\text{Gain} = \frac{V_{in}\left(T - T_0\right)}{\left(E_P - E_0\right)T} = 3.6 = 11.1\ \text{dB}$$

The regulator is configured as an open-loop model in order to measure the Bode response. The inductor, L2, is set to 1H in order to effectively open the loop. The plots in Figures. 4.4, 4.5, and 4.6 show the modulator gain (VM(10)/VM(9) and VP(10) - VP(9), where VM is the magnitude and VP is the phase), the error amplifier gain (V(9)), and the overall loop gain (V(10)), respectively.

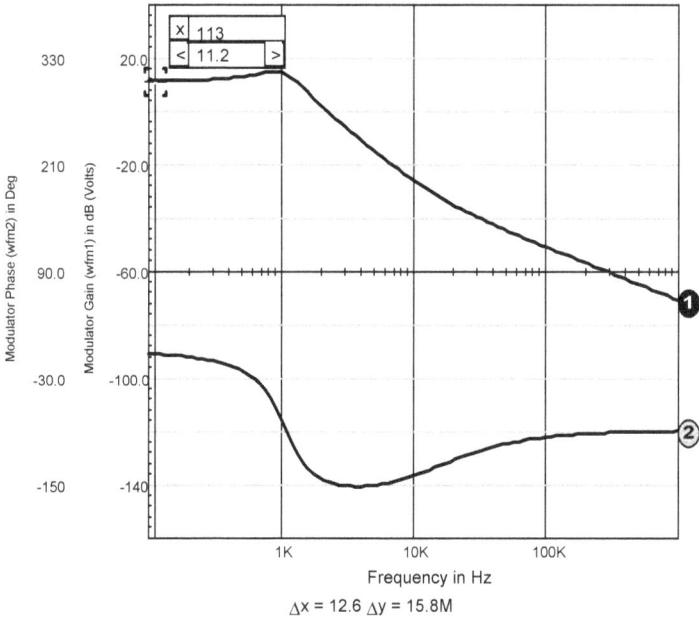

Figure 4.4

Graph of the Modulator Gain and Phase

Note: The waveform division and subtraction to create the waveforms was performed in IntuScope.

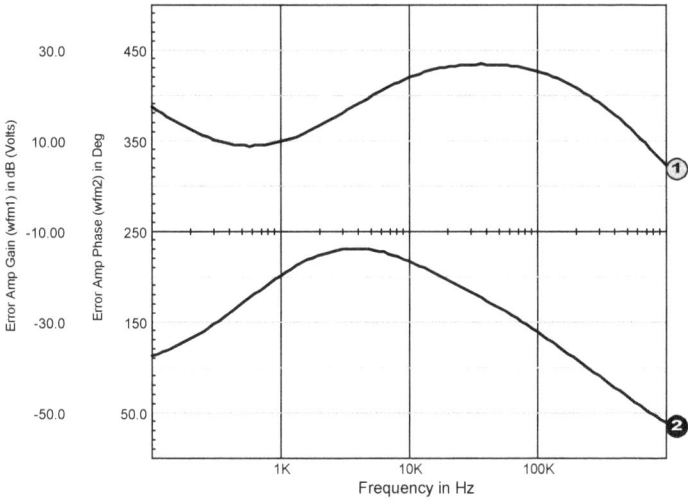

Figure 4.5

Graph for the Error Amplifier Gain (Vdb(9)) and Phase (VP(9))

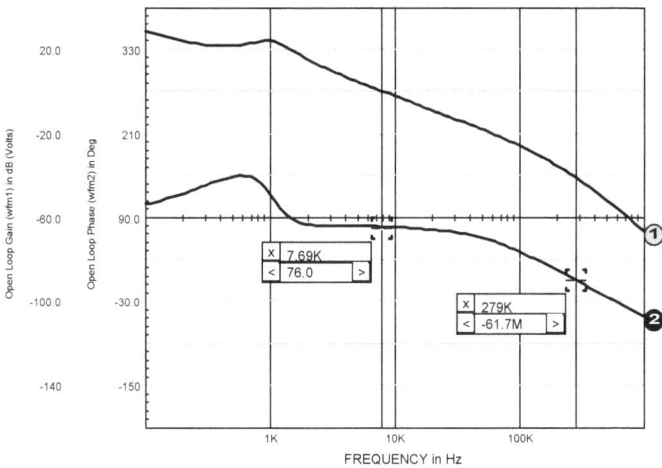

Figure 4.6

Graph of the Open-Loop Gain (Vdb(10)) and Phase (VP(10))

Note: L2 effectively opens the loop.

In the next simulation, the loop is closed in order to simulate the audio susceptibility and load transient characteristics of the converter. The modified schematic is shown in Figure 4.7. Note that L2 has been removed.

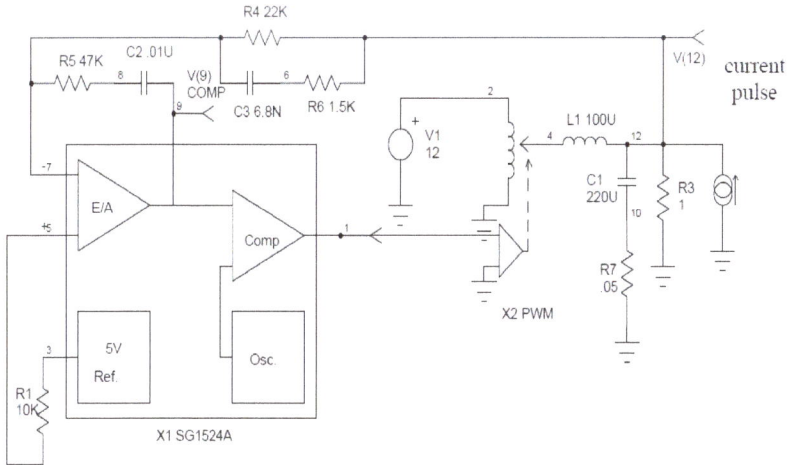

Figure 4.7

Schematic Design for a Closed-Loop Converter

Note: L2 has been removed (see Figure 4.6).

```
1524BCK: TO SIMULATE THE AUDIO SUSCEPTIBILITY AND THE LOAD CHARACTERISTICS OF THE CONVERTER
.OP
.TRAN 1U 5M 0 5U
.AC DEC 20 100HZ 1MEGHZ
.PROBE
* V(9)=COMP
.PRINT AC  V(12)  VP(12)  V(9)  VP(9)
.PRINT TRAN  V(12)
X2 2 0 4 1 0 PWM
V1 2 0 12 AC 1
R1 3 5 10K
L1 4 12 100U
C1 12 10 220U
R3 12 0 1
R4 7 12 22K
R5 7 8 47K
C2 8 9 .01U
C3 7 6 6.8N
R6 6 12 1.5K
R7 10 0 .05
I1 0 12 PULSE 0 1 1U 1U 1U 2.5M 5M
X1 7 5 9 1 3 SG1524A Params: T=10U TO=1U TS=.25U EP=3.5 EO=.5
.END
```

145

The results of the load transient response and audio susceptibility simulations are shown in Figures 4.8 and 4.9, respectively.

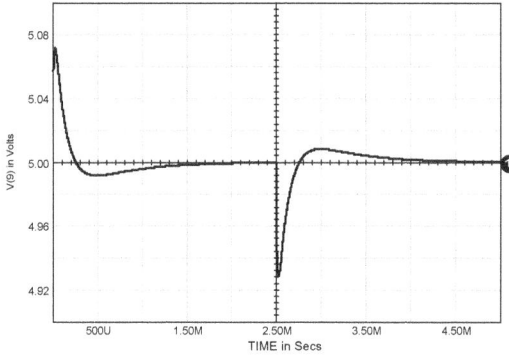

Figure 4.8

Load Transient Response V(12) as the Result of a Current Pulse from I1

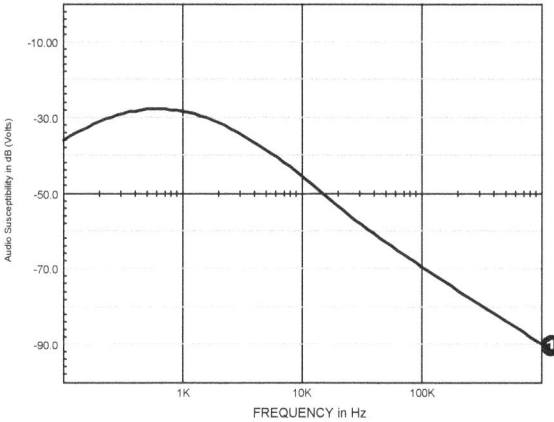

Figure 4.9

Audio Susceptibility Simulation Result from the AC Analysis

Note: V(12) is shown.

Discontinuous Mode Simulation

Although this model is extremely simple to use, it does have one significant drawback. The modulator transfer function is only valid for continuous mode operation. The previous example has an inductor ripple current of approximately 200mA peak-to-peak. This allows the converter to operate at a load current level as low as 100mA but maintains continuous mode operation. Typical ripple currents will more realistically allow operation from 10% to 100% of the load in continuous mode. This model will not produce accurate results for discontinuous mode operation. The graph in Figure 4.10 shows the results of a simulation of the previous circuit with a 50mA load current.

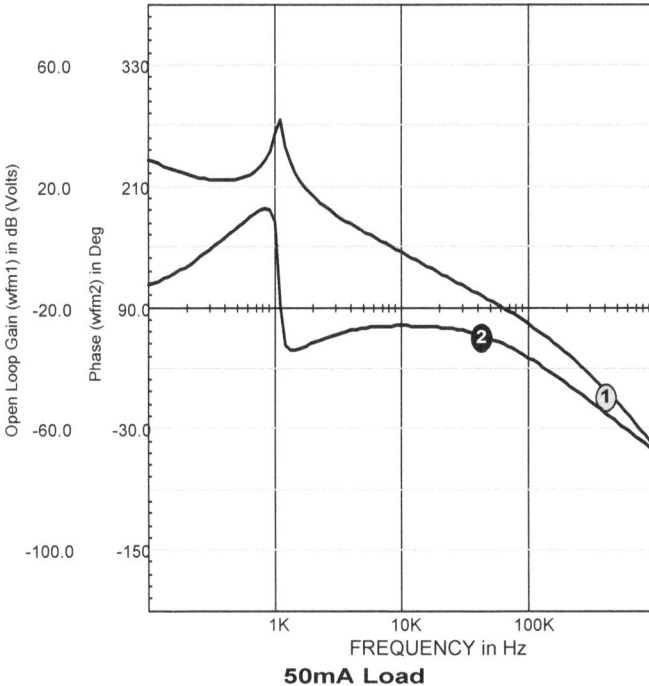

Figure 4.10

Open-Loop Gain and Phase of the Closed-Loop Converter Circuit with a 50-mA Load

A state space model that can simulate continuous and discontinuous mode operation for both current mode and voltage mode converters is included in the AEi Systems Power IC Library for PSpice.

An Improved Buck Subcircuit

An improved buck topology subcircuit, which is based on the peak and valley inductor currents, allows operation in both voltage and current mode with discontinuous and continuous inductor currents. The derivation of the model is shown in Figure 4.11.

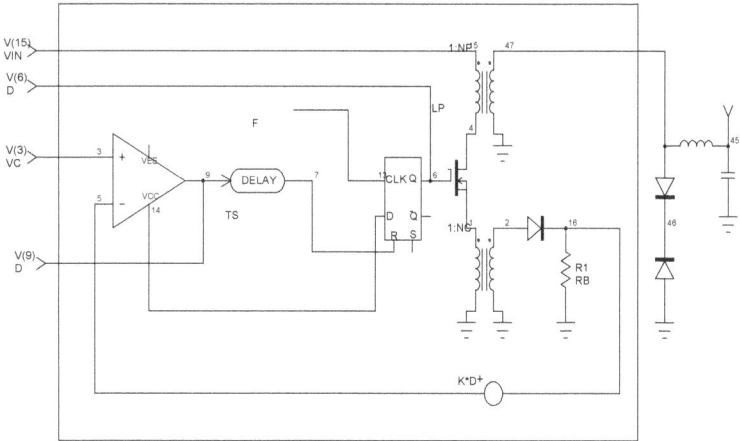

Figure 4.11

Schematic for a Buck Mode Converter that can be used in both Voltage and Current Modes with Discontinuous and Continuous Inductor Currents

Definition of Terms

P_{in}	Converter Input Power	V_c	Control Voltage
L_o	Output Filter Inductance	N_p	Power Xfmr Ratio Ns/Np
I_{min}	Minimum Output Inductor Current	V_o	Converter Output Voltage

148

I_{max} Peak Output Inductor Current I_o Average Output Current

F_{sw} Switching Frequency R_b Current Transformer Burden Resistor

T_s Current Loop Propagation Delay Time N_c Current Xfmr Ratio $1{:}N_c$

T_{on} MOSFET On-Time D Switch On-Time Duty Cycle

D_2 Freewheeling Conduction Duty Cycle D_{max} Max Switch Duty Cycle Limit

V_{in} Converter Input Voltage

Governing Equations

The offset error amplifier output (V_c) controls the peak current in the primary of the power transformer, as sensed by a current transformer with a turns ratio of $1{:}N_c$.

The PWM turns off the switch when the voltage at V_C is equal to the current sense voltage across R_b. The switch will remain on for the delay time of the PWM comparator plus the switch turn-off delay. The total delay time is referred to as T_S.

I_{max} is therefore defined by the control voltage (V_C) as:

$$I_{max} = \frac{V_C N_C}{N_p R_b} + \frac{\left(\left(V_{in} N_P\right) - V_O\right) * T_S}{L_o}$$

Formula 4.1

…which is valid for $V_C > 0$

The on-time of the switch is based upon the voltage across the output inductor and the ($I_{max} - I_{min}$) of the inductor current:

$$T_{on} = \frac{L_o \left(I_{max} - I_{min}\right)}{V_{in} N_p - V_o}$$

Formula 4.2

Relating T_{on} to D:

$$T_{on} = \frac{D}{F_{sw}}$$

Formula 4.3

If we substitute and solve for D, Eq. (4.3) becomes:

$$D = \frac{L_o F_{sw}}{V_{in} N_p - V_o}\left(I_{max} - I_{min}\right)$$

Formula 4.4

During the time for which the switch is off, the current will decay in the output inductor. The minimum current is defined as:

$$I_{min} = I_{max} - \frac{V_o\left(1-D\right)}{L_o F_{sw}} \quad \text{while } I_{min} > 0$$

Formula 4.5

If the converter operates in the discontinuous mode, the inductor current will be zero prior to the end of the switching cycle. If we define the off conduction time through the freewheeling diode as D_2, we can solve for D_2 in terms of $(I_{max} - I_{min})$ as:

$$D_2 = \frac{L_o F_{sw}}{V_o}\left(I_{max} - I_{min}\right)$$

Formula 4.6

The output current from the converter is calculated as:

$$I_o = \left(I_{max} - I_{min}\right)\frac{\left(D+D_2\right)}{2}$$

Formula 4.7

Note: In continuous conduction mode, $D+D_2=1$.

Substituting Eqs. (4.4) and (4.6) into Eq. (4.7) gives:

$$D = \frac{L_o F_{sw}}{2}\left(I_{max}^2 - I_{min}^2\right)\left(\frac{1}{V_o} + \frac{1}{V_{in}N_p - V_o}\right)$$

Formula 4.8

Finally, rearranging Eq. (4.5), we can obtain the value of I_{min}.

Note: In the continuous mode, the value of I_{min} will be positive, whereas in discontinuous mode it will be zero. This allows us to equate the volt-second products across the inductor for intervals of D and D_2, which yields the familiar expression:

$$D = \frac{V_O}{V_{in}N_p}$$

Combining Formulas 4.5 and 4.9 yields:

$$I_{min} = I_{max} - \frac{V_o}{L_o F_{sw}}\left(1 - \frac{V_o}{V_{in}N_P}\right)$$

Formula 4.10

The converter power can be represented on the primary side by equating the input power with the output power:

$$I_{in} = \frac{V_o I_o}{V_{in}}$$

Formula 4.11

Finally, note that by restricting I_{min} to values greater than or equal to zero, both continuous conduction and discontinuous modes will be properly represented.

Adding Slope Compensation

The schematic in Figure 4.12 shows the addition of an external ramp that provides slope compensation to the model.

The D output of the subcircuit is provided for this purpose. The D output is a voltage equivalent of the duty cycle, so that a ramp is defined as $K*D$, where K is the peak voltage of the ramp at a duty cycle of 1. K may also be described as the slope of the ramp divided by the switching frequency.

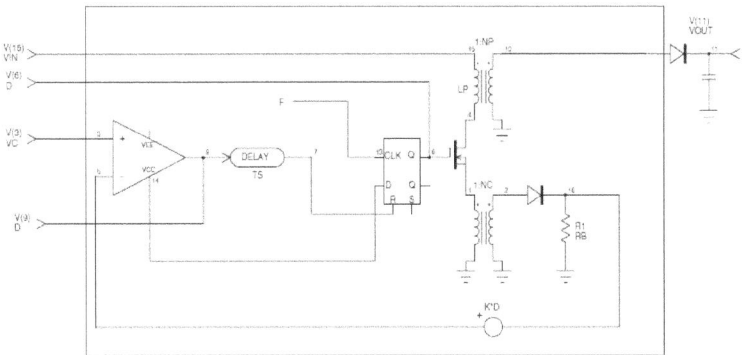

Figure 4.12

Buck Mode Converter with the Addition of an External Ramp

Although we do not have access to the internal nodes that are required in order to add the ramp, we can rotate it through the comparator and easily add it externally.

A nonlinear arbitrary dependent source (Berkeley SPICE 3 B element) or PSpice E element is used to provide the multiplication $K*D$. The schematic in Figure 4.13 shows the implementation of the external slope compensation ramp of the subcircuit.

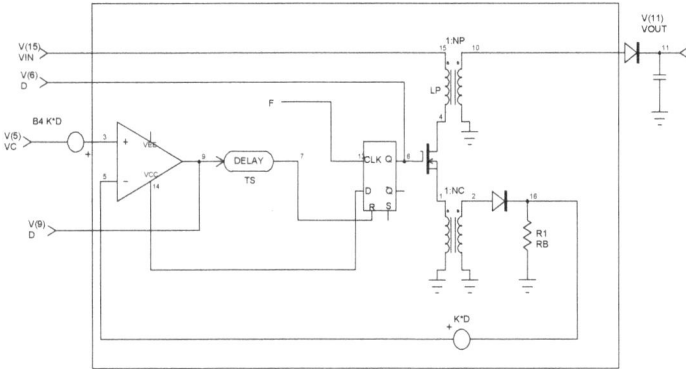

Figure 4.13

Implementation of the External Slope Compensation Ramp to the Subcircuit

Voltage Mode Control

If we use a further extension of the circuit shown in Figure 4.13, voltage mode control (also called duty cycle control) can be implemented. In this case, there is no current sensed, so that RB will ideally be set to zero. *RB cannot be set to zero* because it will result in a divide-by-zero error within the subcircuit. It may, however, be set to a very low value such as 1 mΩ or less, if necessary. If we set K to 1, the result will be a duty cycle that is equal to the control voltage V_c. The modulator gain can also be represented in this subcircuit by setting K to $1/V_r$, where V_r is the peak-to-peak voltage of the ramp. Within the subcircuit, V_c is bounded between 0 and 1 V. In order to use this limiting function, it is recommended that you set K to 1 and add the modulator gain externally.

Improved SG1524A Buck Regulator

The example in Figure 4.14 uses the buck mode subcircuit to model the buck regulator example (Figure 4.3).

153

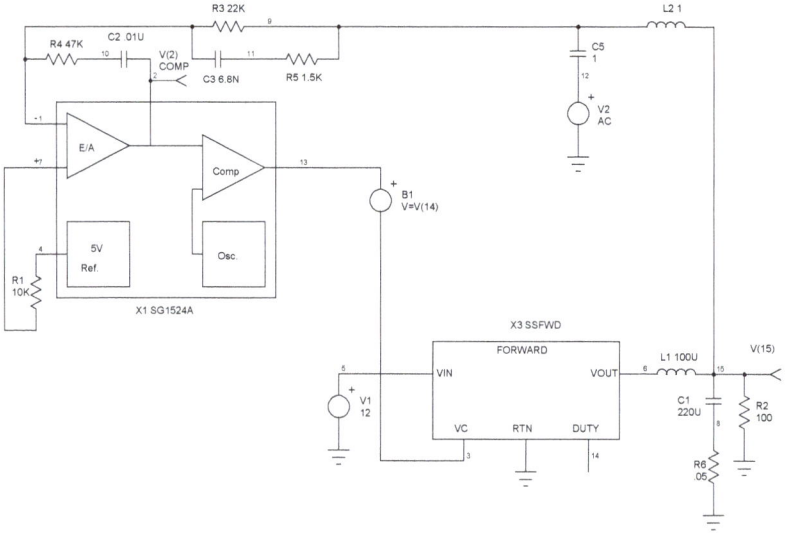

Figure 4.14

The Buck Mode Subcircuit (Forward) is used in a Buck Regulator Simulation

```
1524BCK3: A NEW BUCK MODE SUBCIRCUIT
.AC DEC 25 100HZ 1000KHZ
*  V(2)=COMP
.PRINT AC  V(15)  VP(15)  V(2)  VP(2)
.PROBE
V1 5 0 12
R1 4 7 10K
L1 6 15 100U
C1 15 8 220U
R2 15 0 100
R3 1 9 22K
R4 1 10 47K
C2 10 2 .01U
C3 1 11 6.8N
L2 9 15 1
V2 12 0 AC 1
R5 11 9 1.5K
R6 8 0 .05
X3 5 0 3 6 14 SSFWD Params: L=100U NC=1 NP=1 F=100K DMAX=.9 RB=1M TS=.25U
EB1 13 3 Value={ V(14) }
C5 9 12 1
X1 1 7 2 13 4 SG1524A Params: T=10U TO=1U TS=.25U EP=3.5 EO=.5
.END
```

The results of the simulation are shown in Figure 4.15. Note the excellent agreement between this model and the previously used

PWM switch model.

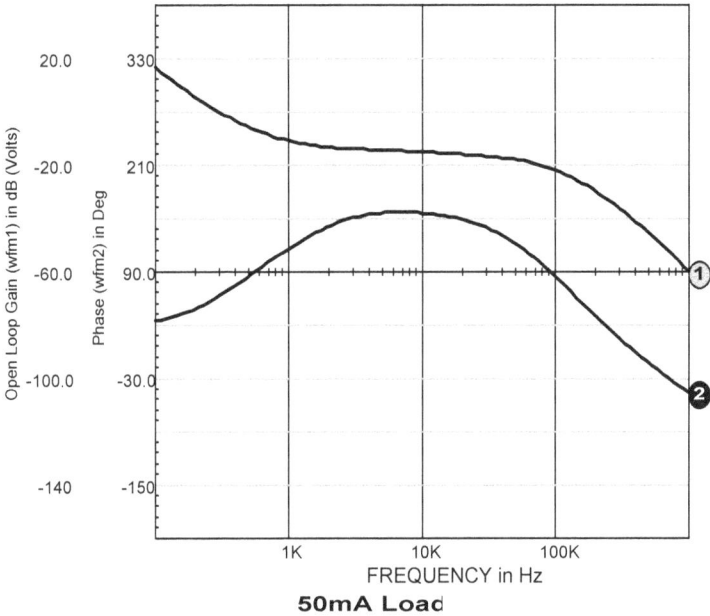

Figure 4.15

Graph of the Open-Loop Gain and Phase, Node 15

The circuit was resimulated with a 50mA load current, which caused it to operate in discontinuous conduction mode. The results of the simulation are shown in Figure 4.16.

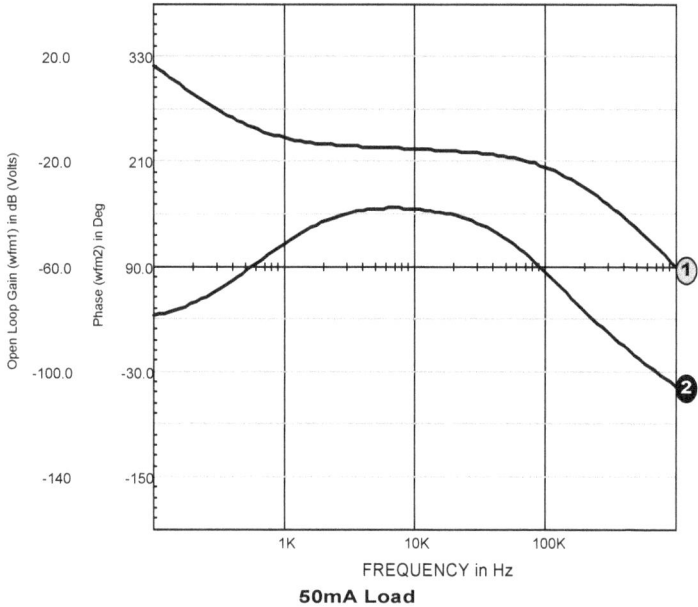

Figure 4.16

Graph of the Open-Loop Gain and Phase with a 50mA Load

Note the drastic difference in the phase gain plot compared with that of the PWM switch. The improved model correctly shows the reduction in modulator gain and also correctly shows that the modulator is represented by a single pole rather than two poles, as in the continuous conduction mode. From the operating voltages in the schematic, it is also evident that the improved model correctly shows that the duty cycle is significantly reduced as a result of the discontinuous operation. The graph in Figure 4.17 shows the result of the modulator gain using the improved model.

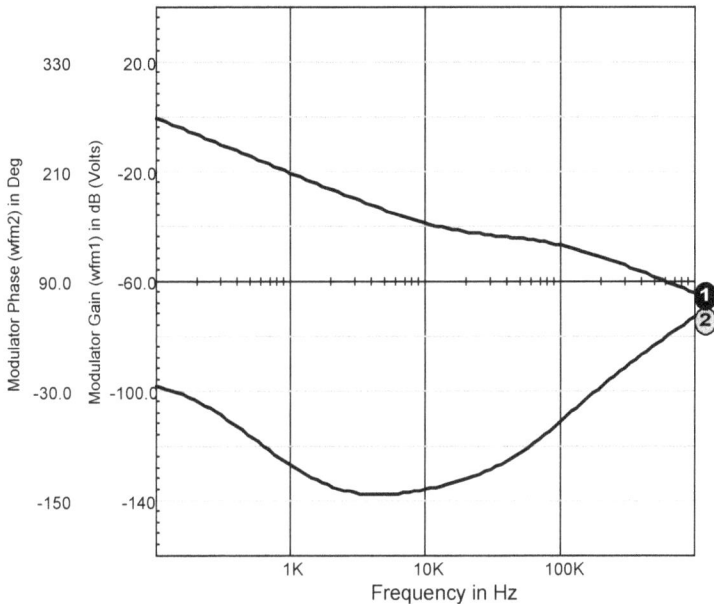

Figure 4.17

Result of the Modulator Gain using the New Model

Transient Model

The Power IC Model Library for PSpice also includes transient-based models of many pulse width modulators, including the UC1524A, which is identical to the SG1524A.

The next example shows the application of the nonlinear switching transient models to simulate the previous buck regulator circuit (see Figure 4.18). The transient model properly models the output ripple, propagation delay times, and cycle-by-cycle switching effects. The disadvantage to the transient models is the increased simulation time and the difficulty in simulating frequency domain characteristics such as phase-gain analysis and audio susceptibility.

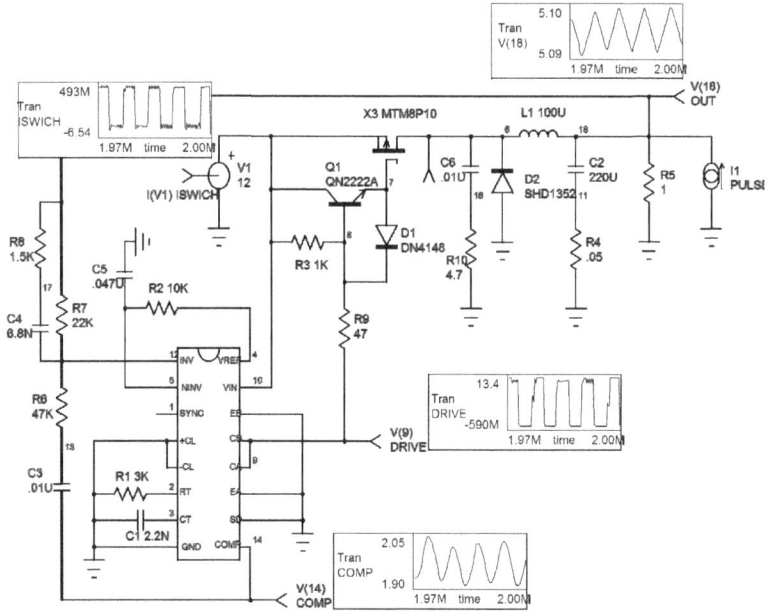

Figure 4.18

Application of the Transient Subcircuits to Simulate the Previous Buck Regulator

```
TRAN1524: TO SHOW THE APPLICATION OF THE TRANSIENT SUBCIRCUIT
.TRAN .2U 10M 5M .05U UIC ; Load Step
*.TRAN .2U 5M 0 .05U UIC ; Startup
.PROBE
.OPTION GMIN=1N ABSTOL=10U VNTOL=10U RELTOL=.01 ITL4=100
* V(6)=SWITCH
* V(15)=OUT
* I(V1)=ISWICH
* V(9)=DRIVE
* V(14)=COMP
.PRINT TRAN V(6) V(15) I(V1) V(9)
.PRINT TRAN V(14)
R1 2 0 3K
C1 3 0 2.2N
R2 5 4 10K
V1 10 0 12
Q1 10 8 7 QN2222A
R3 10 8 1K
D1 7 8 DN4148
D2 0 6 SHD1352
L1 6 15 100U
C2 15 11 220U
R4 11 0 .05
R5 15 0 1
R6 12 13 47K
C3 13 14 .01U
R7 12 15 22K
C4 12 17 6.8N
R8 17 15 1.5K
C5 5 0 .047U
R9 8 9 47
C6 6 16 .01U
R10 16 0 4.7
X3 6 7 10 MTM8P10
I1 0 15 PULSE 0 1 5.001M 1U 1U 2.5M 5M ; Load Step
* I1 0 15 1 ; Startup
X1 12 5 1 0 0 2 3 0 14 0 0 9 9 0 10 4 UC1524A
.END
```

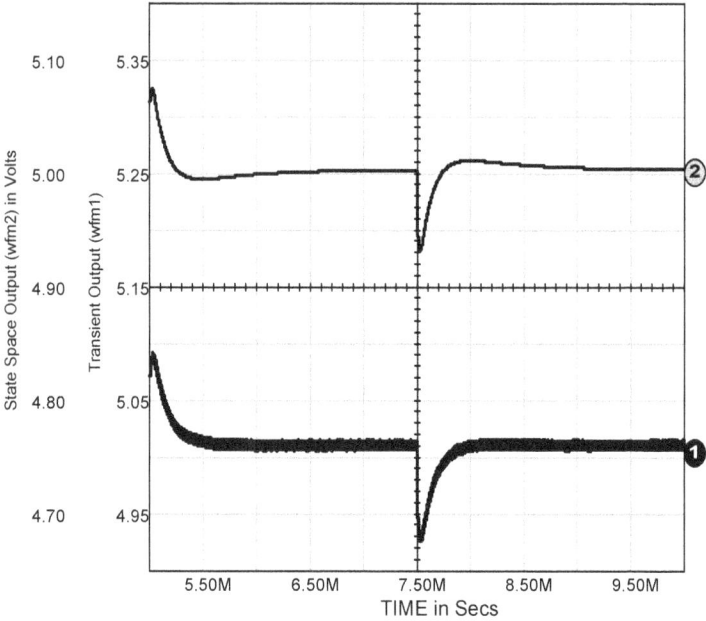

Figure 4.19

Transient Step Load Response

The graph in Figure 4.19 displays the results of the transient step load response. The upper trace is the result of the state space model, and the lower trace is the result of the transient simulation. Note that the transient model shows a slightly lower Q, as evidenced by the reduced undershoot that results from the MOSFET's on resistance. Also note that the transient model includes the output ripple. The waveforms in Figure 4.18 show the MOSFET's voltage and output ripple.

When I ran this simulation on a 75MHz Pentium computer, it required approximately 2 hours of simulation time. On a P4 3GHz computer, it ran somewhat faster, taking 4 min 9.42 s.

The simulation speed has obviously improved, although the transient simulation will always be considerably slower than the state space model, which runs in less than a tenth of a second.

Why do we bother using transient models? The transient

model allows us to view important considerations of the real hardware. In this case, the concern was the "cheap and dirty" high side driver circuit. The transient simulation allowed us to view the topological aspects of the circuit as well as the MOSFET switching speed. The transient model was also used to perform a simulation at a light load current of 50mA. According to the state space model, the converter should operate in discontinuous conduction mode. The snubber was removed from the Schottky diode in order to make the discontinuity easier to see.

The operating duty cycle under this condition is approximately 25%, which agrees with the state space model. A final simulation shows the turn-on of the buck regulator in order to establish the functionality of the soft-start circuit, which comprises R2 and C5.

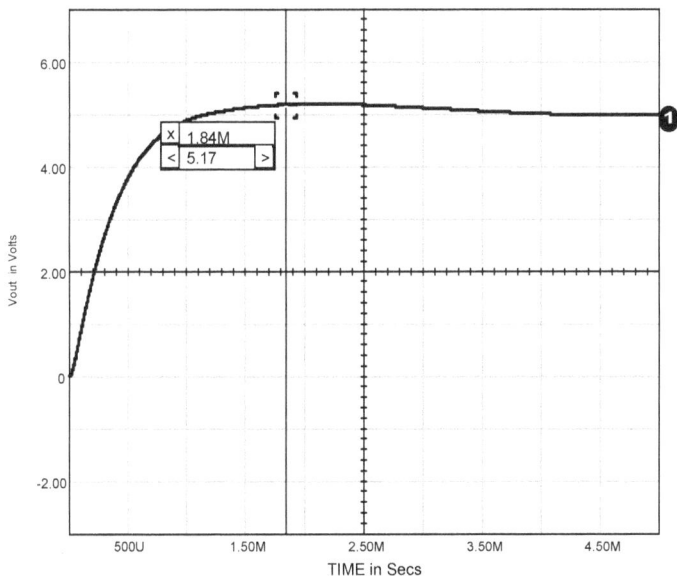

Figure 4.20

Turn-On Response of the Output Voltage, V(15), using the Nonlinear Transient Model

The buck regulator reached a maximum voltage of 5.17V (see

Figure 4.20), which equates to approximately 3% overshoot. Although this is generally acceptable, the soft-start time can be increased in order to eliminate the overshoot. For comparison purposes, the turn-on simulation was also performed using the new state space and the transient models (see Figures 4.21 and 4.22). The results are as follows:

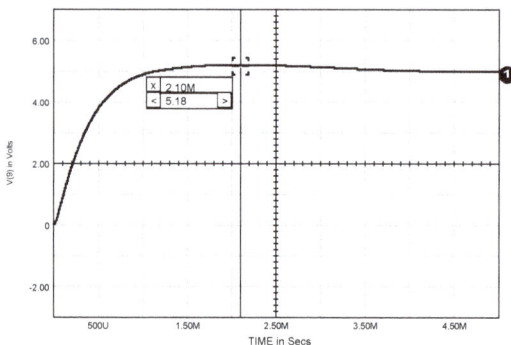

Figure 4.21

Turn-On Response of the Output Voltage, V(15), using the State Space Model

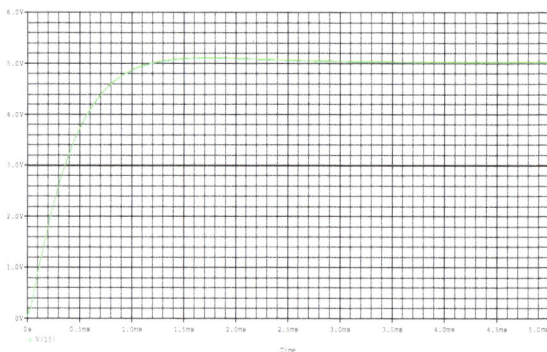

Figure 4.22

Turn-On Response of the Output Voltage, V(15), using the Transient Model

Chapter 5

Flyback Converters

THE FLYBACK CONVERTER has long been popular for low-power applications. The major attraction of the flyback topology is its low component count. At higher power levels, the output capacitor ripple current is often too great to deal with using conventional, low-cost capacitors. Dynamic response is also limited in continuous conduction mode, because of a right-half-plane (RHP) zero in the transfer function.

In the flyback topology, energy is stored in a power inductor (which often has multiple windings, as in a transformer) during the on-time of the switch. During the off-time of the switch, the energy is delivered to the load. The flyback topology is often used in both discontinuous and continuous conduction modes and can be successfully controlled using current mode or voltage converters.

A Flyback Subcircuit

A simplified functional schematic diagram of the flyback subcircuit is shown in Figure 5.1. It is included in the Power IC Model Library for PSpice available from AEi Systems. It is a universal subcircuit that is capable of simulating the flyback regulator in both the continuous and discontinuous modes of operation with either voltage mode or current mode control. The derivation of the model is as follows:

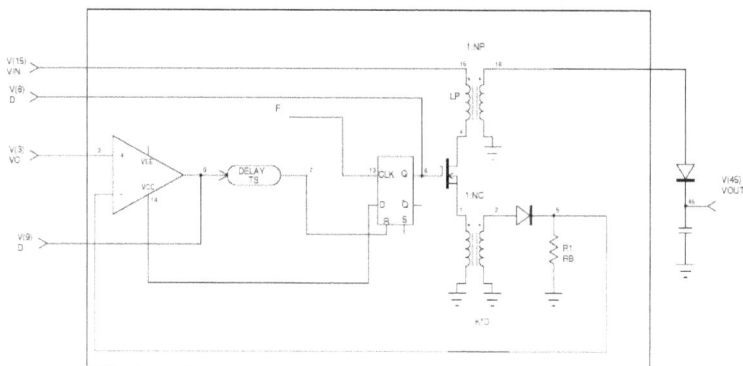

Figure 5.1

Flyback Subcircuit Schematic that can be used in both Voltage and Current Modes with Discontinuous and Continuous Inductor Currents

Defined Terms

Pin	Converter Input Power	Vc	Offset Error Amp Output
Lm	Pwr Xfmr Magnetizing	Np	Power Xfmr Ratio
Imin	Minimum Primary Current	Vout	Subcircuit
Imax	Peak Primary Current	Iout	Average Output Current
Fsw	Switching Frequency	Rb	Current Transformer Burden
η	Efficiency Factor	Nc	Current Xfmr Ratio
Ts	Propagation Delay	D	Converter Duty Cycle
Ton	MOSFET On-Time	Pout	Converter Output Power
Vin	Converter Input Voltage		

Governing Equations

$$P_{out} = P_{in} * \eta$$

$$P_{in} = \frac{1}{2} L_m \left(I_{max}^2 - I_{min}^2 \right) F_{sw}$$

I_{max} is defined by the control Voltage V_C as:

$$I_{max} = \frac{V_C N_C}{Rb} + \frac{V_{in} T_s}{L_m}$$

The MOSFET on-time is calculated as:

$$T_{on} = \frac{L_m \left(I_{max} - I_{min} \right)}{V_{in}}$$

...since $T_{on} = D/F_{sw}$

$$D = \frac{L_m F_{sw} \left(I_{max} - I_{min} \right)}{V_{in} N_P - V_{out}}$$

During the MOSFET off-time, the primary current falls as:

$$I_{max} - I_{min} = \frac{V_{out} \left(1 - D \right)}{N_P L_m F_{sw}} \quad while \quad I_{max} - I_{min} \geq 0$$

Substituting equations:

$$I_{min} = I_{max} - \frac{V_{out}}{N_P} \left(1 - \frac{L_m F_{sw}}{V_{in} \left(I_{max} - I_{min} \right)} \right)$$

…which can be further simplified as:

$$I_{min} = I_{max} - \frac{V_{out}}{N_P L_m F_{sw}\left(1 + \dfrac{V_{out}}{N_P V_{in}}\right)} \quad while \quad I_{min} \geq 0$$

Substituting equations:

$$I_{out} = \frac{L_m F_{sw}\left(I_{max}^2 - I_{min}^2\right)}{2}\left(\frac{1}{V_{out}} + \frac{1}{V_{in} N_P - V_{out}}\right)\eta$$

…and the duty cycle can be calculated as:

$$D = \frac{L_m F_{sw}\left(I_{max} - I_{min}\right)}{V_{in} N_P - V_{out}}$$

The following circuit is a simple representation, using the new subcircuit, of a dual output flyback converter with a separate transformer winding for voltage regulation. The flyback subcircuit essentially replaces the PWM switch model discussed in Chapter 4.

Dual Output Flyback Converter

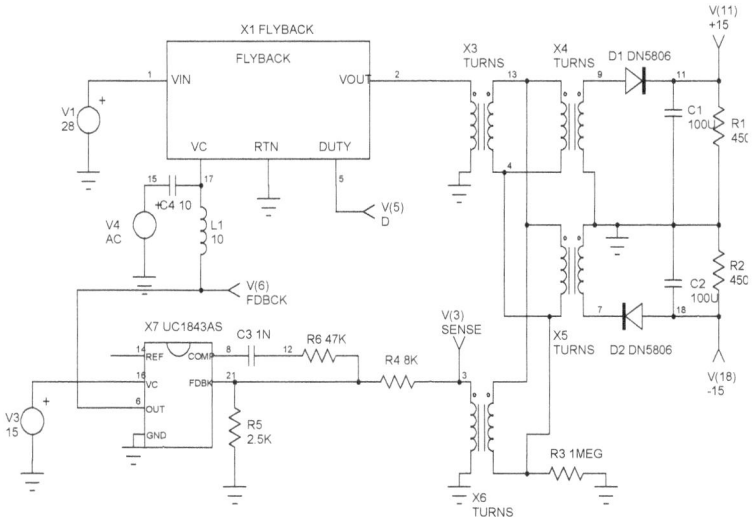

```
FLY1: DUAL OUTPUT FLYBACK CONVERTER
*SPICE_NET
*INCLUDE POWERSS.LIB
*INCLUDE XFMR.LIB
*INCLUDE MAGNETIC.LIB
*INCLUDE DIODE5.LIB
.OPTION GMIN=1N ALTINIT=10
*.TRAN 10U 2M
.AC DEC 25 100 1MEG
.DC V1 18 38 .1
*ALIAS  V(11)=+15
*ALIAS  V(3)=SENSE
*ALIAS  V(6)=FDBCK
*ALIAS  V(18)=-15
*ALIAS  V(5)=D
.PRINT AC  V(11) VP(11) V(3) VP(3)
.PRINT AC  V(6) VP(6)
.PRINT TRAN V(3) V(18) V(5)
.PRINT DC V(17)
V1 1 0 28 AC 1
X3 2 0 13 4 TURNS {NUM=18 }
X4 9 0 13 4 TURNS {NUM=18 }
X5 0 7 13 4 TURNS {NUM=18 }
X6 3 0 13 4 TURNS {NUM=12 }
D1 9 11 DN5806
D2 18 7 DN5806
C1 11 0 100U
C2 0 18 100U
R1 11 0 15
R2 0 18 15
R3 4 0 1MEG
X7 8 21 0 6 16 14 UC1843AS
R4 3 21 8K
R5 21 0 2.5K
C3 8 12 1N
R6 12 21 47K
V3 16 0 15
L1 17 6 1p
C4 15 17 1p
V4 15 0 AC 1
X1 1 0 17 2 5 FLYBACK {L=20U NC=100 NP=1 F=250K EFF=1 RB=10 TS=.25U}
.END
```

Figure 5.2

Schematic Design and Netlist for a Dual-Output Flyback Converter

The results of the gain-phase measurement of the flyback converter are shown below for a 30mA load and a 1A load on each output, respectively. The circuit has a bandwidth of 7kHz with a phase margin of 75 degrees with a 1 Amp load. At a 30mA load, the performance is quite different due to the discontinuous operation. The 34kHz would likely be a problem for most applications. The converter would either require a preload, or the 1 A load bandwidth would have to be reduced. This would sacrifice performance.

Note: L1 and C4 are used to break the loop for the open loop measurement. Voltage source V4 is the injection signal. This method allows the DC path to be closed via L1, while the AC information is removed (essentially) by the very low frequency filter created by L1 and C4.

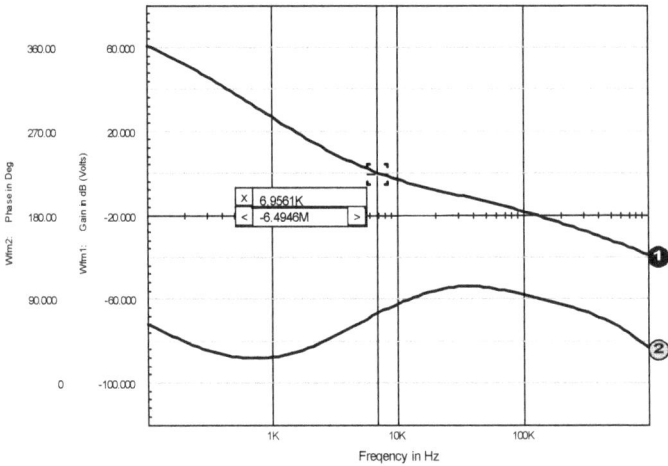

Figure 5.3

Gain-Phase Bode Plot of the Dual-Output Flyback Converter with 1A Load on each Output

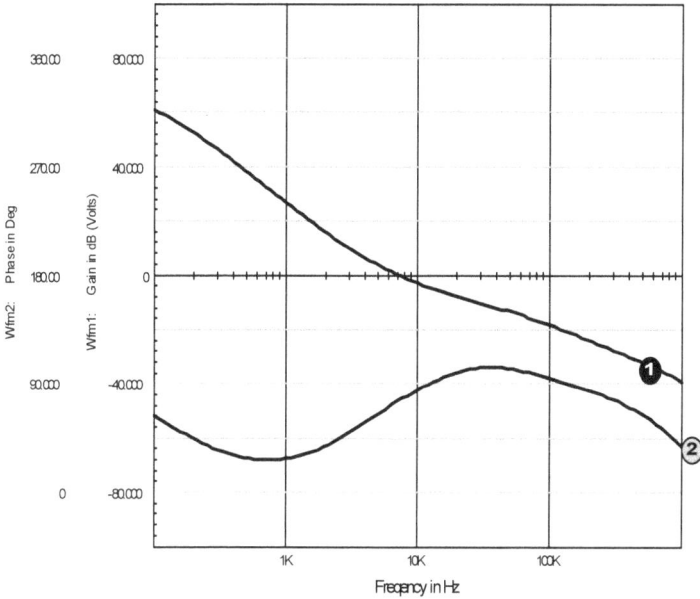

Figure 5.4

Gain-Phase Bode Plot of the Dual-Output Flyback Converter with a 30mA Load on each Output

Audio Susceptibility

The same SPICE model can be used to evaluate closed loop performance parameters, such as audio susceptibility. To use the model for these evaluations, the inductor, capacitor and AC voltage source can be left in the circuit. This is accomplished by changing the value of L1 to 1pH, and C4 to 1pF. In order to simulate the audio susceptibility performance, an AC source statement must also be added to the input voltage source, V1.

The results of the Audio Susceptibility simulation are shown in the graph below.

169

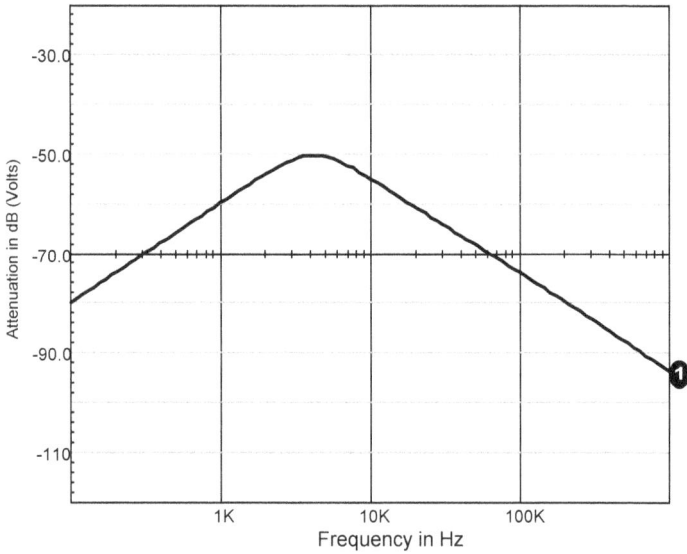

Figure 5.5

Audio Susceptibility Simulation Results

Feedforward Improvements

The flyback converter has a peak input current that varies with input voltage.

This can be seen by sweeping the input voltage and monitoring the control voltage or the output of the error amplifier.

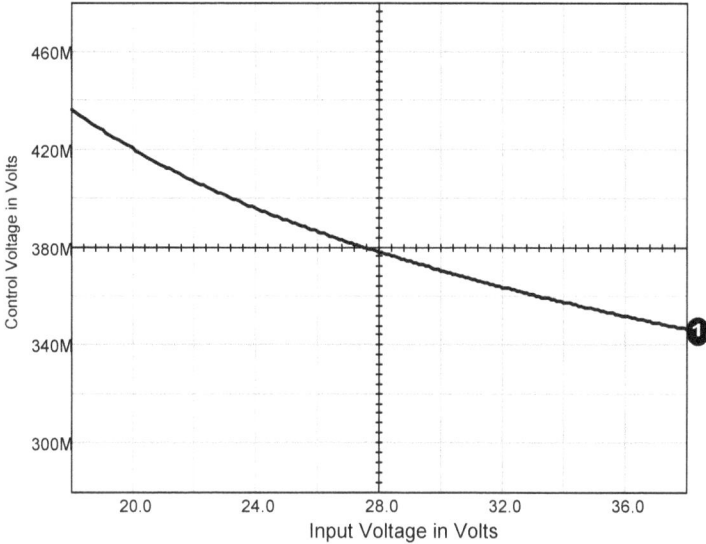

Figure 5.6

Graph Showing the Nonlinear Relationship between the Input Voltage and the Control Voltage

While this curve is not linear, the audio susceptibility of the flyback converter can still benefit from feedforward compensation. This is most easily added via a simple resistor connected from the input voltage to the current sense pin of the PWM IC. We can add a feedforward signal in series with the control pin of the subcircuit to accomplish the same effect.

The schematic showing the incorporation of the feedforward signal is shown in Figure 5.7.

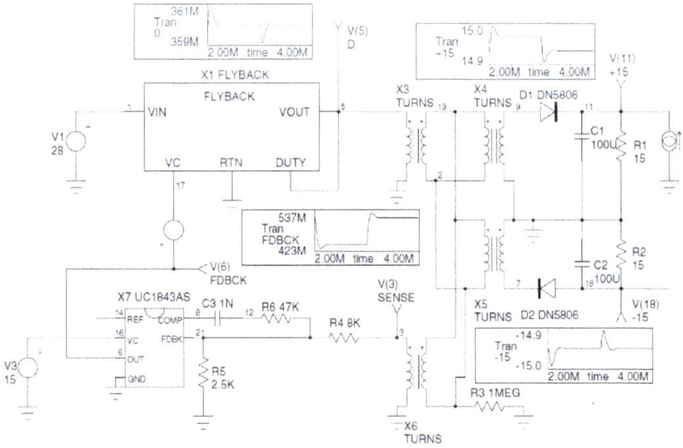

Figure 5.7

Feedforward Signal Schematic and Netlist

The improvement in Audio Susceptibility is shown in Figure 5.8. Note that the feedforward signal improves the audio susceptibility performance by more than 20dB. In several applications, I have been able to use this feedforward technique rather than adding a linear regulator, to obtain the necessary attenuation. There are several benefits. There is no reduction in efficiency performance, as would occur with the addition of a linear regulator. Also, the converter can be made smaller and less expensively without the linear regulator.

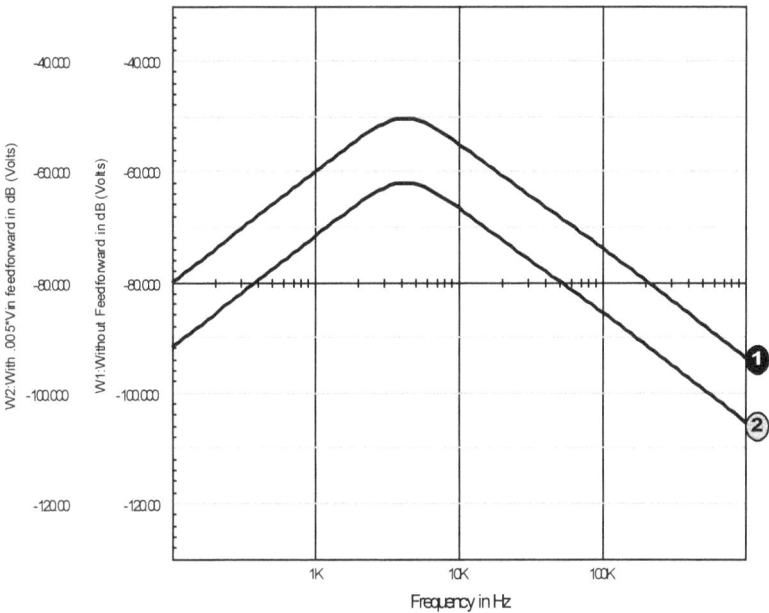

Figure 5.8

Improvement in Audio Susceptibility Graph

Flyback Transient Response

The transient response of the flyback converter is unaffected by the addition of the feedforward signal. The following transient simulation shows an overlay of a 0.5A step on the +15V output with and without the feedforward signal.

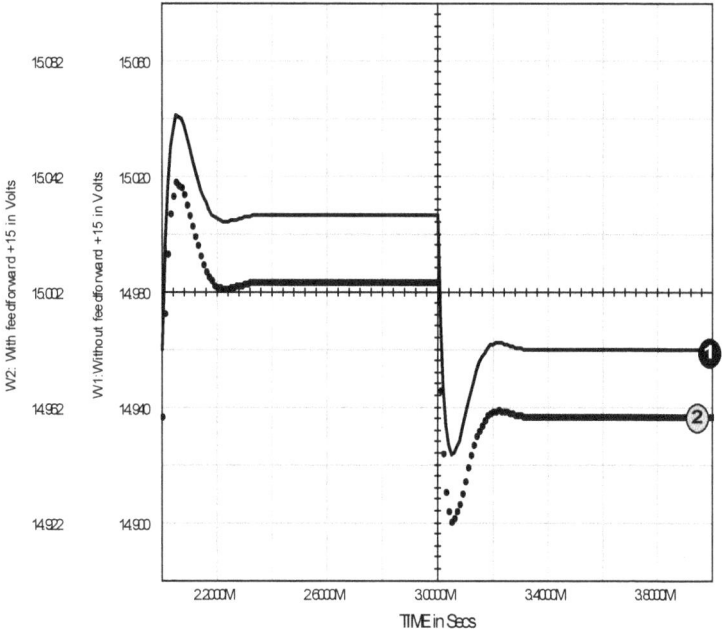

Figure 5.9

**Transient Response Simulation Results with the
Unaffected Flyback Converter**

To calculate the DC output resistance we use the following equations:

$$\Delta I_l = \frac{15(.64)}{25u(250Khz)} = 1.536\,Amps$$

$$I_{Pk} = \frac{I_O}{D'} + \frac{\Delta I_l}{2} = \frac{0.833}{.64} + \frac{1.536}{2} = 2.069\,Amps$$

$$I_{rms} = \frac{I_O}{\sqrt{D'}} = \frac{0.833}{\sqrt{.64}} = 1.04\,Amps$$

$$I_{cap} = I_O \sqrt{\frac{1}{D'} + D} = 0.833 \sqrt{\frac{1}{.64} + .36} = 1.15 \, Amps$$

$$P_{loss} = \frac{1}{2} L_l^2 I_{pk}^2 F_S + I_{rms}^2 DCR + I_{cap}^2 ESR =$$

$$\frac{1}{2} (350nH)(2.07)^2 \, 250kHz + (1.04)^2 .1 + (1.15)^2 .03 = 0.335W$$

$$R_{eff} = \frac{P_{loss}}{I_O^2} + Rd = \frac{0.188}{(0.833)^2} + 0.12 = 0.483 + .12 = 0.603 Ohms$$

The resulting 0.6Ω is a good approximation of the DC output resistance. Based on our example, the load regulation from 10% to 100% load would be:

$$\Delta V = 0.833 * 0.9 * 0.6 = 0.45 volts$$

The actual data which was recorded for the converter was 0.49V. Obviously, the resistance is nonlinear and dependent upon input voltage, but this is a good estimate.

The output resistance has been added in the SPICE model below in order to evaluate the effect on transient response.

$$R_{eff} = \frac{P_{loss}}{I_O^2} + Rd$$

From the previous simulation, we can obtain the nominal duty cycle of 0.36 with an input voltage of 28 Volts, or we could calculate it as:

$$D = 1 - \frac{V_{in}}{V_O}$$

The delta inductor current can be calculated based on the output voltage and D'...

$$\Delta I_l = \frac{V_{out} D'}{L_S F_S}$$

The peak secondary current is calculated as:

$$I_{pk} = \frac{I_O}{D'} + \frac{\Delta I_l}{2}$$

The secondary RMS current can be approximated by:

$$I_{rms} = \frac{I_O}{\sqrt{D'}}$$

The output capacitor RMS ripple current is calculated as:

$$I_{cap} = I_O \sqrt{\frac{1}{D'} + D}$$

The effects of the diode forward drop can best be approximated by evaluating the difference in forward voltage at two output currents of interest as:

$$R_d = \frac{\Delta Vf}{\Delta I_O}$$

The parameters from the power supply design are listed in the following table.

L_1	350 μH	I_{out}	0.833 A
L_s	25 μH	F_s	250 kHz
ESR	0.03 Ω	DCR	0.1 Ω
D	0.36	D'	0.64
N	1	R_{eff}	0.12 Ω

Simulating Regulation

One of the more difficult simulations to perform is the DC regulation of the flyback converter. The regulation and, more importantly, the cross-regulation of a flyback converter is a function of the parasitic leakage inductance of the power transformer, the output rectifier characteristics and the output capacitor ESR.

These losses can be viewed in simple terms as linear power losses. While this is not entirely true, it will generally provide reasonably accurate results. The one characteristic that will not show up is the large voltage at the output under light load or no-load conditions. This does not generally pose a problem because there is a protection or limiting device (such as a zener diode) present to make this voltage predictable.

The following example is from an actual dual output 15 Volt power supply which was designed recently. Given the following parameters, we will calculate the regulation for incorporation into our SPICE model.

Regulation Definitions

L_1	Power transformer secondary leakage inductance	I_{out}	Output DC current
L_s	Power transformer secondary inductance	F_s	Switching frequency
ESR	Output capacitor ESR	DCR	Transformer secondary resistance
D	Duty cycle	D'	1 Duty cycle
N	power transformer turns ratio	I_{rms}	RMS secondary current
I_{pk}	Peak secondary current	ΔI_1	Secondary inductor current delta
R_d	Effective diode resistance	R_{eff}	Effective average resistance
I_{cap}	Output capacitor RMS current		

The total loss of the secondary can be calculated as:

$$P_{loss} = \frac{1}{2} L_1 I_P^2 F_s + I_{rms}^2 DCR + I_{cap}^2 ESR$$

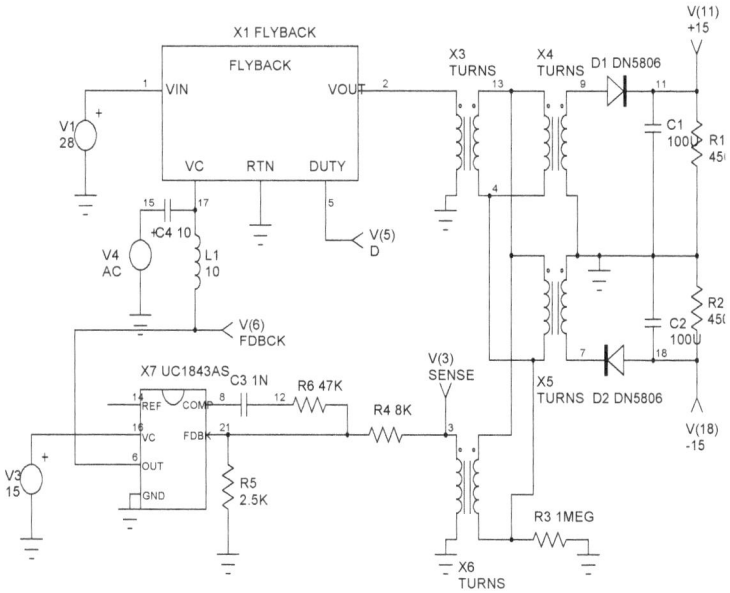

Figure 5.10

Dual-Output 15 Volt Power Supply Schematic

```
FLY1: DUAL OUTPUT 15U POWER SUPPLY
*SPICE_NET
*INCLUDE POWERSS.LIB
*INCLUDE XFMR.LIB
*INCLUDE MAGNETIC.LIB
*INCLUDE DIODE5.LIB
*.OPTION GMIN=1N ALTINIT=10
.TRAN 10U 4M 2M
*ALIAS  U(11)=+15
*ALIAS  U(3)=SENSE
*ALIAS  U(6)=FDBCK
*ALIAS  U(18)=-15
*ALIAS  U(5)=D
.PRINT AC  U(11)  UP(11)  U(3)  UP(3)
.PRINT AC  U(6)  UP(6)
.PRINT TRAN  U(11)  U(3)  U(18)  U(5)
U1 1 0 28
X3 2 0 13 4 TURNS {NUM=18 }
X4 9 0 13 4 TURNS {NUM=18 }
X5 0 7 13 4 TURNS {NUM=18 }
X6 3 0 13 4 TURNS {NUM=12 }
D1 10 11 DN5806
D2 18 15 DN5806
C1 11 0 100U
C2 0 18 100U
R1 11 0 15
R2 0 18 15
R3 4 0 1MEG
X7 8 21 0 6 16 14 UC1843AS
R4 3 21 8K
R5 21 0 2.5K
C3 8 12 1N
R6 12 21 47K
U3 16 0 15
B1 6 17 U=.005*U(1)
R7 9 10 .6
R8 7 15 .6
I3 0 11 PULSE 0 .5 .1U .1U .1U 1M 2M
X1 1 0 17 2 5 FLYBACK {L=20U NC=100 NP=1 F=250K EFF=1 RB=10 TS=.25U}
.END
```

The simulation results are shown below along with the previous transient simulation results in order to see the drastic effect of the output resistance.

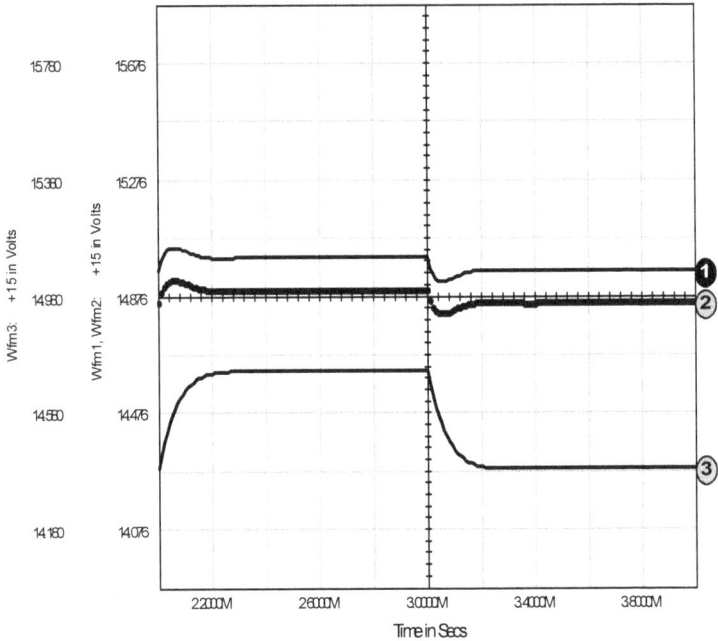

Figure 5.11

Transient Analysis Showing the Drastic Effect of the Output Resistance

Time Domain Model

The next simulation shows the basic configuration for a transient model of an off-line flyback converter. The transient model allows us to investigate details within the converter, such as peak switch current, harmonic content, output ripple voltage and many other phenomena which would not be observable using a state space model.

While this model is somewhat simplified, it can easily be upgraded even further. Upgrades could include a nonlinear core model for the power transformer, an input EMI filter, multiple outputs, transformer leakage inductance, etc.

In most cases, it is recommended that you start with a basic power supply representation such as this and then add the required details. In fact, each piece can be simulated separately before they are all put together.

Using this approach you will have more assurance that the final model will converge, and you can make any necessary changes to the subsections taking advantage of the superior simulation speed.

Obviously, as the model complexity increases, the run time will also increase, thus making investigation of the behavior of each subsection more costly.

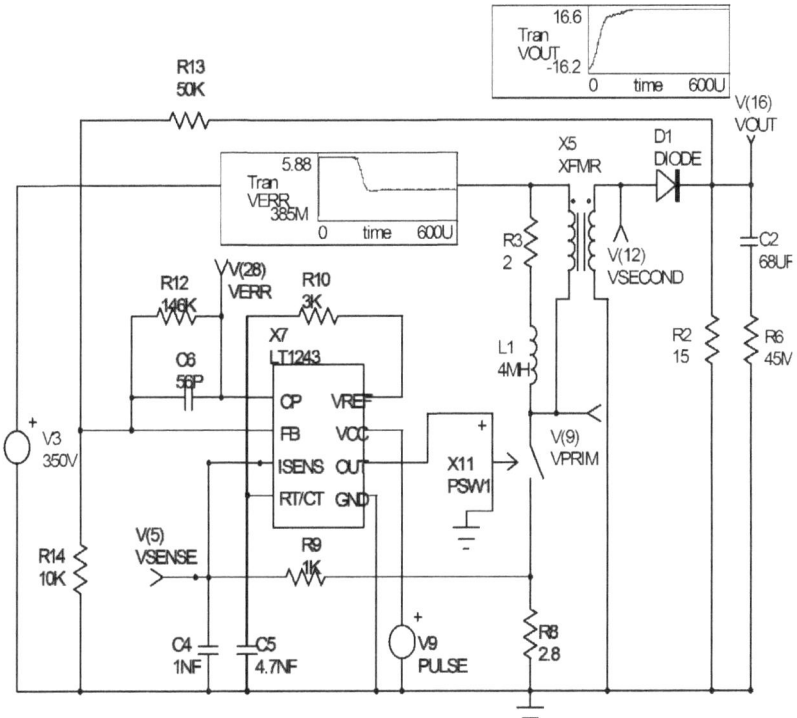

```
LT1243: OFF-LINE FLYBACK CONVERTER
*SPICE_NET
*INCLUDE DEVICE.LIB
*INCLUDE POWER.LIB
.TRAN 0.1US 0.6MS .1MS 100NS UIC
.OPTIONS METHOD=GEAR MINSTEP=50NS MINBREAK=-1 RELTOL=.01 ITL1=300 ITL4=300
.PRINT TRAN @U3[I] @D1[ID]
*ALIAS  V(9)=VPRIM
*ALIAS  V(16)=VOUT
*ALIAS  V(12)=VSECOND
*ALIAS  V(17)=ISENSE
*ALIAS  V(28)=VERR
.PRINT TRAN  V(9)  V(16)  V(12)  V(17)
.PRINT TRAN  V(28)
V3 2 0 350V
R2 16 0 15
C2 16 3 68UF IC=-14.8V
R3 1 2 2
X5 2 9 12 0 XFMR {RATIO=-0.05 }
R6 3 0 45M
D1 12 16 DIODE  OFF
.MODEL DIODE D (TT=1NS CJO=1PF RS=1M)
X7 28 21 17 27 0 11 15 25 LT1243
R8 14 0 2.8
V9 15 0 PULSE 0 15 0 1U
R9 17 14 1K
C4 17 0 1NF
C5 27 0 4.7NF
R10 27 25 3K
R12 21 28 146K
C6 21 28 56P
R13 21 16 50K
R14 21 0 10K
X9 9 14 11 0 PSW1 {RON=.1 VON=5 VOFF=3 ROFF=1E6 }
L1 1 9 4MH IC=0
.END
```

Figure 5.12

**Schematic for an Off-Line Flyback Converter using a
PWM IC Model Capable of Showing all Key Transient
Effects**

Note: The top-level netlist is also shown.

The simulation results of the transient model are shown below:

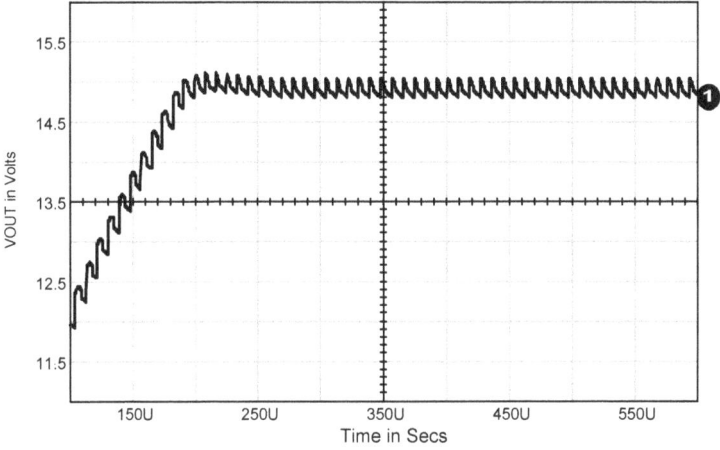

Figure 5.13

Transient Model Results

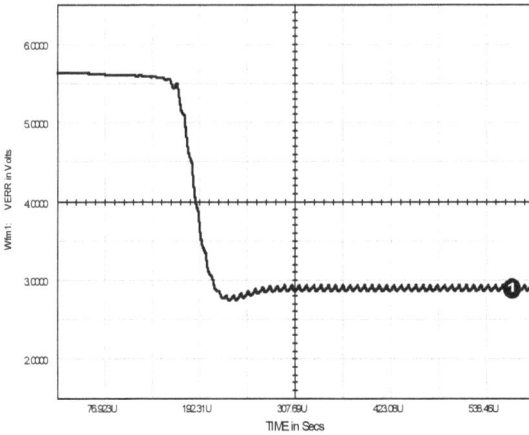

Figure 5.14

Transient Model Results

Adding Slope Compensation

The schematic in Figure 5.15 shows the addition of an external ramp to provide slope compensation to the model. The D output of the subcircuit is provided for this purpose. The D output is a voltage equivalent of the duty cycle, so a ramp is defined as K*D where K is the peak voltage of the ramp at a duty cycle of 1. K can also be described as the slope of the ramp divided by the switching frequency.

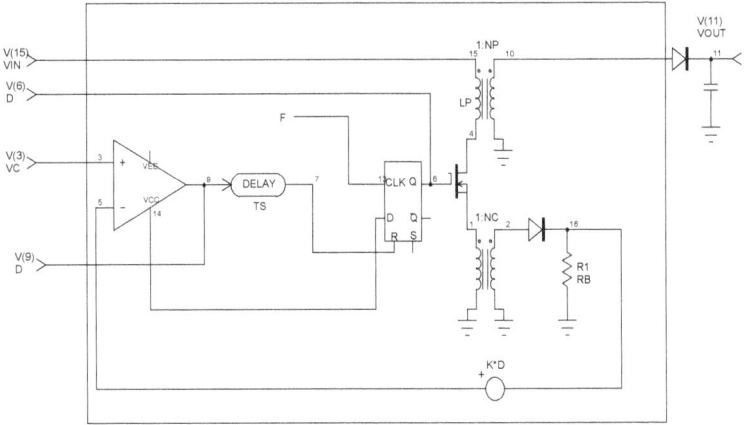

Figure 5.15

Schematic of the Subcircuit with the Addition of an External Ramp

Although we don't have access to the internal nodes required to add the ramp, we can rotate it through the comparator and easily add it externally. A non-linear dependent source (B element) is used to provide the multiplication of K*D. The schematic in Figure 5.16 shows the implementation of the slope compensation ramp which is external to the subcircuit.

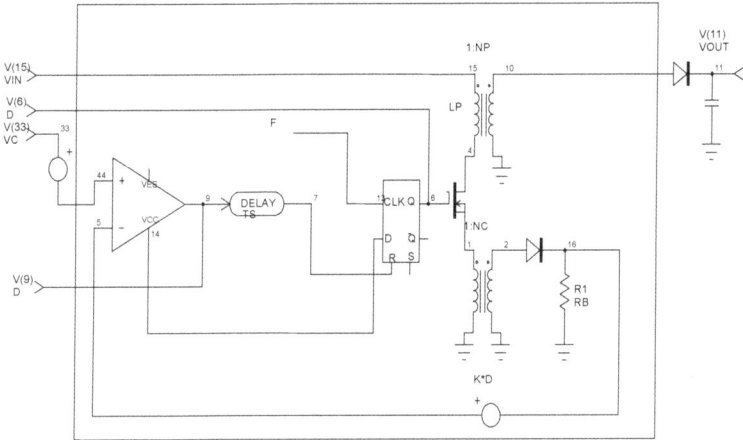

Figure 5.16

Schematic of the Subcircuit with the Addition of an External Ramp using a Nonlinear Dependent Source

Voltage Mode Control

Using a further extension of the circuit above, voltage mode control (also called duty cycle control) can be implemented. In this case, there is no current sensed, so RB would ideally be set to zero.

However, RB can not be set to zero because it would result in a "divide by zero error" within the subcircuit.

It can, however, be set to a very low value such as 1mΩ or lower, if necessary. Setting K to 1 will result in a duty cycle which is equal to the control voltage, Vc. The modulator gain may also be represented in this subcircuit by setting K equal to 1/Vr, where Vr is the peak-to-peak voltage of the ramp. Within the subcircuit, Vc is bounded between 0 and 1 Volt. In order to use this limiting function, it is recommended that you set K to 1 and that you add the modulator gain externally.

Chapter 6

Low Dropout Linear Regulator

POWER CONVERTERS TYPICALLY have multiple outputs. In some cases, the regulation is good enough that post regulation is not required. In many applications, the regulation requirement demands the use of post regulators for the secondary outputs.

Simple three terminal regulators may be used in the vast majority of applications, however, many applications are sensitive to the efficiency of the converter. A good example of this can be seen in the notebook computer, and other battery powered equipment.

The following circuit demonstrates a MOSFET low dropout regulator. The MOSFET is controlled by a TL431 shunt regulator IC. The use of the MOSFET reduces the minimum input-to-output differential voltage (headroom) from a value of 1.5 to 2V in a typical three terminal regulator, to the product of the output current and the MOSFET's on resistance.

It is possible to reduce the headroom requirement to tens of mV in many cases. The operation of the circuit is very simple and straightforward.

The circuit uses the MOSFET as a source follower. This causes the dominant pole to occur at the corner frequency which is created by the source impedance, $1/G_{FS}$, and the output capacitor. A second high frequency pole exists at the corner frequency which is created by the MOSFET's C_{ISS} and its driving impedance (the 1kΩ resistor in parallel with the 10kΩ bias resistor).

The compensation adds a low frequency pole and a zero at the dominant pole frequency. At low currents, the IRF140 has a G_{FS} of approximately 4 millimhos. This translates to a source resistance of 0.25Ω. The dominant pole frequency is therefore at:

$$\frac{1}{2\,\pi\,(.25)(33uF)} = 19{,}000Hz$$

The zero which is added by the compensation is at a frequency of:

$$\frac{1}{2\,\pi\,(2.49k)(3.3nF)} = 19{,}000Hz$$

Since the bandwidth is relatively low, the high frequency pole from C_{ISS} is not canceled. If greater bandwidth is necessary, this pole may be canceled via the placement of a small capacitor across the 5.49kΩ divider resistor.

Note: This circuit requires a bias voltage for the MOSFET gate, which is at least several volts greater than the output voltage. In most power converters, this bias voltage is available. In cases where the bias voltage is not available, a CMOS charge pump circuit is often used to generate it.

The following circuit was used to simulate the transient response, turn-on, headroom and ripple rejection performance of the low dropout regulator. The results are shown below:

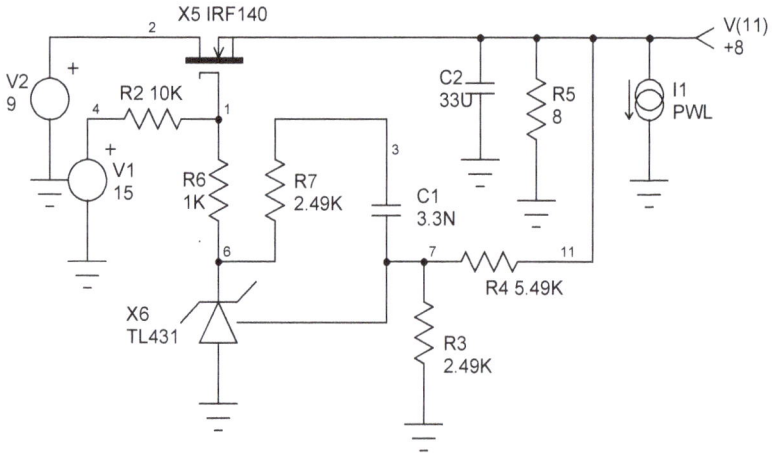

Figure 6.1

Schematic of a Low Dropout Regulator

```
LDO: LOW DROPOUT REGULATOR LDO1.CIR
.AC DEC 10 100HZ 1000KHZ
.DC V2 5 10 .1
.TRAN 1U 1M UIC
*INCLUDE POWMOS.LIB
*INCLUDE REG.LIB
*ALIAS  V(11)=+8
.PRINT AC  V(11)  UP(11)
.PRINT DC  V(11)
.PRINT TRAN  V(11)
V1 4 0 15
R3 7 0 2.49K
R4 7 11 5.49K
R5 11 0 8
V2 2 0 9 AC 1
X5 2 1 11 IRF140
X6 6 0 7 TL431
R6 1 6 1K
C1 3 7 3.3N
R7 3 6 2.49K
I1 11 0 PWL 0 0 500U 0 510U 2 750U 2 + 760U 0
C2 11 0 33U
R2 1 4 10K
.END
```

Headroom

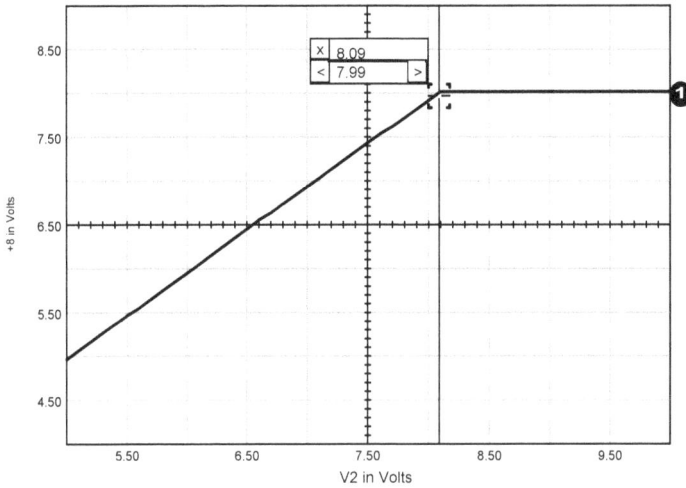

Figure 6.2

Headroom Measurement Graph

The headroom measurements indicate that the dropout voltage (the minimum voltage across the pass element) at 1A is 90mV. The use of a MOSFET with a lower on resistance will further reduce the headroom.

Transient Response

The graph below shows the response to a 2A step load. The circuit has a recovery time of approximately 50μsec, and a transient impedance of 10mΩ.

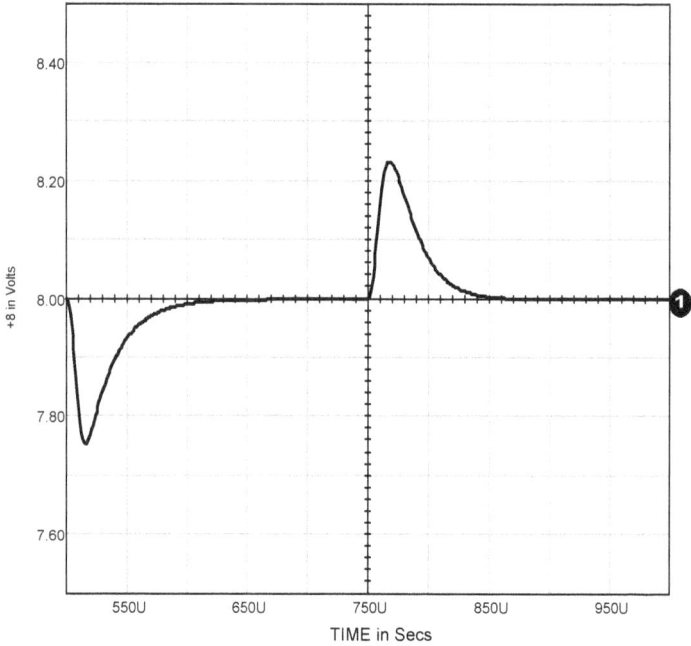

Figure 6.3

Response Curve Generated by a 2A Step Change in the Load

Ripple Rejection

The ability of the linear regulator to reject input perturbations (such as ripple) is shown below. This characteristic is equivalent to the CS-0X audio susceptibility requirements of the military standard, MIL-STD-461. The ripple rejection is primarily a function of the closed loop bandwidth of the regulator.

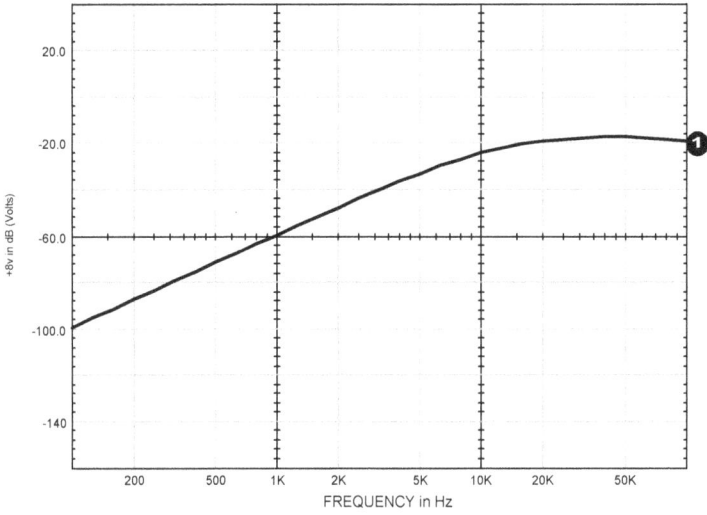

Figure 6.4

Frequency Domain Ripple Rejection Analysis Results

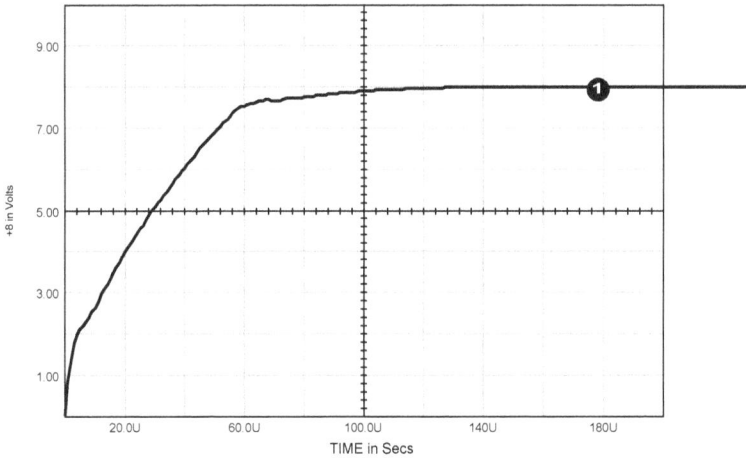

Figure 6.5

Transient Turn-On Response of the Linear Regulator

Control Loop Stability

Feedback stability is an important issue for all closed loop systems. The simple modification which has been added to the circuit below (L1, C1) allows us to measure the open loop gain and phase of the system while the circuit loop is still closed. This method is very similar to the method which is used by most modern network analyzers, such as the Veneable™ and the Hewlett Packard model 3577.

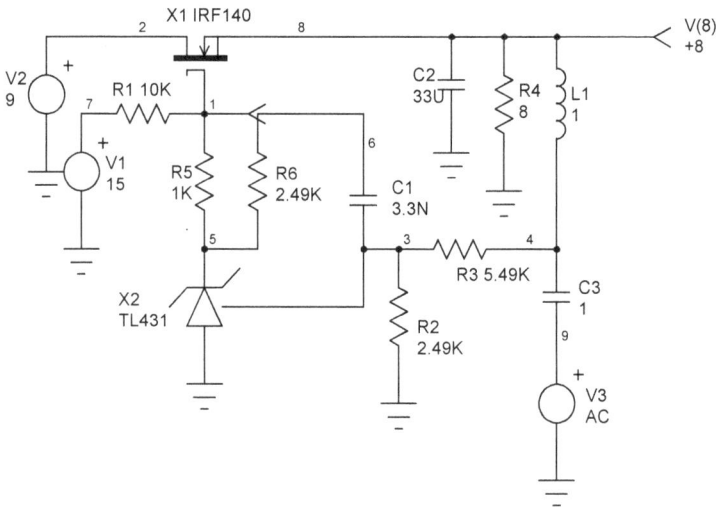

Figure 6.6

Feedback Stability Schematic uses a Large Value Inductor and Capacitor to Allow Closed Loop Measurements

```
LDO2: LOW DROPOUT REGULATOR
.AC DEC 10 100HZ 1MEG
*INCLUDE POWMOS.LIB
*INCLUDE REG.LIB
*ALIAS  V(8)=+8
.PRINT AC  V(8)  VP(8)  V(1)  VP(1)
V1 7 0 15
R2 3 0 2.49K
R3 3 4 5.49K
R4 8 0 8
V2 2 0 9
X1 2 1 8 IRF140
X2 5 0 3 TL431
R5 1 5 1K
C1 6 3 3.3N
R6 6 5 2.49K
C2 8 0 33U
C3 4 9 1
L1 8 4 1
V3 9 0 AC 1
R1 1 7 10K
.END
```

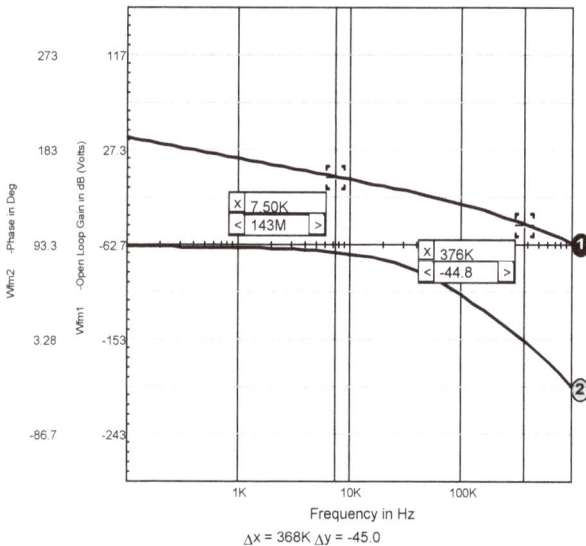

Figure 6.7

Bode Plot of the Feedback Loop

Figure 6.7 shows the Bode plot of the feedback loop. The graph indicates a 7.5kHz bandwidth with a phase margin of nearly 90 degrees, and a gain margin of 45dB.

The simulation results of the MOSFET LDO are extremely dependent on the accurate representation of the MOSFET G_{FS} over the operating load current range. In many cases the models provided by the manufacturer (which are also the models included in most simulator libraries) may not accurately represent this parameter. The next example is a similar regulator, designed to provide 2.5V output at up to 1 Amp. The simulations were performed with two MOSFET models. The first model is provided by the manufacturer and is available as a free download from their website. I wrote the second MOSFET model using measured data for the device and implementing it in a new MOSFET subcircuit topology that I expect to publish in the near future. (This model is included in the new PSPICE Power Library, available from AEi Design Systems). The regulator was also constructed so that the correlation results between the measured data using the two MOSFET models could be shown. Figure 6.8 shows the schematic of the example regulator.

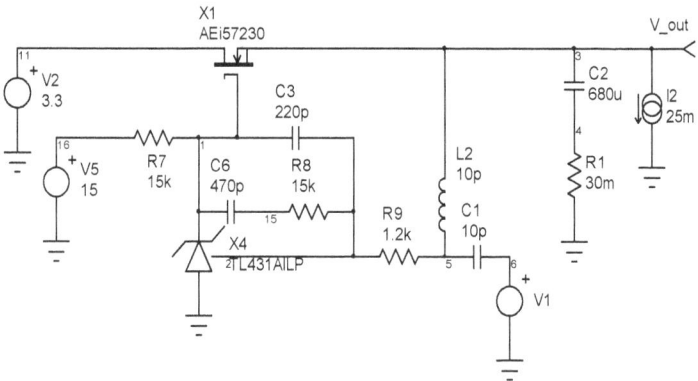

Figure 6.8

2.5V LDO Circuit

```
LDO: LOW DROPOUT REGULATOR LDO3.CIR
.TRAN .1u 1m .5m 1u
.OPTIONS abstol=1E-8 method=GEAR
.OPTIONS gmin=1E-9 icstep=40
.PRINT  TRAN V_out
C3 1 2 100p
X1 11 1 3 AEI57230 {  }
L2 5 3 10p
C1 5 6 10p
V1 6 0 AC=1
R1 4 0 30m
V2 11 0 DC=3.3 AC=1
C2 3 4 680u
I2 3 0 DC=25m PULSE 1m 1 100u .1u .1u 250u 500u
V5 16 0 DC=15
R7 16 1 15k
X4 1 0 2 TL431AILP {  }
C6 1 15 470p
R8 15 2 15k
R9 2 5 1.2k
.END
```

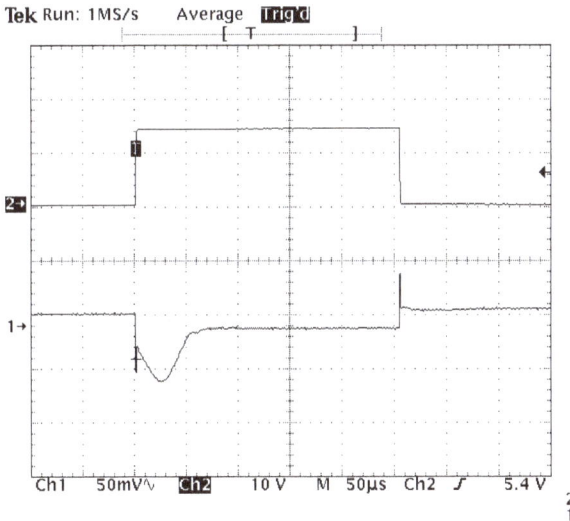

Figure 6.9

Measured Pulse Load Response

❶ v(3)   ❸ v(3)#b

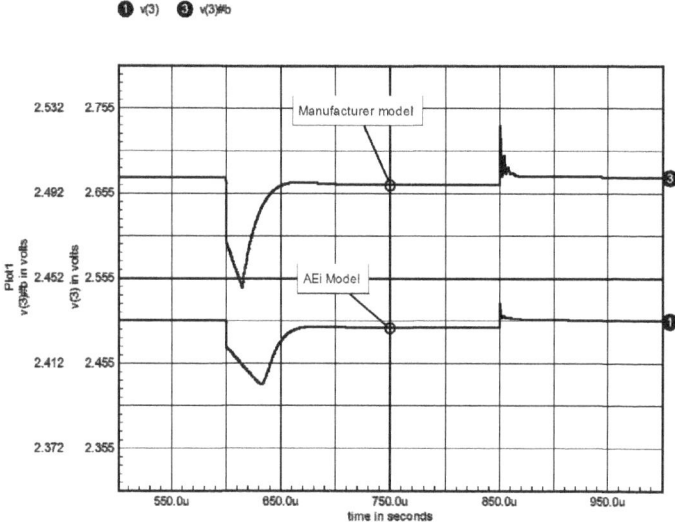

Figure 6.10

Simulated Pulse Load Response

The models show significantly different responses, while the AEi model is much closer to the measured response. The only difference between the two simulations is the MOSFET model. Measurements were made of the MOSFET transconductance at various load currents and the results were compared with the results from the two models. These results are shown below.

Id	Measured Result			Manufacturer model results			Aei model results		
	Vgs	Reff	Gfs	Vgs	Reff	Gfs	Vgs	Reff	Gfs
1mA	3.25	148.784	0.007	4.44	1	1.000	3.210	156.000	0.006
2mA	3.34	77.243	0.013	4.44	0.645	1.550	3.320	78.300	0.013
5mA	3.45	36.653	0.027	4.45	0.447	2.237	3.470	31.470	0.032
10mA	3.57	17.257	0.058	4.45	0.351	2.849	3.570	15.820	0.063
25mA	3.7	7.357	0.136	4.45	0.261	3.831	3.720	6.406	0.156
50mA	3.82	3.621	0.276	4.46	0.221	4.525	3.830	3.250	0.308
100mA	3.93	1.799	0.556	4.46	0.19	5.263	3.940	1.667	0.600
200mA	4.03	0.940	1.064	4.49	0.168	5.952	4.060	0.868	1.152
500mA	4.15	0.449	2.228	4.53	0.149	6.711	4.230	0.383	2.611

Measured and simulated results are shown for loop gain measurements at 1mA and 1A load currents. These results are shown in Figures 6.11 and 6.12 respectively. All of the simulations use the AEi MOSFET model.

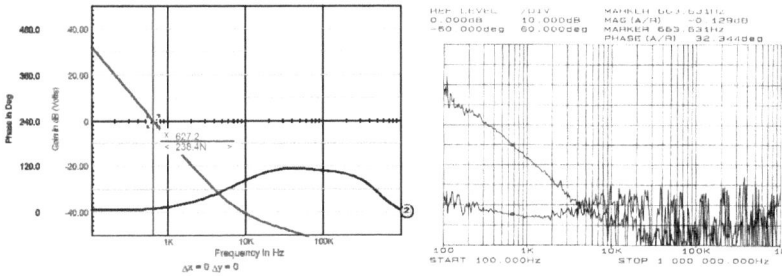

Figure 6.11

Loop Gain Results—1mA Load

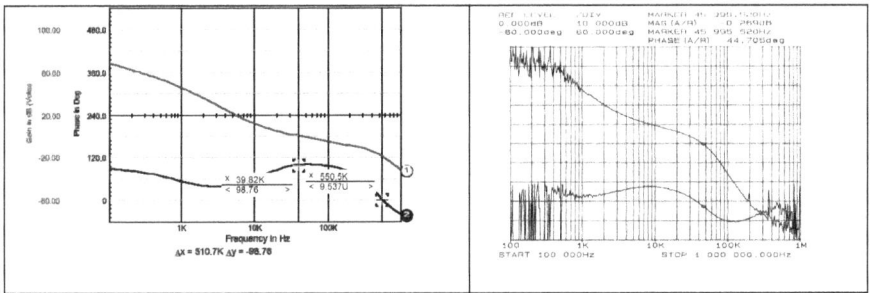

Figure 6.12

Loop Gain Results—1A Load

These results show that the regulator loop gain bandwidth varies from approximately 650Hz at 1mA to 45kHz at 1Amp representing a multiplying factor of 69 all due to the MOSFET transconductance.

The AEi model proved to be quite accurate over the entire load current range.

A similar effect exists with Bipolar Junction Transistors. The transconductance of the BJT device is much more predictable, making it a somewhat simpler simulation.

The transconductance of a BJT device is:

$$Gfs = \frac{1}{re' + R}$$

Where *ré* is defined by Shockley's relation:

$$re' = \frac{26mV}{Ie}$$

…and R is the internal bulk resistance of the emitter. The BJT Spice models are generally very accurate since the model topology is fixed, and there is really only one variable controlling G_{FS}. The BJT generally results in a higher frequency pole, due to the higher G_{FS}, however the MOSFET regulator can operate with a lower input-output differential voltage.

There are also several low dropout voltage regulators that utilize a PNP transistor or a P-Channel MOSFET. These configurations can often operate with a single supply voltage and the BJT version can operate with an input-output voltage differential as low as a few hundred millivolts, depending on VCE_{SAT}. An example of a PNP BJT voltage regulator is shown in Figure 6.13.

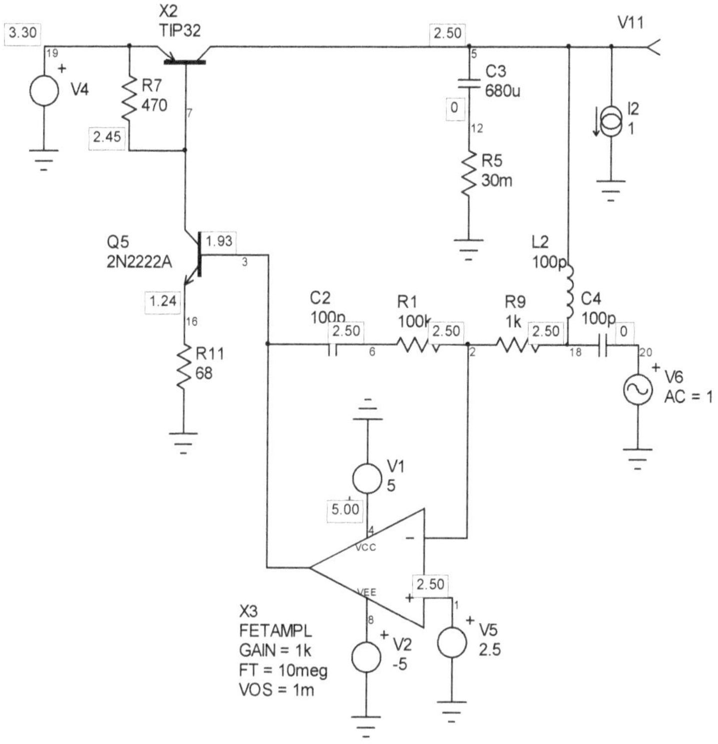

Figure 6.13

PNP BJT Regulator Circuit

```
PNP_LDO.cir
.AC DEC 20 10 1meg
.OPTIONS abstol=1E-8 itl1=1000 method=GEAR
.OPTIONS autotol=-2 icstep=40
.PRINT  AC Vdb(V11) phase(V11)
X3 4 2 3 1 8 OPA27B {  }
X1 5 7 19 SI4463DY {  }
V1 1 0 DC=-5
R1 2 6 10k
C2 6 8 1n
ILoad 5 0 DC=1
V2 3 0 DC=3.3
Q2 7 8 9 QN2222A
U3 4 0 DC=2.5
U4 19 0 DC=3.3
C3 5 12 680u
R5 12 0 30m
R7 19 7 4.7k
L2 5 18 100
C4 18 20 100
V6 20 0 AC=1
R9 2 18 1k
R11 9 0 100
.END
```

In this case the PNP transistor is driven by a current source (Q5). If we look at the Base of Q5 as the control voltage then the transfer function from V_C to V_{OUT} is:

$$Vout \approx \frac{Vc}{R11} \cdot \frac{Hfe_{X2}}{Zout}$$

Where Z_{OUT} is the impedance of the output capacitor (and its ESR) along with the external load impedance. In this configuration the transfer function is not dependent on the transconducance of the output transistor, but primarily on the H_{FE} of the output transistor. The transistor H_{FE} is dependent on the load current, the operating temperature and the relatively wide initial production tolerances. Nuclear radiation will also have a significant impact on H_{FE}.

Driving the output transistor from a voltage rather than a

current changes the transfer function to:

$$Vout \approx Vc \cdot \frac{Gfs}{Zout}$$

...which is dependent on the transistor GFS. A final and more complicated configuration using a P-Channel MOSFET is shown in Figure 6.14.

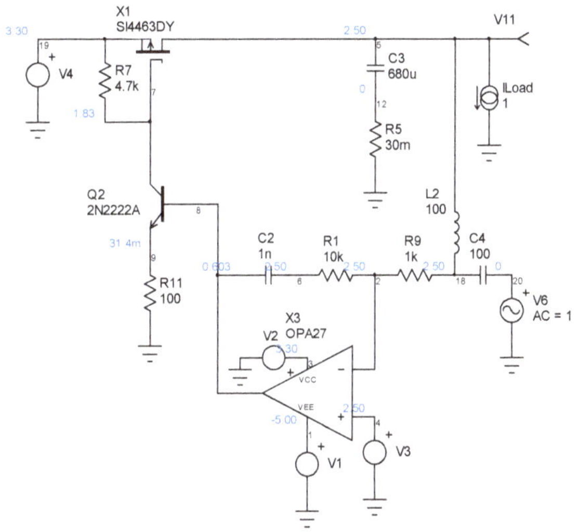

Figure 6.14

P-Channel MOSFET Regulator Circuit

```
PNP_LDO.cir
.AC DEC 20 10 1meg
.OPTIONS abstol=1E-8 itl1=1000 method=GEAR
.OPTIONS autotol=-2 icstep=40
.PRINT  AC Vdb(V11) phase(V11)
X3 4 2 3 1 8 OPA27B {  }
X1 5 7 19 SI4463DY {  }
V1 1 0 DC=-5
R1 2 6 10k
C2 6 8 1n
ILoad 5 0 DC=1
V2 3 0 DC=3.3
Q2 7 8 9 QN2222A
V3 4 0 DC=2.5
V4 19 0 DC=3.3
C3 5 12 680u
R5 12 0 30m
R7 19 7 4.7k
L2 5 18 100
C4 18 20 100
V6 20 0 AC=1
R9 2 18 1k
R11 9 0 100
.END
```

Considering the Base of Q2 as the control voltage, V_C then we can see that the current through Q2 is a function of the Gate-Source voltage required to obtain the output current, which is a non-linear variable.

The *ré* of Q2 is a function of this current, and influences the voltage gain of the loop. The relationship is:

$$Vout = Vc \cdot \frac{R7}{R11 + re'} \cdot Gfs \cdot Zout$$

For clarity, I left out that there is also a pole created by the input capacitance of the MOSFET, C_{ISS}. By inspection of this equation it is clear that the gain term is dependent on the operating current of Q2, which is dependent on the load current, G_{FS} and the threshold voltage of the MOSFET.

There are also two poles, one from C_{ISS} and the other from the output capacitor. Loop Gain plots are shown in Figure 6.15 for load currents of 1mA and 1Amp. You can see that there is a 3 decade change in bandwidth as a result of the load current change and also that the circuit is not stable at 1mA load.

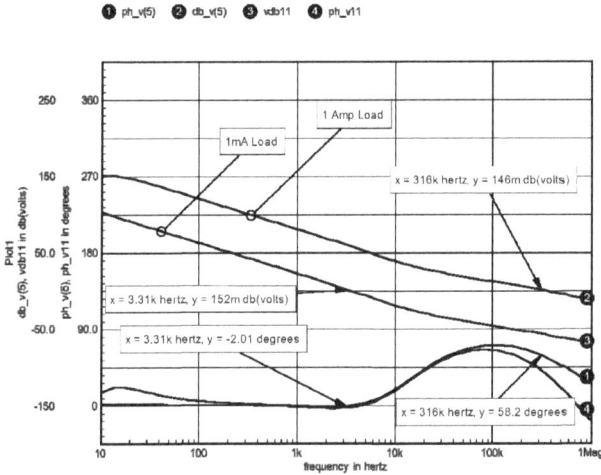

Figure 6.14

P-Channel MOSFET Regulator Loop Gain

The poor stability at 1mA is also evident in the output impedance of the regulator, shown in Figure 6.15.

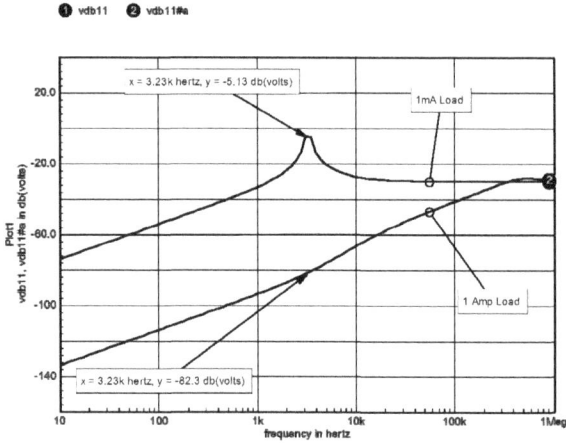

Figure 6.15

P-Channel MOSFET Regulator Output Impedance

This circuit can be stabilized over a wide operating load current, however it is important to consider the effects of the MOSFET and the driving transistor on the overall regulator stability. In any case the very large variations make is a difficult and certainly less than ideal choice as well as a significant challenge to simulate.

The most common topology of the three terminal regulator uses an NPN Bipolar Junction transistor (BJT) as the output series pass element. Some of the newer devices use power MOSFETs, which would then be very similar to the example shown in Figure 6.8. The basic structure of the most common three terminal voltage regulator is shown in Figure 6.16.

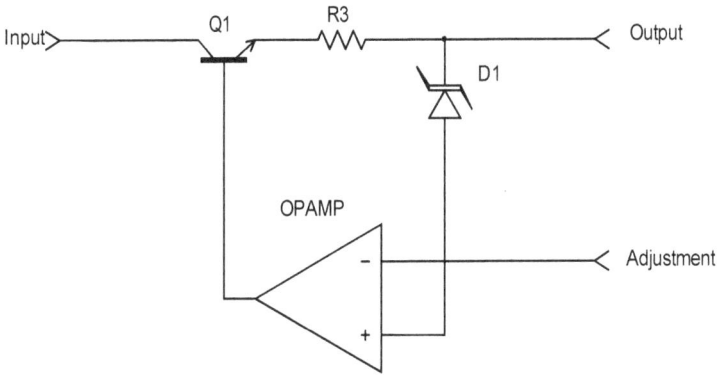

Figure 6.16

Typical Three Terminal Regulator

The output transistor, Q1 has an effective emitter resistance that is related to the emitter current by Shockley's equation:

$$re' = \frac{26mV}{Ie}$$

This relationship is valid at low emitter currents and at higher currents re is limited by the internal bulk resistances of the transistor as well as any external resistors, such as emitter current limit sense resistors. At very low currents, an upper resistance limit may be imposed due to the use of a base-emitter resistor. The overall resistance, including these limits is defined by the term R_{EFF}.

The effect of this R_{EFF} resistance is to combine with the output capacitor resulting in a frequency pole in the feedback path that is defined by:

$$\text{Fpole} = \frac{1}{2 \cdot \pi \cdot \text{Reff} \cdot \text{Cout}}$$

This frequency pole is in addition to the typical dominant pole compensation of the voltage regulator which results in conditional stability of the voltage feedback loop. This additional pole is further complicated by the fact that it has a load dependent corner frequency and also that it is proportional to load capacitance. Devices may also vary from manufacturer to manufacturer since the internal feedback loop characteristics are generally not specification controlled.

The use of a MOSFET in place of a BJT has a similar effect, but Shockley's equation does not apply. The effective resistance of the MOSFET device is typically much greater than that of the BJT.

An example circuit was constructed as shown in Figure 6.17. A 0 to 100mA step load was applied in addition to the 2.2K resistor load in order to see the effects of the moving frequency pole and the poor resulting phase margin.

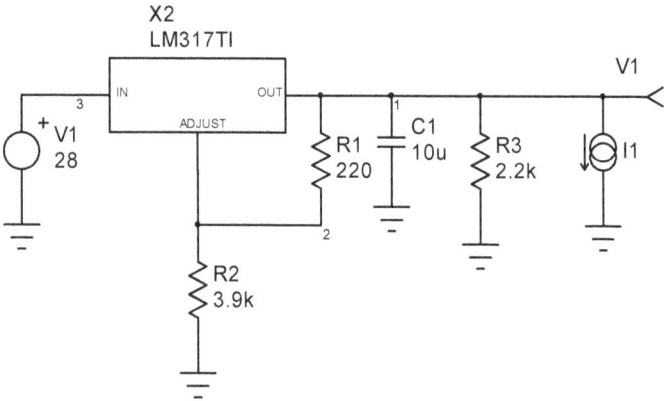

Figure 6.17

LM317 Three Terminal Regulator Test Circuit

```
LM317TI.cir
.TRAN 1u 10m 0 10u
.PRINT  TRAN V1
C1 1 0 10u
R1 1 2 220
R2 2 0 3.9k
R3 1 0 2.2k
V1 3 0 DC=28
I1 1 0 PULSE 0 .1 2m 1u 1u 5m 10m
X2 3 2 1 LM317TI {  }
.END
```

The measured step load response is shown in Figure 6.18 and the SPICE model simulation result is shown in Figure 6.19.

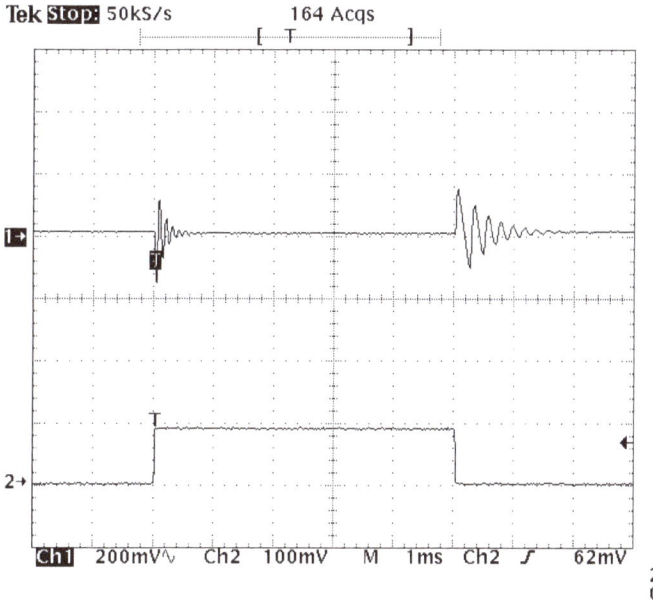

Figure 6.18

LM317 Three Terminal Regulator Test Circuit Response

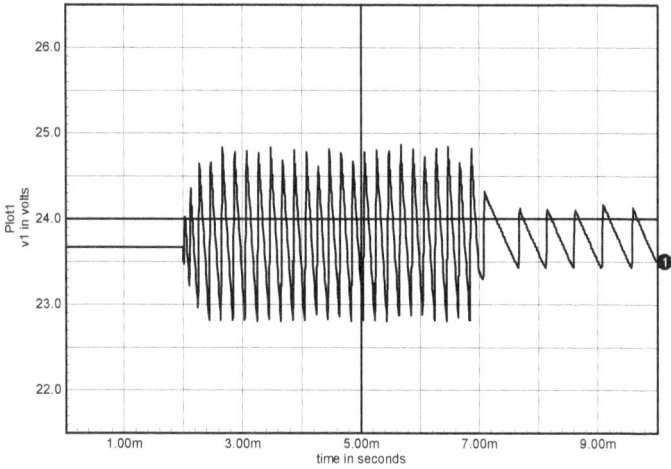

Figure 6.19

LM317 Three Terminal Regulator Simulated Response

While the models do not agree all that well, both the measured result and the simulated result indicate poor stability. The loop gain of the test circuit was measured with only the 2.2KΩ load resistor. The measured result is shown in Figure 6.20.

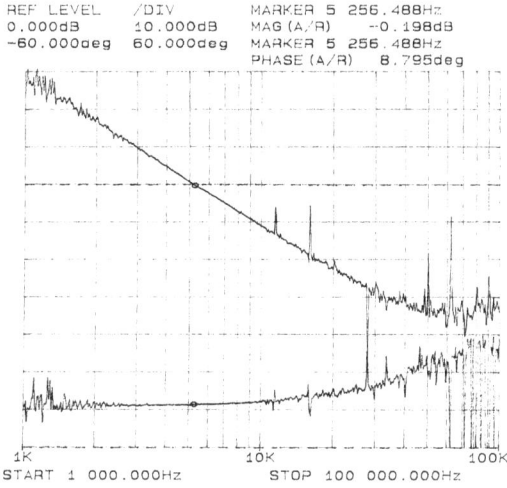

Figure 6.20

Three Terminal Regulator Test Circuit with 2.2K Load

Chapter 7

DC-to-AC Conversions

WHILE MOST OF this book has been dedicated to the modeling and simulation of DC-to-DC converters, there are applications such as Uninterruptible Power Supplies (UPS) that convert a DC input voltage to a sinusoidal AC output voltage. The basis of the conversion is very similar to the conversion of a DC input voltage to a DC output voltage.

One of the more difficult aspects of DC-to-AC conversion is obtaining a regulated, low distortion sine wave reference. Several example circuits which demonstrate different techniques for generating sine wave references are contained in this chapter.

Using SPICE to Generate a Sine ROM

The following example demonstrates an unusual task for SPICE. This example is the result of an actual design for a three phase sine wave reference (only one phase is shown). The circuit simulates a single bit pulse code representation of a sine wave. The implementation is accomplished using a microprocessor which generates a 4 bit word. One bit is used for each of the three phase references, while the 4th bit is used to generate a synchronization pulse which is required by other circuits. The microprocessor functions as a crystal oscillator and counter. This implementation allows the microprocessor to support functions such as programmable frequency, which are used to support 50, 60 and 400 Hz outputs. Much of the protection circuitry is also realized by the microprocessor.

The fundamental problem is the generation of a bit pattern for the sine wave reference. The first circuit below shows a novel approach for generating the bit pattern for a single phase. The same circuit is easily extended to three phases (or any other number of phases).

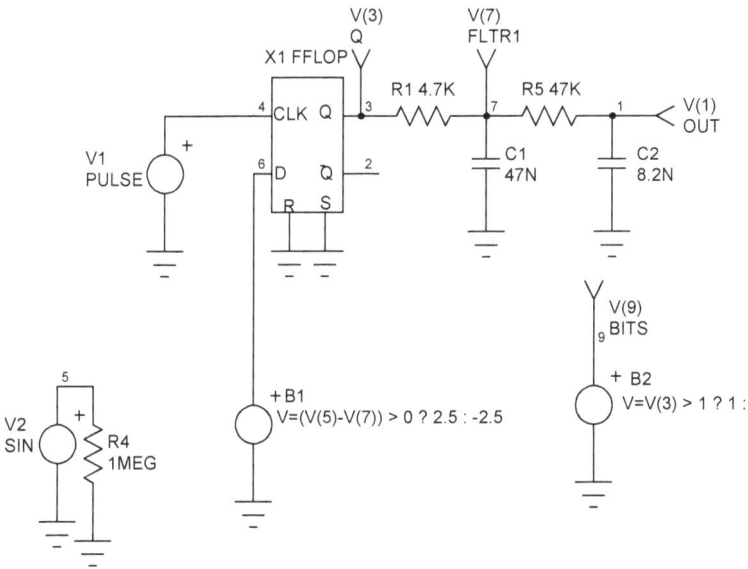

```
SINE.CIR: BIT PATTERN GENERATOR
*INCLUDE STEVES.LIB
*INCLUDE POWER.LIB
.OPTIONS LONE=2.5 LZERO=-2.5 + LTHRESH=0 RELTOL=.01
.TRAN 9.766U 9M UIC
.FOUR 400HZ U(1)
*ALIAS  U(1)=OUT
*ALIAS  U(3)=Q
*ALIAS  U(9)=BITS
*ALIAS  U(7)=FLTR1
.PRINT TRAN  U(1)  U(3)  U(9)  U(7)
R1 3 7 4.7K
C1 7 0 47N IC=0
U1 4 0 PULSE -2.5 2.5 10N 10N 10N 5U + 9.766U
U2 5 0 SIN 0 1.5 400
R4 5 0 1MEG
R5 7 1 47K
C2 1 0 8.2N IC=0
B1 6 0 U=(U(5)-U(7)) > 0 ? 2.5 : -2.5
B2 9 0 U=U(3) > 1 ? 1 : 0
X1 4 6 0 0 2 3 FFLOP
.END
```

Figure 7.1

**Schematic and Netlist Showing a Novel Approach for
Generating a Bit Pattern**

The pulse generator, V1, is used as the clock. Since we will generate 256 values in the table, this clock is 256 times greater than the output frequency. Flip flop, X1, was created using Boolean logic expressions. It latches the data between clock pulses. V2 is a sine wave which is used as a reference in the circuit. R1, R5, C1, and C2 filter the pulse coded waveform and reconstruct the sine wave. B1 is a simple comparator that sets the output bit high if the sine wave output is lower than the sine wave reference value, or sets the output bit low if the sine wave output is higher than the sine wave reference value. B2 shifts the level of the bit values to a zero-one format (If V(3) is greater than 1 than V(9) is set to 1V otherwise V(9) is set to 0V).

The SPICE .FOUR analysis is performed on the sine wave output in order to place the total harmonic distortion in the output table. The circuit was simulated several times, with different amplitude values for V2. The lowest distortion occurs with the values listed in Figure 7.1. As we look at the output data in IntuScope, we can see the bit patterns and the sine wave output at each filter stage. Note that more sophisticated filters could produce lower distortion, as could more values in the data table. The waveforms below show the sine wave output and the one-zero bit pattern which is produced by B2.

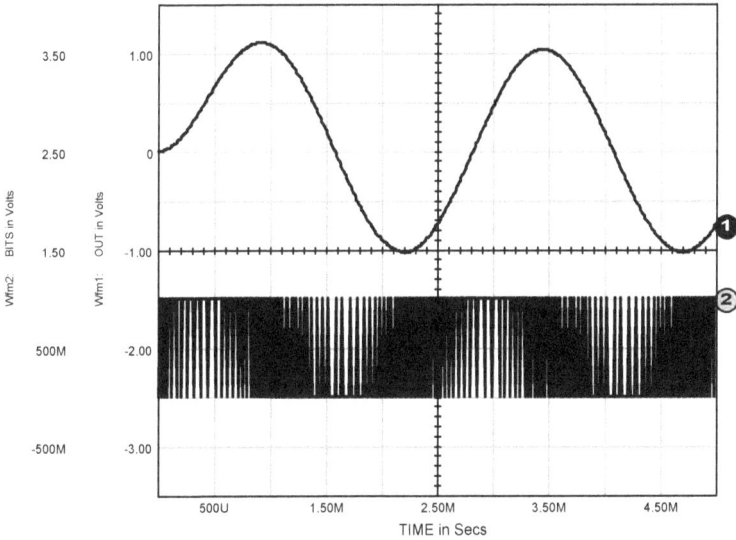

Figure 7.2

Sinewave Output and Bit Pattern Produced by the Circuit in Figure 7.1

Notice that the circuit starts with initial voltages of zero. For that reason, two cycles are simulated and the data for the Fourier analysis is extracted only from the second cycle so that the transient residues are eliminated.

While this demonstrates the circuit operation, it does not produce the data in a desirable format. A section of the output listing is shown below.

```
**** 04/22/05 11:14:34 ******* PSpice 10.0.0 (Jan 2003) *******
     SINE: BIT PATTERN GENERATOR
****    FOURIER ANALYSIS          TEMPERATURE =  27.000 DEG C
     *********************************************************
FOURIER COMPONENTS OF TRANSIENT RESPONSE V(1)
DC COMPONENT = 7.470631E-04
```

HARMONIC NO	FREQUENCY (HZ)	FOURIER COMPONENT	NORMALIZED COMPONENT	PHASE (DEG)	NORMALIZED PHASE (DEG)
1	4.000E+02	1.035E+00	1.000E+00	1.704E+02	0.000E+00
2	8.000E+02	1.618E-03	1.564E-03	5.586E+01	-2.850E+02
3	1.200E+03	9.813E-04	9.482E-04	1.264E+02	-3.849E+02
4	1.600E+03	6.173E-04	5.965E-04	1.679E+02	-5.139E+02
5	2.000E+03	1.506E-03	1.456E-03	6.730E+01	-7.849E+02
6	2.400E+03	3.724E-04	3.599E-04	-1.354E+02	-1.158E+03
7	2.800E+03	5.308E-04	5.129E-04	-1.345E+02	-1.328E+03
8	3.200E+03	2.945E-04	2.846E-04	-7.875E+01	-1.442E+03
9	3.600E+03	2.342E-04	2.263E-04	1.356E+02	-1.398E+03

```
     TOTAL HARMONIC DISTORTION =  2.518698E-01 PERCENT

**** 04/22/05 11:14:34 ******* PSpice 10.0.0 (Jan 2003) *******
     SINE: BIT PATTERN GENERATOR

****    TRANSIENT ANALYSIS         TEMPERATURE =  27.000 DEG C

     *********************************************************

TIME     V(1)     V(3)     V(9)     V(7)

0.000E+00  1.601E-15 -1.383E-04  0.000E+00  4.617E-09
9.766E-06  1.248E-03  2.312E+00  1.000E+00  9.912E-02
```

Figure 7.3

SPICE Transient Data (below) and Fourier Results (above) for the Simulation in Figure 7.2

The distortion analysis results are displayed along with the output data in the output file. In order to obtain the table in the desired format, we will re-simulate a modified version of the circuit. The .Options Numdgt=0 setting causes the output to be displayed in the output file using no decimal places (integer values only). The results will display properly in the IsSpice real time display when the simulation is run; however, the data in IntuScope will appear to be incorrect since it is read from the output file, which has only integer values. Only two columns of data will appear in the output file. The first column is the bit pattern and the second column is the index number. The numbers are displayed in exponential format. Via the search and replace command found in most text editors, we can clean up the two values that are present. Replace 1e+000 with 1, and replace 0e+000 with 0. The result will be a bit pattern as shown in the partial output file below.

```
SINE2.CIR: MODIFIED BIT PATTERN GENERATOR
*INCLUDE STEVES.LIB
*INCLUDE POWER.LIB
.OPTIONS LONE=2.5 LZERO=-2.5 LTHRESH=0 RELTOL=.01 NUMDGT=0
.TRAN 9.766U 4.99M 2.5M UIC
*ALIAS  V(9)=BITS
.PRINT TRAN V(9)
R1 3 7 4.7K
C1 7 0 47N IC=0
V1 4 0 PULSE -2.5 2.5 10N 10N 10N 5U 9.766U
V2 5 0 SIN 0 1.5 400
R2 5 0 1MEG
R3 7 1 47K
C2 1 0 8.2N IC=0
B1 6 0 V=(V(5)-V(7)) > 0 ? 2.5 : -2.5
B2 9 0 V=V(3) > 1 ? 1 : 0
X1 4 6 0 0 2 3 FFLOP
.END
```

TIME	V(9)	INDEX
	0	0
	1	1
	1	2
	0	3
	1	4
	1	5
	0	6
	1	7
	1	8
	1	9
	0	10

Figure 7.4

Partial Output File Listing after the Transient Data has been Manipulated

The left column is our bit pattern (which has 256 values) and the right column is the index (think of the index as an address).

This bit pattern can now be coded into ROM. In order to achieve a three phase bit pattern, the circuit can be copied three times and the sine wave reference can be replaced by a three phase reference. The result will be 3 columns of bit data and an index column.

State Machine Modeling

The IsSpice simulator has the ability to model digital functions using a state machine model (See Chapter 8). State machine models allow very fast simulation of large digital systems. The state machine model in Figure 7.5 ran in .48 seconds, compared with 3.0 second for Figure 7.1! For comparison purposes this same circuit took 79 seconds in the first edition of this book!

While this is a very simple circuit, it does illustrate the power and speed improvements which can be attained. In general, the greater the complexity of the digital circuit, the greater the benefit provided by the state machine model. The following example uses the output data from the previous example in order to create a state machine model for an 8 bit counter with a 256 x 1 bit ROM.

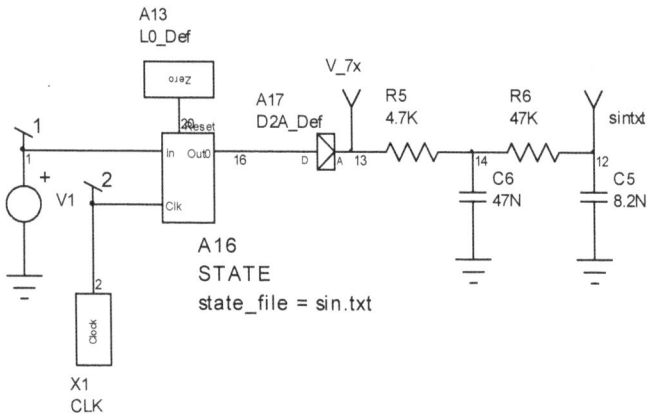

```
NEWSINE.cir
.TRAN 9.766u 10m 0 UIC
.FOUR 400 v(12)
.PRINT  TRAN U_7x
.PRINT  TRAN sintxt
X1 2 CLK { FREQ=102.4K DUTY=50 }
V1 1 0 DC=0
C5 12 0 8.2N
R5 13 14 4.7K
R6 14 12 47K
A13 20 L0_DefA5
.MODEL L0_DefA5 D_pulldown( load=1.0P)
A17 [ 16 ] [ 13 ] D2A_DefA8
in_high=3.00 rise_delay=1N fall_delay=1N
.MODEL D2A_DefA8 dac_bridge( out_low=-2.5 out_high=2.5
+ out_undef=0.0E+000 t_rise=1.0N t_fall=1.0N
+ input_load=1.0P)
C6 14 0 47N
A16 [ 1_Din ] 2 20 [ 16 ] STATEA20
.MODEL STATEA20 d_state( clk_delay=1n reset_delay=1n
+ state_file=sin.txt reset_state=0 input_load=1p clk_load=1p
+ reset_load=1p)
A16_Din_1 [  1] [  1_Din] A2D
.MODEL A2D adc_bridge( in_low=0.600
.END
```

Figure 7.5

Schematic and Netlist for the Sinewave Generator using a State Machine Model

Referring to the netlist, the state machine model is described by the .Model Sinst line. Various delays are shown along with a pointer (state_file=sin.txt) to the file containing the state definition table. The state file model parameter is actually like any other SPICE model parameter except that instead of being a number, its value is that of a file name. The A elements describe either digital elements or "bridges". The bridges act like translation devices. They convert signals between the various analog and digital elements. These "SPICE" extensions, included in IsSpice, were taken from XSPICE, a public domain version of SPICE 3 that includes a digital logic simulator extension [36].

Selected from Output File

Fourier analysis for v(12):

No. Harmonics: 10, THD: 0.264578 %, Gridsize: 200, Interpolation Degree: 1

HARMONIC NO	FREQUENCY (HZ)	FOURIER COMPONENT	NORMALIZED COMPONENT	PHASE (DEG)	NORMALIZED PHASE (DEG)
1	4.00E+02	1.06E+00	-4.37E+01	1.00E+00	0.00E+00
2	8.00E+02	1.77E-03	-1.94E+01	1.67E-03	2.43E+01
3	1.20E+03	9.58E-04	-1.60E+02	9.03E-04	-1.17E+02
4	1.60E+03	6.71E-04	2.45E+01	6.33E-04	6.82E+01
5	2.00E+03	1.65E-03	6.69E+01	1.56E-03	1.11E+02
6	2.40E+03	4.15E-04	1.29E+01	3.91E-04	5.66E+01
7	2.80E+03	5.52E-04	1.53E+02	5.21E-04	1.96E+02
8	3.20E+03	3.43E-04	-6.41E-02	3.23E-04	4.36E+01
9	3.60E+03	2.49E-04	-7.86E+00	2.35E-04	3.58E+01

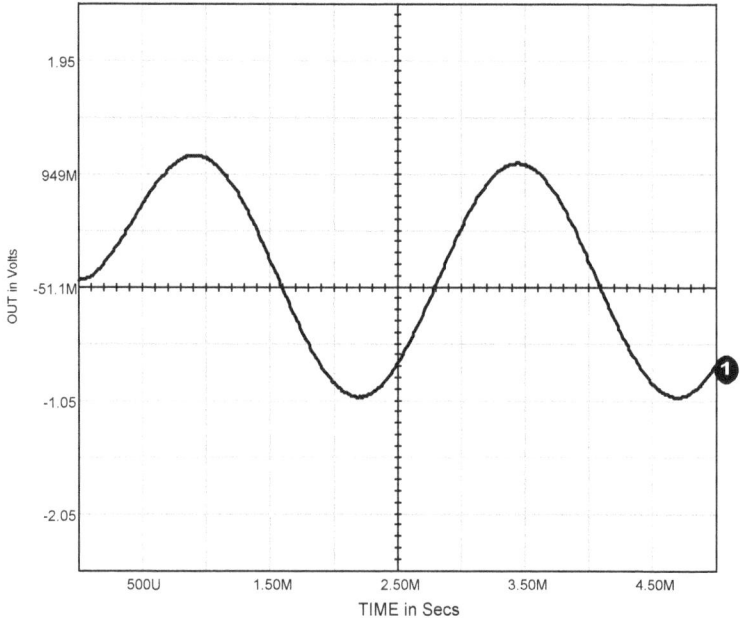

Figure 7.6

Fourier Analysis (top) and Transient Response (bottom) of the Sin ROM Circuit in Figure 7.5

218

Using the Sine Reference to Drive a Power Stage

The sine reference is useful for generating a reference signal for applications such as a UPS (Uninterruptible Power Supply), but it is also capable of directly driving a power stage.

The following circuit demonstrates the use of the bit code pattern to directly drive a push-pull converter stage.

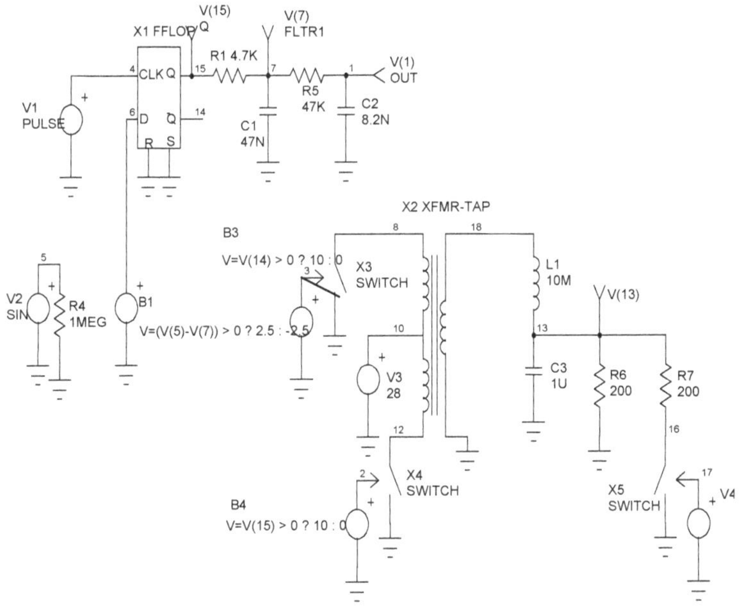

Figure 7.7

A Push-Pull Converter Driven by the State Machine Sine ROM

Notice the distorted waveform and the "spike" at 3.15msec, which was generated by the step load.

A second simulation was performed using the identical circuit, but the input voltage was 28V, as opposed to the 24V input in the first simulation. The output voltages of both simulations are shown in the following graph.

These two simulations show the two major drawbacks of this

simple circuit. The first is the relatively high output impedance which results from the output filter. The second is the inability to regulate the output voltage against input voltage changes.

The circuit is still useful, however, it should be restricted to applications where the input voltage is stabilized (or the regulation of the output isn't a concern) and the load is relatively static.

Such applications may include ballasts, motors, and lamps.

```
UPS.CIR
*INCLUDE STEVES.LIB
*INCLUDE POWER.LIB
.OPTIONS LONE=2.5 LZERO=-2.5 LTHRESH=0 RELTOL=.01
.TRAN 9.766U 10M UIC
.FOUR 400HZ U(13)
*INCLUDE DEVICE.LIB
*ALIAS  U(1)=OUT
*ALIAS  U(15)=Q
*ALIAS  U(7)=FLTR1
.PRINT TRAN  U(1)  U(15)  U(7)  U(13)
R1 15 7 4.7K
C1 7 0 47N IC=0
U1 4 0 PULSE -2.5 2.5 10N 10N 10N 5U 9.766U
U2 5 0 SIN 0 1.5 400
R5 7 1 47K
C2 1 0 8.2N IC=0
B1 6 0 U=(U(5)-U(7)) > 0 ? 2.5 : -2.5
X2 18 0 8 11 10 XFMR-TAP {RATIO=.1 }
X4 10 0 2 SWITCH
U3 11 0 24
L1 18 13 10M
C3 13 0 1U
R6 13 0 200
X3 8 0 12 SWITCH
R4 5 0 1MEG
B3 12 0 U=U(14) > 0 ? 10 : 0
B4 2 0 U=U(15) > 0 ? 10 : 0
R7 13 16 200
X5 16 0 17 SWITCH
U4 17 0 PWL 0 10 3.125M 10 3.15M 0
X1 4 6 0 0 14 15 FFLOP
.END
```

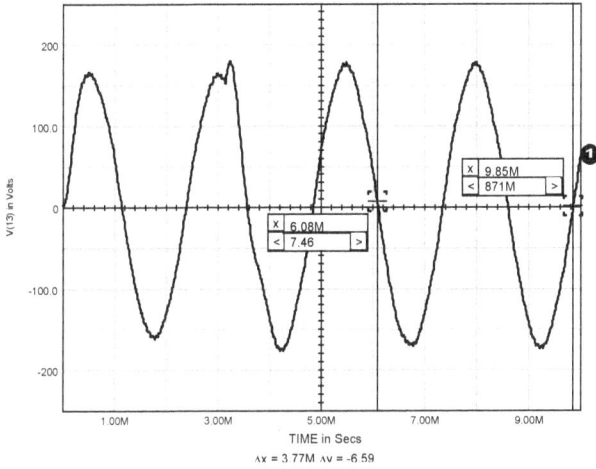

Figure 7.8

Output of the Push-Pull Converter of Figure 7.7

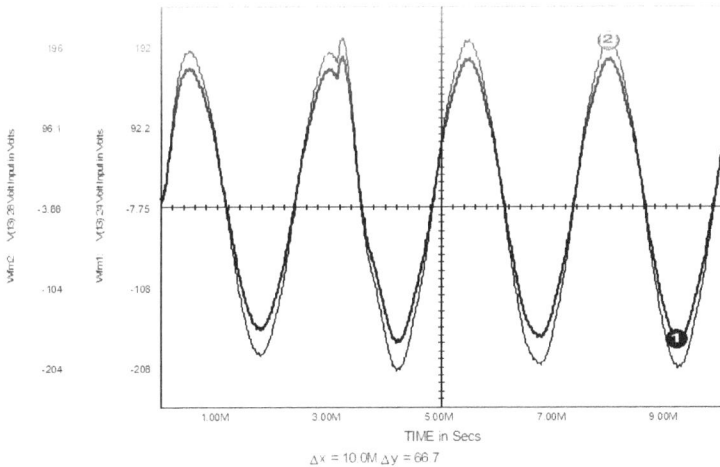

Figure 7.9

Output of the Push-Pull Converter using 24 and 28 Volt Inputs

Improving the Sine Wave Power Circuit

Both of the weaknesses of the simple circuit in Figure 7.7 can be easily overcome. The following circuit uses the sine reference voltage, V(5), and compares it with the actual output voltage, V(19). This approach uses the same algorithm as we used to create the reference which stabilized the output voltage. The result is greatly improved regulation with respect to both line and load changes.

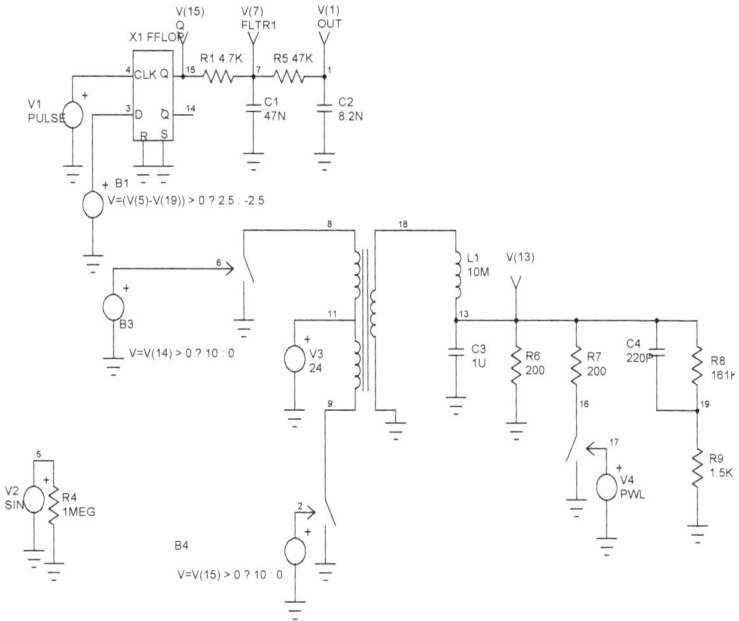

```
UPS_COMPARE.CIR USE THE SINE REFERENCE
*AND COMPARE IT WITH THE
*OUTPUT VOLTAGE.
*INCLUDE STEVES.LIB
*INCLUDE POWER.LIB
.OPTIONS LONE=2.5 LZERO=-2.5 + LTHRESH=0 RELTOL=.01
.TRAN 9.766U 10M UIC
.FOUR 400HZ V(13)
*INCLUDE DEVICE.LIB
*INCLUDE DIODE3.LIB
*ALIAS  V(1)=OUT
*ALIAS  V(15)=Q
*ALIAS  V(7)=FLTR1
.PRINT TRAN  V(1)  V(15)  V(7)  V(13)
R1 15 7 4.7K
C1 7 0 47N IC=0
V1 4 0 PULSE -2.5 2.5 10N 10N 10N 5U |+ 9.766U
V2 5 0 SIN 0 1.5 400
R4 5 0 1MEG
R5 7 1 47K
C2 1 0 8.2N IC=0
B1 6 0 V=(V(5)-V(19)) > 0 ? 2.5 : -2.5
X2 18 0 8 11 10 XFMR-TAP {RATIO=.1 }
X4 10 0 2 SWITCH
V3 11 0 24
L1 18 13 10M
C3 13 0 1U
R6 13 0 200
X3 8 0 12 SWITCH
B3 12 0 V=V(14) > 0 ? 10 : 0
B4 2 0 V=V(15) > 0 ? 10 : 0
R7 13 16 200
X5 16 0 17 SWITCH
V4 17 0 PWL 0 10 3.125M 10 3.15M 0
R8 13 19 161K
R9 19 0 1.5K
C4 13 19 220P
X1 4 6 0 0 14 15 FFLOP
.END
```

Figure 7.10

Schematic and Netlist for the Push-Pull Converter with Improved Regulation. B1 compares the Sinewave Reference with the Output Voltage

The output voltage is now sensed by R8, R9, and C4. The purpose of C4 is to cancel one of the two poles of the output filter. The comparator, B1, now compares the sine wave reference to the output of the power stage rather than the output of the flip-flop (V(7)), as in Figure 7.7. The results are shown below.

Note: There is a drastic improvement in the dynamic transient response. The waveform is no longer highly distorted as a result of the transient. Also note that the spike which was created by the load switching is much smaller, and recovers more quickly. The results also demonstrate the improved regulation against line changes. As in the previous circuit, the input voltage was simulated at 24 V and 28 V. The improved circuit is useful in applications in which the output regulation and/or waveform are important.

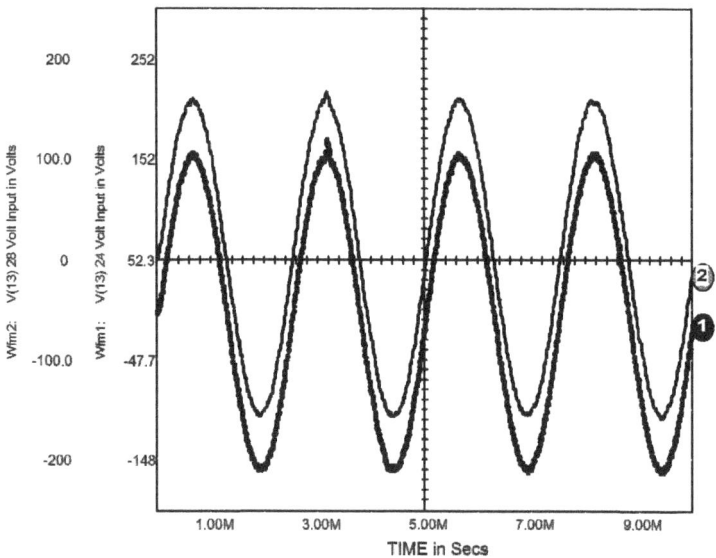

Figure 7.11

Output of the Improved Push-Pull Converter

Powering Nonlinear Loads

One of the greatest problems with DC-to-AC converters is the non-linear load. The non-linear load is often a rectifier circuit which may be found in most power supplies. A typical example is the power supply which is used in a personal computer. If the DC-to-AC converter is used as a UPS for a personal computer, it is likely that the power supply input circuit will contain a simple rectifier and filter. The circuits below demonstrate the behavior of both the original circuit (see Figure 7.7), as well as the improved circuit (see Figure 7.10), when used to power a non-linear load.

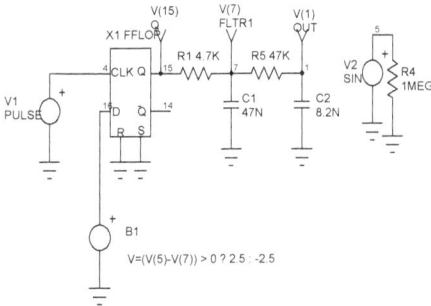

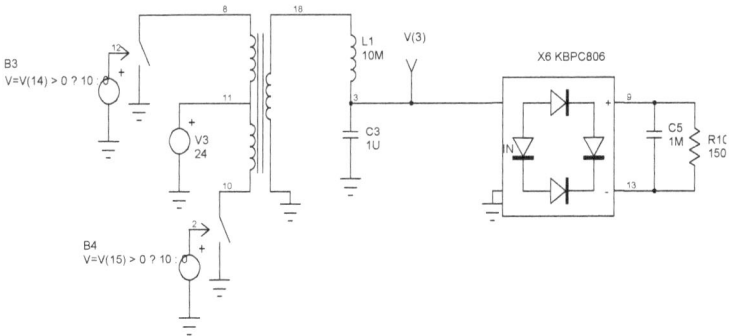

```
UPS_NONLINEAR.CIR: POWER A NON-LINEAR LOAD
*INCLUDE STEVES.LIB
*INCLUDE POWER.LIB
.OPTIONS LONE=2.5 LZERO=-2.5 + LTHRESH=0 RELTOL=.01
.TRAN 9.766U 10M UIC
.FOUR 400HZ V(13)
*INCLUDE DEVICE.LIB
*INCLUDE DIODE3.LIB
.PRINT TRAN V(9,13)
.VIEW TRAN V(9,13)
*ALIAS  V(1)=OUT
*ALIAS  V(15)=Q
*ALIAS  V(7)=FLTR1
.PRINT TRAN  V(1)  V(15)  V(7)  V(3)
R1 15 7 4.7K
C1 7 0 47N IC=0
V1 4 0 PULSE -2.5 2.5 10N 10N 10N 5U + 9.766U
V2 5 0 SIN 0 1.5 400
R4 5 0 1MEG
R5 7 1 47K
C2 1 0 8.2N IC=0
B1 6 0 V=(V(5)-V(19)) > 0 ? 2.5 : -2.5
X2 18 0 8 11 10 XFMR-TAP {RATIO=.1 }
X4 10 0 2 SWITCH
V3 11 0 24
L1 18 3 10M
C3 3 0 1U
X3 8 0 12 SWITCH
B3 12 0 V=V(14) > 0 ? 10 : 0
B4 2 0 V=V(15) > 0 ? 10 : 0
R8 3 19 161K
R9 19 0 1.5K
C4 3 19 220P
X6 3 0 9 13 KBPC806
C5 9 13 1M IC=140
R10 9 13 150
X1 4 6 0 0 14 15 FFLOP
.END
```

Figure 7.12a

Schematic of the Push-Pull Converter Driving a Non-Linear Load

Note: The original configuration is similar to Figure 7.7.

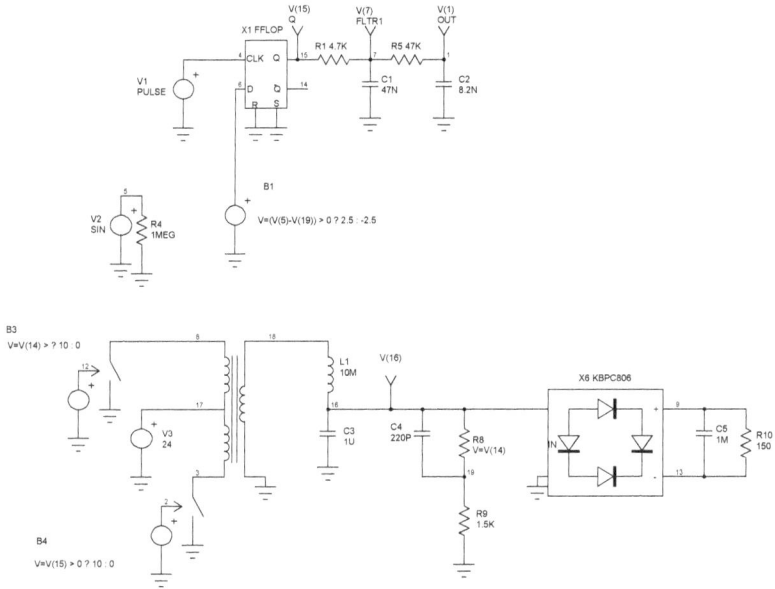

```
UPS3.CIR
*INCLUDE STEVES.LIB
*INCLUDE POWER.LIB
.OPTIONS LONE=2.5 LZERO=-2.5 + LTHRESH=0 RELTOL=.01
.TRAN 9.766U 10M UIC
.FOUR 400HZ V(13)
*INCLUDE DEVICE.LIB
*INCLUDE DIODE3.LIB
.PRINT TRAN V(9,13)
.VIEW TRAN V(9,13)
*ALIAS  V(1)=OUT
*ALIAS  V(15)=Q
*ALIAS  V(7)=FLTR1
.PRINT TRAN  V(1)  V(15)  V(7)  V(16)
R1 15 7 4.7K
C1 7 0 47N IC=0
V1 4 0 PULSE -2.5 2.5 10N 10N 10N 5U + 9.766U
V2 5 0 SIN 0 1.5 400
R4 5 0 1MEG
R5 7 1 47K
C2 1 0 8.2N IC=0
B1 6 0 V=(V(5)-V(19)) > 0 ? 2.5 : -2.5
X2 18 0 8 11 10 XFMR-TAP + {RATIO=.1 }
X4 10 0 2 SWITCH
V3 11 0 24
L1 18 16 10M
C3 16 0 1U X3 8 0 12 SWITCH
B3 12 0 V=V(14
B4 2 0 V=V(15) > 0 ? 10 : 0
R8 16 19 V=V(14) > 0 ? 10 : 0
R9 19 0 1.5K
C4 16 19 220P
X6 16 0 9 13 KBPC806
C5 9 13 1M IC=140
R10 9 13 150
X1 4 6 0 0 14 15 FFLOP
.END
```

Figure 7.12b

Schematic of the Push-Pull Converter Driving a Non-Linear Load

Note: This improved configuration is similar to Figure 7.10.

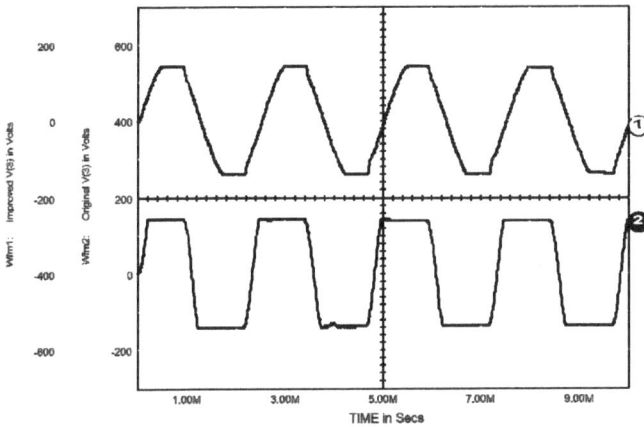

Figure 7.13

Simulation Results of Figure 7.12b (waveform 1) and Figure 12a (waveform 2)

The upper trace shows the result of our improved circuit, while the lower trace shows the results of the original circuit. Both of the simulations resulted in the same peak output amplitude, which has been reduced to 142 Volts as a result of the high current demand by the non-linear load.

The major difference between the two circuits is the output wave shape. The improved circuit maintains the sinusoidal wave shape throughout the waveform, with the exception of the flattened peaks. The original circuit produces a square wave as a result of the unloaded condition which occurs throughout the waveform, except at the peaks. The end result is a major difference in the RMS amplitude (108 and 127 Volts, respectively).

The increased RMS voltage of the original circuit can easily cause the saturation of transformers within the load. The increased RMS voltage may also stress other components which are sensitive to the RMS content of the load.

Three Phase Sine Reference

The circuit example in Figure 7.14 demonstrates a three phase sine wave reference using the mixed mode simulation techniques. A 6-stage shift register is used to generate 3 quasi-square waves which are exactly 120 degrees apart. Each quasi-square wave has a conduction angle of 120 degrees.

The 120 degree quasi-square waveform has the advantage of having no third harmonic content. Each quasi-square wave is filtered by a second order active low pass filter. The quasi-square waves are created by averaging 2 square waves which are phase shifted by 60 degrees.

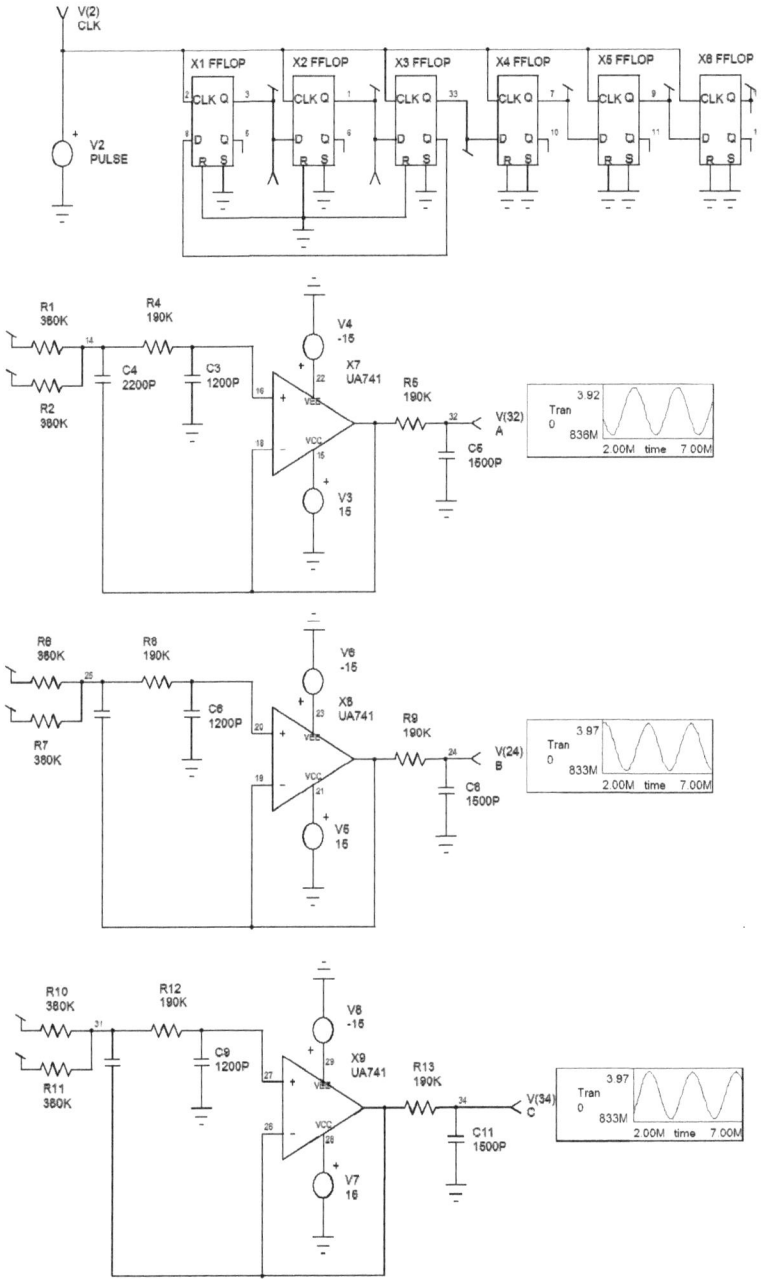

```
3PHASE.CIR A THREE PHASE SINE WAVE
.OPTIONS LONE=5 LZERO=0
.TRAN 1U 7M 2M UIC
*INCLUDE STEVES.LIB
*INCLUDE LIN.LIB
*INCLUDE NONLIN.LIB
*INCLUDE POWER.LIB
.FOUR 500HZ V(32)
*ALIAS  V(3)=Q1
*ALIAS  V(1)=Q2
*ALIAS  V(2)=CLK
*ALIAS  V(32)=A
*ALIAS  V(24)=B
*ALIAS  V(30)=C
.PRINT TRAN  V(3)  V(1)  V(2)  V(32)
.PRINT TRAN  V(24)  V(30)  V(33)
X2 2 3 0 0 6 1 FFLOP
X3 2 1 0 0 8 33 FFLOP
V2 2 0 PULSE 0 5 100N 10N 10N 100U 333.33U
X4 2 33 0 0 10 7 FFLOP
X5 2 7 0 0 11 9 FFLOP
X6 2 9 0 0 12 13 FFLOP
R1 3 14 380K
R2 1 14 380K
X7 18 16 18 15 22 UA741
V3 15 0 15
V6 23 0 -15
R8 25 20 190K
C6 20 0 1200P
C7 25 19 2200P
R9 19 24 190K
C8 24 0 1500P
R10 9 31 380K
R11 13 31 380K
X9 4 27 26 28 29 UA741
V7 28 0 15
V8 29 0 -15
R12 31 27 190K
C9 27 0 1200P
C10 31 26 2200P
R13 26 30 190K
C11 30 0 1500P
X1 2 8 0 0 5 3 FFLOP
.END
```

Figure 7.14

Schematic and Netlist for a 3-Phase Sinewave Reference

The Fourier results from the output file are shown in Figure 7.15. Note that as a result of the quasi-square waveform, the first significant harmonic is the fifth harmonic. The sine wave output distortion can be further reduced by the use of a higher order active filter (which will reduce the corner frequency of the existing filters) or replacement of the quasi-square waveform with a more sophisticated waveform in order to eliminate several additional harmonics.

Care must be taken in the placement of the filters, since component tolerances can easily alter the angles between phases. A Monte Carlo simulation can be performed in order to analyze the effect of component tolerances on the phase angles (and amplitudes) of the sine wave outputs.

FOURIER COMPONENTS OF TRANSIENT RESPONSE V(32)

DC COMPONENT = 2.475499E+00

HARMONIC NO	FREQUENCY (HZ)	FOURIER COMPONENT	NORMALIZED COMPONENT	PHASE (DEG)	NORMALIZED PHASE (DEG)
1	5.000E+02	1.430E+00	1.000E+00	2.003E+01	0.000E+00
2	1.000E+03	1.102E-03	7.704E-04	8.055E+01	4.049E+01
3	1.500E+03	3.476E-04	2.430E-04	1.483E+02	8.822E+01
4	2.000E+03	8.351E-04	5.839E-04	-9.185E+01	-1.720E+02
5	2.500E+03	4.363E-03	3.051E-03	-3.703E+00	-1.038E+02
6	3.000E+03	4.820E-04	3.370E-04	1.227E+02	2.568E+00
7	3.500E+03	4.187E-03	2.928E-03	-7.488E+01	-2.151E+02
8	4.000E+03	7.734E-04	5.408E-04	8.985E+01	-7.038E+01
9	4.500E+03	3.807E-04	2.662E-04	1.590E+02	-2.129E+01

TOTAL HARMONIC DISTORTION = 4.398894E-01 PERCENT

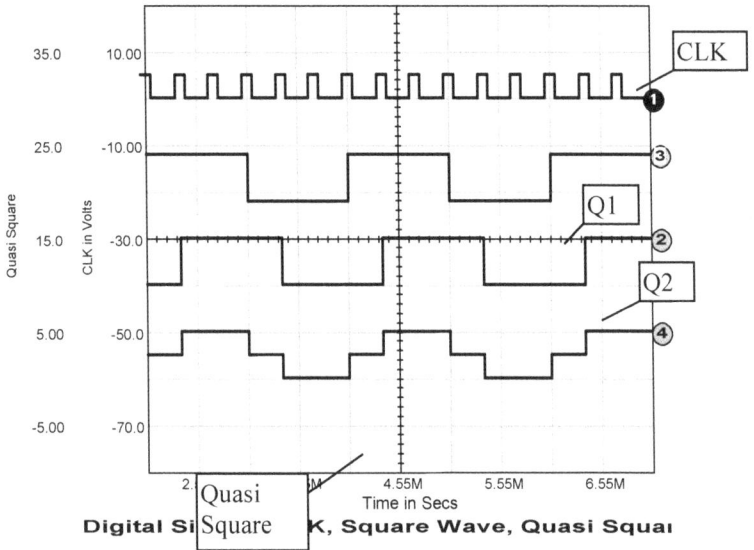

Figure 7.15

Digital Signals Showing a Single Phase

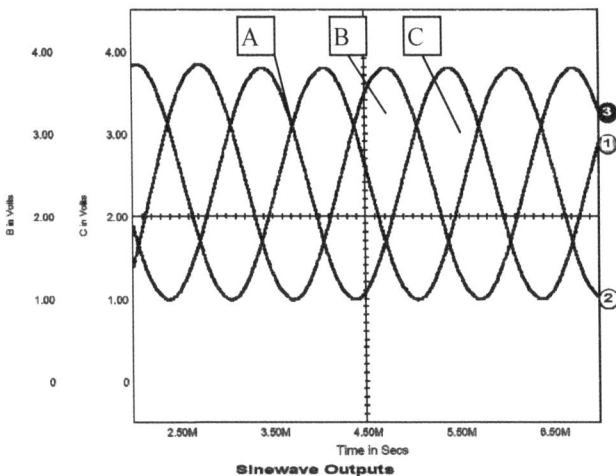

Figure 7.16

Results for the Phase Sinewave Referenced Circuit in 7.14

An Improved Stepped Waveform

The circuit in Figure 7.17 demonstrates another stepped waveform. While the 120 degree conduction angle of the circuit in Figure 7.14 eliminated the third harmonic, this waveform can eliminate all harmonics up to the eleventh harmonic. Resistors R1 through R5 form a "cheap and dirty" D/A converter, while the amplifier circuit is configured as a bandpass filter. This circuit can be used as a reference circuit but is also widely used in power stages as well. When used in a power stage, the stepped waveform is generally created by summing the outputs of several transformers, each of which is driven by a separate phase shifted power converter.

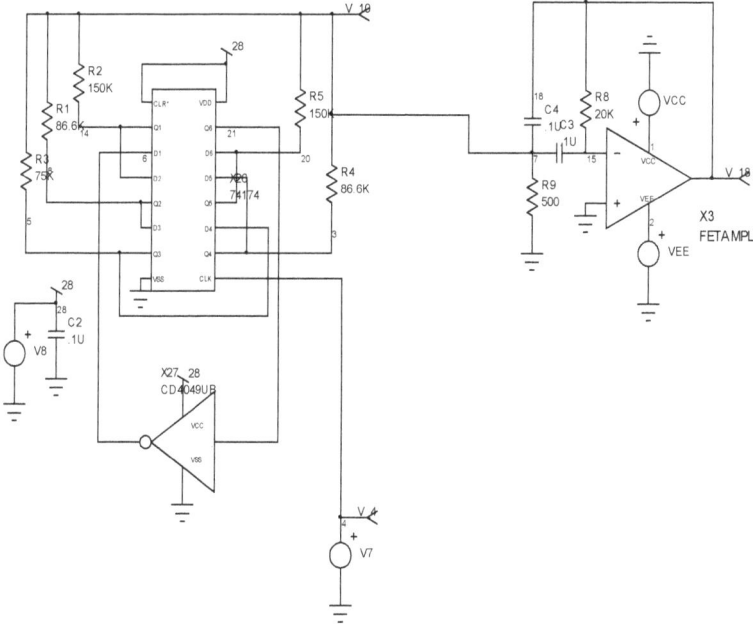

```
STAIRSINE.CIR
.TRAN 1u 10m 5m UIC
.CONTROL
SET NFREQS=25
.endc
.FOUR 500 v(18)
.PRINT   TRAN V_4
.PRINT   TRAN V_18
.PRINT   TRAN V_10
C2 28 0 .1U
VCC 1 0 DC=15
VEE 2 0 DC=-15
C3 15 7 .1U
R1 7 8 86.6K
C4 7 18 .1U
R2 7 14 150K
V7 4 0 PULSE 0 5 0 .1U .1U 83.33U 166.66U
R3 7 5 75K
V8 28 0 PULSE 0 5
R4 7 3 86.6K
R5 7 20 150K
X26 28 14 6 14 8 8 5 0 4 3 5 20 3 20 21 28 74174X26 {   }
R8 15 18 20K
X27 21 6 28 0 CD4049UB {   }
R9 7 0 500
X3 15 0 18 1 2 FETAMPL { GAIN=1k FT=1meg VOS=1m }
.END
```

Figure 7.17

**Schematic and Netlist for an Improved Stepped
Waveform**

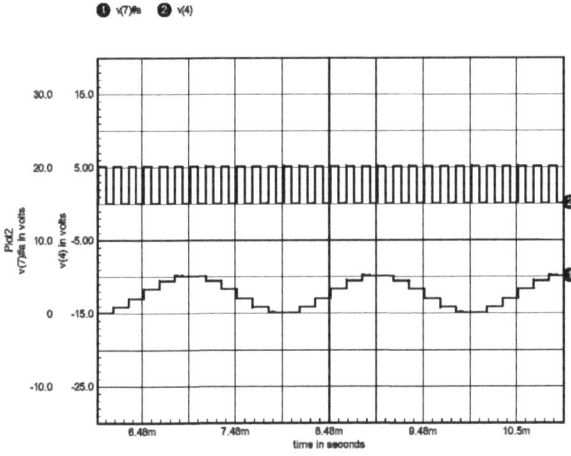

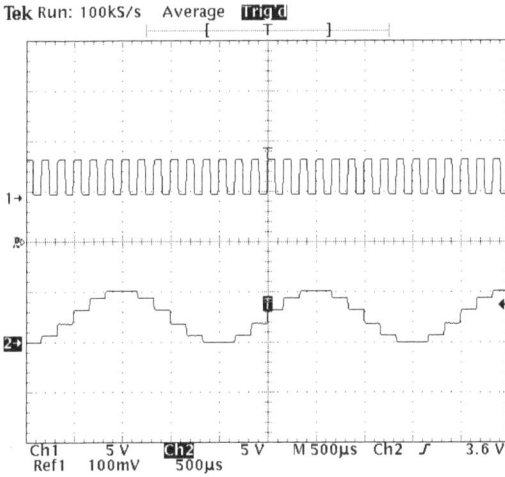

Figure 7.18

Measured and Simulated Unfiltered Output (Node 7 with Filter Disconnected)

❸ v(18)

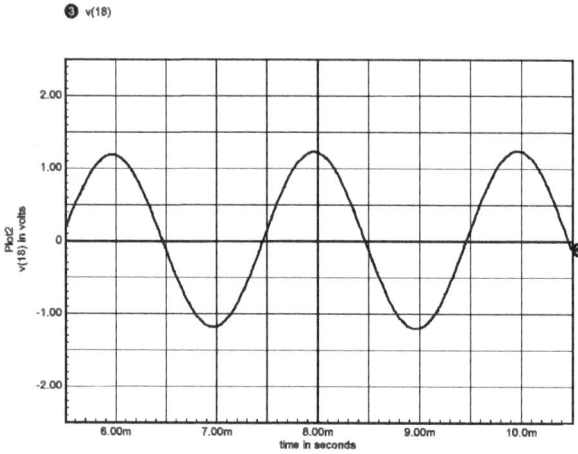

Figure 7.19

Filtered Output (Node 7 with Filter Disconnected)

A Full Bridge Harmonic Neutralized Inverter

There are many other configurations and bit patterns that can greatly reduce the harmonic content of a power train. The schematic in Figure 7.20 demonstrates a full-wave H-Bridge circuit that minimizes the harmonic content up to the ninth harmonic. In this circuit a PWLGEN model is used to simulate the contents of a ROM. The PWLGEN model reads a text file which is a continuous PWL statement. The model allows the waveform to be repeating. Although not an advantage in this case, one of the benefits of the PWLGEN model is that an arbitrary waveform can be generated, whereas the State Machine model in Figure 7.5 is limited to a digital value (1 or zero). The output switches, which are generally either Mosfets or IGBT's are simulated using switches in order to simplify and speed up the simulation. A measurement was made on a prototype of the full bridge inverter for comparison with the simulated results. A Spectrum Analysis plot was also made from the prototype and the result is shown in Figure 7.22.

Switched-Mode Power Supply Simulation with SPICE

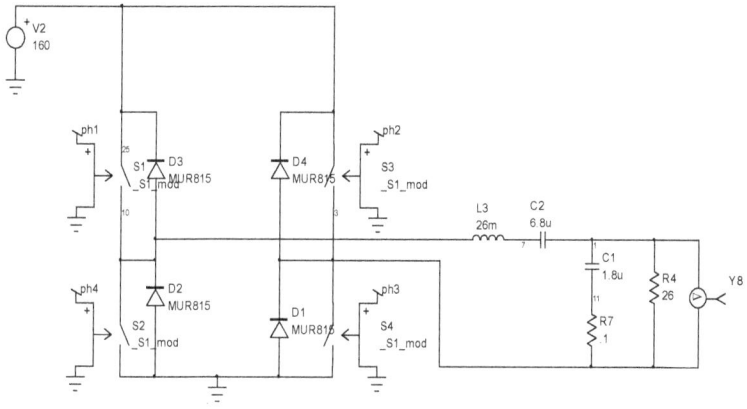

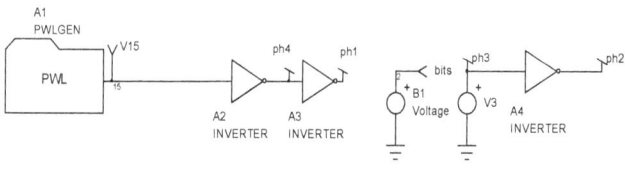

```
64SAMPLE.CIR
.TRAN .5u 30m 10m 10u UIC
.FOUR 400 v(1,3)
.OPTIONS abstol=1E-8 itl4=1000 method=TRAP
.OPTIONS gmin=10n reltol=0.005
.PRINT  TRAN V15
.PRINT  TRAN bits
.PRINT  TRAN Y8
S1 25 10 ph1 0 _S1_mod
.MODEL _S1_mod SW VT=3 VH=.1 RON=.02 ROFF=1meg
S2 10 0 ph4 0 _S1_mod
S3 25 3 ph2 0 _S1_mod
S4 3 0 ph3 0 _S1_mod
A2 15_Din ph4_Dout INVERTERA2
A3 ph4_Din ph1_Dout INVERTERA3
A4 ph3_Din ph2_Dout INVERTERA4
L3 10 7 26m
C1 1 11 1.8u
D1 0 3 MUR815
R4 1 3 26
A1 15 PWLGENA1
.MODEL PWLGENA1 vsrc_pwl( input_file=64s.txt repeat=TRUE)
V2 25 0 DC=160
R7 11 3 .1
D2 0 10 MUR815
D3 10 25 MUR815
D4 3 25 MUR815
B1 2 0 V=v(10,3)
V3 ph3 0 PULSE 0 5 0 .1u .1u 1.25m 2.5m
C2 7 1 6.8u
.END
```

Figure 7.20

Harmonic Neutralized Full Bridge Inverter Schematic and Netlist

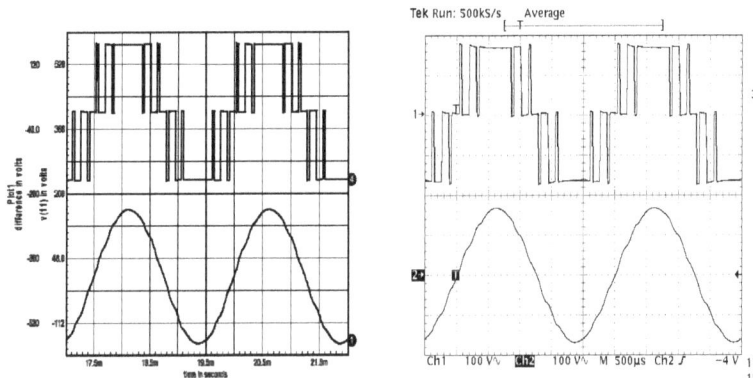

FOURIER COMPONENTS OF TRANSIENT RESPONSE V(1.3)

DC COMPONENT = -1.955657E-03

HARMONIC NO	FREQUENCY (HZ)	FOURIER COMPONENT	NORMALIZED COMPONENT	PHASE (DEG)	NORMALIZED PHASE (DEG)
1	4.000E+02	1.620E+02	1.000E+00	-6.901E+00	0.000E+00
2	8.000E+02	9.838E-02	6.072E-04	-2.742E+01	-1.362E+01
3	1.200E+03	2.878E-01	1.776E-03	1.033E+02	1.240E+02
4	1.600E+03	7.250E-02	4.475E-04	-1.498E+02	-1.222E+02
5	2.000E+03	1.002E-01	6.185E-04	6.752E+01	1.020E+02
6	2.400E+03	4.970E-02	3.068E-04	1.647E+02	2.061E+02
7	2.800E+03	6.924E-02	4.274E-04	8.369E+01	1.320E+02
8	3.200E+03	2.986E-02	1.843E-04	1.192E+02	1.744E+02
9	3.600E+03	1.042E-01	6.434E-04	-6.238E+01	-2.784E-01

TOTAL HARMONIC DISTORTION = 2.197904E-01 PERCENT

Figure 7.21

**Fourier and Graphical Result of the Full Bridge Inverter
Simulation of Figure 20**

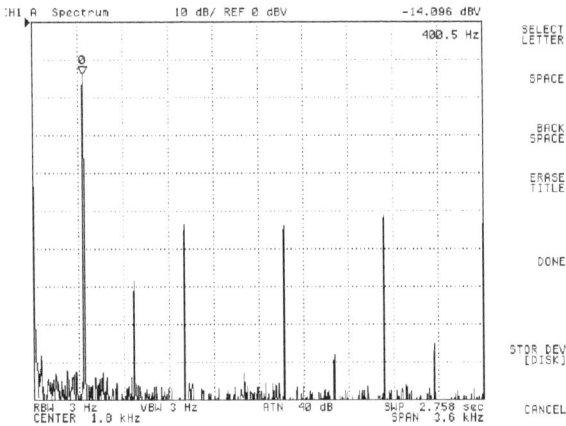

Figure 7.22

Spectrum Analysis of the Full Bridge Inverter of Figure 20

A Half Bridge Harmonic Neutralized Inverter

In a similar fashion, many of the harmonics can be eliminated in a half-bridge configuration. Using a 128 bit digital pattern, most of the third, fifth and seventh harmonic can be minimized. The ninth harmonic however is substantially larger than the half bridge configuration or even larger than a square wave. Fortunately, the ninth harmonic is easily minimized by the output filter, though the result is not as good as the full bridge circuit. Higher bit counts could further reduce the harmonic content.

The half-bridge configuration is often used in three phase transformerless conversions, where a full bridge circuit is not possible. The half-bridge configuration is also generally much less expensive since it uses half the number of MOSFETs and drivers.

The output voltage is generally regulated by controlling the DC input which feeds the half-bridge circuit.

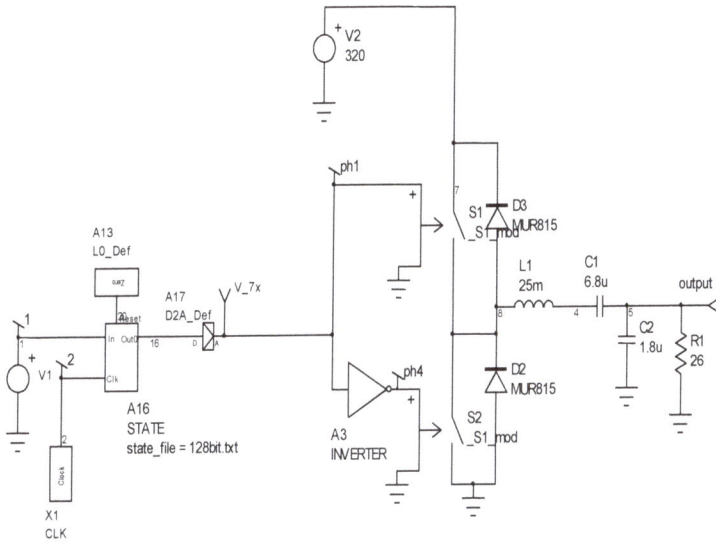

Figure 7.23

Harmonic Neutralized Half Bridge Inverter Schematic and Netlist

● v(5)   ● v(ph1)

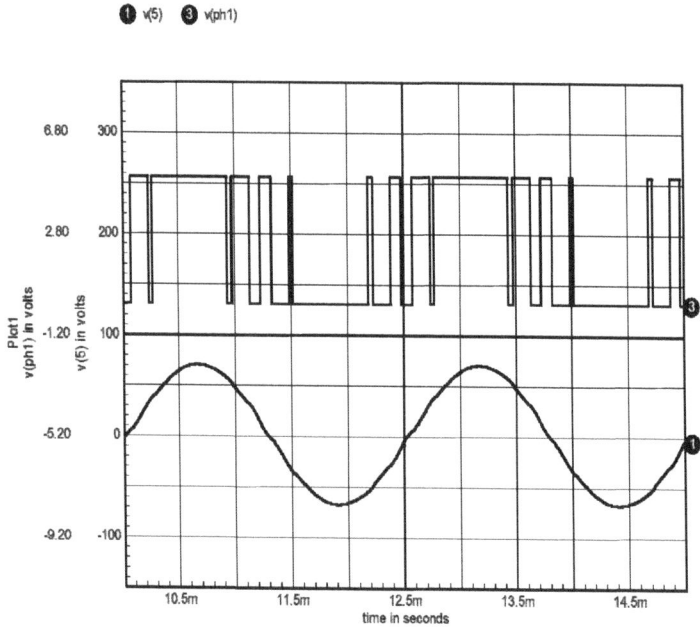

Fourier analysis for v(5):

No. Harmonics: 10, THD: 0.929872 %, Gridsize: 200, Interpolation Degree:1

Harmonic	Frequency	Magnitude	Phase	Norm. Mag	Norm. Phase
0	0	0.000802049	0	0	0
1	400	69.0061	-6.8934	1	0
2	800	0.00413678	17.1877	5.99481e-005	24.0811
3	1200	0.152741	86.0766	0.00221344	92.97
4	1600	0.00195197	46.8701	2.8287e-005	53.7635
5	2000	0.0586701	76.1783	0.000850217	83.0717
6	2400	0.0015346	64.6708	2.22386e-005	71.5643
7	2800	0.0260316	-108.27	0.000377237	-101.38
8	3200	0.00110158	79.6249	1.59635e-005	86.5184
9	3600	0.61989	69.068	0.00898312	75.9614

Figure 7.24

Fourier and Graphical result of the Full Bridge Inverter of Figure 7.23

A PWM Inverter

The PWM inverter compares a control voltage with a triangle waveform, which is at the switching frequency. The switching frequency is much higher than the fundamental output frequency. Integrated circuit devices such as the UC3637 offer all of the functions required, including a variable dead time control to avoid overlapping of the upper and lower switches. This controller is often used in motor control applications, but also can be used for audio switching amplifiers, ultrasonics or UPS applications. A simple example is shown in Figure 7.25. This example uses a very low switching frequency in order to provide a visual representation of the switched output. A simple two stage RC filter is used to filter the output. In a typical application, the output filter would be an LC filter and the UC3637 would be used to drive a power stage.

PWM amplifiers are also available as hybrid devices and more recently as monolithic integrated circuit devices. In these devices, the entire control circuit and output stage are contained in a very small package. A good example of this type of device is the SA-12 device, which is manufactured by Apex. Apex also provides SPICE model support for these devices.

Switched-Mode Power Supply Simulation with SPICE

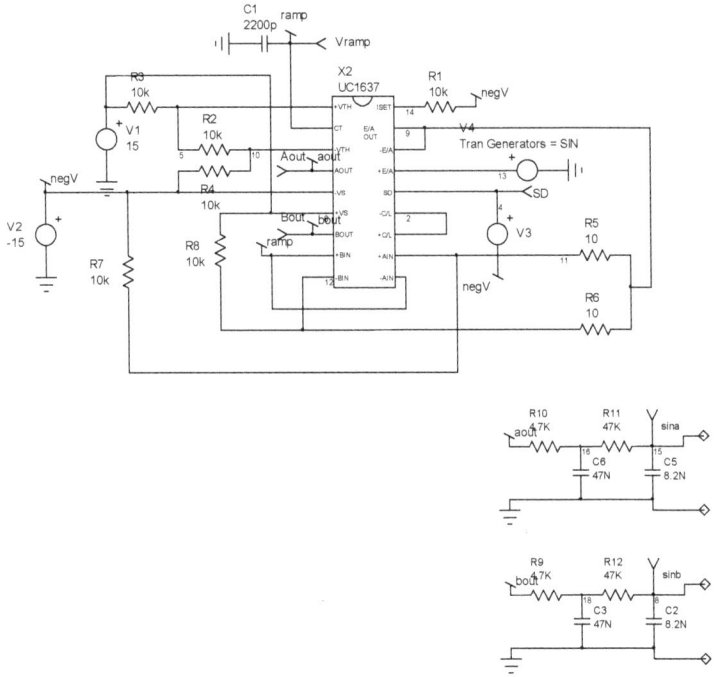

```
PWM_Inverter.cir Setup1
.TRAN .5u 15m 5m 1u UIC
.FOUR 400 v(15) v(16) v(15,bout)
.OPTIONS abstol=1E-8 method=TRAP
.OPTIONS gmin=1E-10 reltol=0.001
.PRINT  TRAN Vramp
.PRINT  TRAN Aout
.PRINT  TRAN SD
.PRINT  TRAN Bout
.PRINT  TRAN sinb
.PRINT  TRAN sina
C2 8 0 8.2N
R1 14 negV 10k
C1 0 ramp 2200p
V1 6 0 DC=15
V2 negV 0 DC=-15
R2 10 5 10k
R3 6 5 10k
R4 10 negV 10k
R5 11 9 10
R6 12 9 10
R7 11 negV 10k
R8 6 12 10k
V4 13 0 SIN 0 4.5 400
V3 4 negV PULSE 0 3m 150u
X2 5 ramp 10 aout negV 6 bout ramp 12 ramp 11 2 2 4 13 9 9
+ 14 UC1637X2 {   }
R9 bout 18 4.7K
R12 18 8 47K
C3 18 0 47N
C5 15 0 8.2N
R10 aout 16 4.7K
R11 16 15 47K
C6 16 0 47N
.END
```

Figure 7.25

PWM Inverter Schematic and Netlist

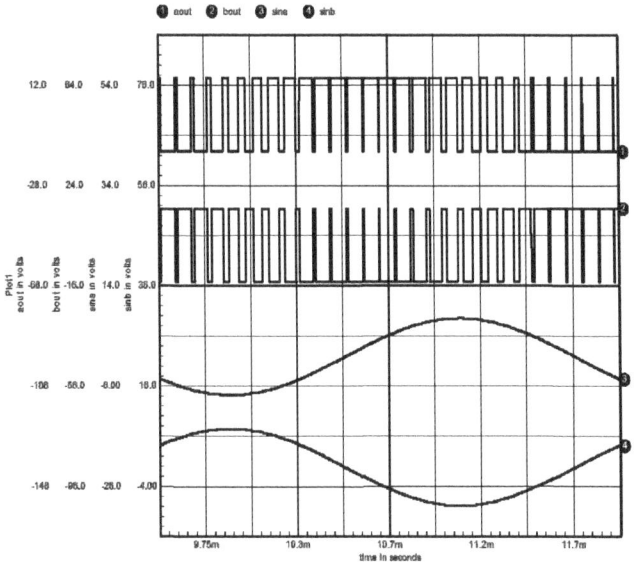

Figure 7.26

PWM Inverter Simulation Results

Chapter 8

Power Factor Correction (PFC)

THERE HAS BEEN a growing interest in power factor correction. In fact, the European Union implemented a directive, EN61000-3-2 which controls the harmonic content and power factor of many products that are sold to European countries. There are several important reasons for this control.

- Poor power factor results in reduced efficiency, which increases the cost of electricity.

- More importantly many devices suffer from harmonically rich waveforms. A good example of this is motors, which may overheat as a result of harmonics.

- In the case of three phase motors the harmonics can result in significant neutral current, which can also result in overheating and ultimately in motor failure.

Typical switching power supplies rectify the input power and utilize a capacitor filter in order to provide a DC bus voltage. The typical power factor if such a conversion is approximately 0.6. Linear regulated power supplies generally use a transformer to step down the AC input voltage and rectify the secondary voltage and then utilize a capacitor filter to create the DC voltage to the input of the regulator stage. The transformer improves the power factor of the input just slightly from the typical switching power supply. Phase controlled power supplies utilize either SCR's or Triacs to control the conduction angle of the input, which is then filtered using an L-C type filter. This can result in a power factor that is even lower than the typical switching power supply.

Power Factor (PF) is defined as the ratio of watts to volt amperes:

$$PF = \frac{Watts}{Volts * Amps}$$

Single Phase Transformer Rectifier

Figure 8.1 shows a typical single phase rectifier filter circuit. The results of the input current, input voltage and input Watts are shown in Figure 8.2.

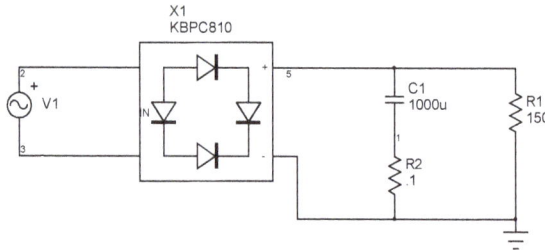

```
PFC1
.TRAN 10u 104m 54m .1m UIC
.FOUR 60 I(v1)
.OPTIONS method=GEAR
.PRINT  TRAN V3
X1 2 1 4 0 KBPC810 {   }
V1 2 1 SIN 0 165 60
C1 4 3 1000uF IC=100
R1 4 0 150
R2 3 0 .1
.END
```

Figure 8.1

Single Phase Rectifier Filter Schematic and Netlist

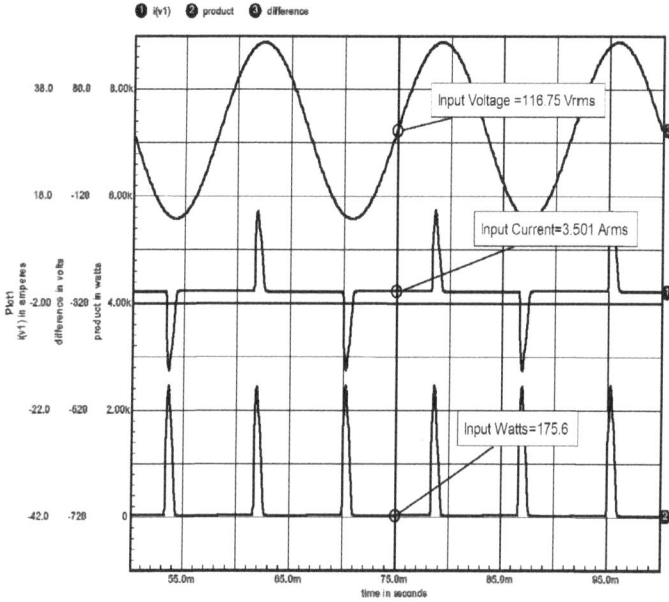

Figure 8.2

Single Phase Rectifier Filter Waveforms

In this example, the power factor is calculated as:

$$PF = \frac{175.45}{3.501*116.75} = 0.429$$

Power factor is largely dependent on the input source impedance and the characteristics of the output capacitor. Poor power factor creates a rich harmonic content of the input current. Figure 8.3 shows a spectral plot.

❷ mag(fft(temp))

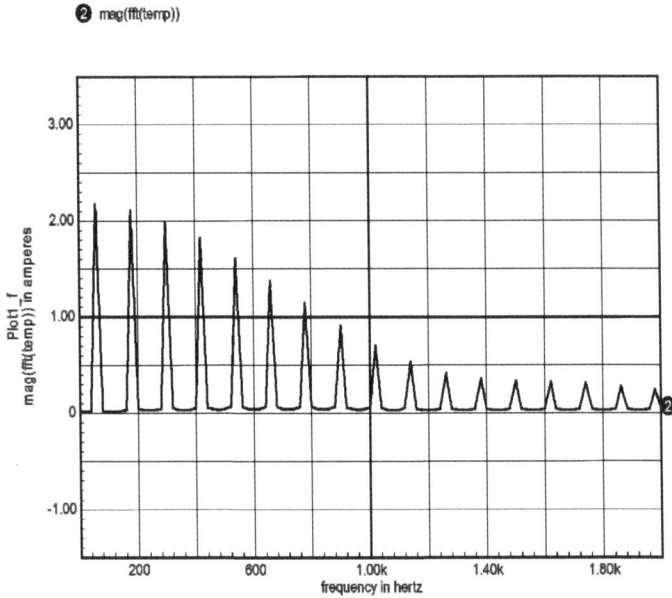

Figure 8.3

Single Phase Rectifier Filter Input Current Spectrum

If the single-phase circuit were to have an LC output filter rather than a capacitor filter the input current would have a much larger conduction angle. In the extreme case where an infinite inductance would be present the conduction angle would be 180 degrees for each rectifier and the input current would approach a square wave. In this case the power factor would increase to unity and the input current harmonic content would be that of a square wave:

$$Iharmonic = \frac{Ifundamental}{harmonicnumber}$$

...for the odd harmonics.

Three Phase Transformer Rectifier

There are many configurations of three phase rectifiers. In the simplest case, a full wave rectifier is used in conjunction with a single three phase bridge rectifier. The resulting ripple frequency is six times the input AC frequency and the power factor is generally approximately 0.7.

A better configuration, using both delta and wye secondaries results in a ripple frequency that is twelve times the AC frequency. The power factor of this configuration is generally approximately 0.8.

More sophisticated approaches utilize even more secondaries in order to produce higher ripple frequencies and better power factor. An example of a three-phase delta-wye configuration is shown in Figure 8.4.

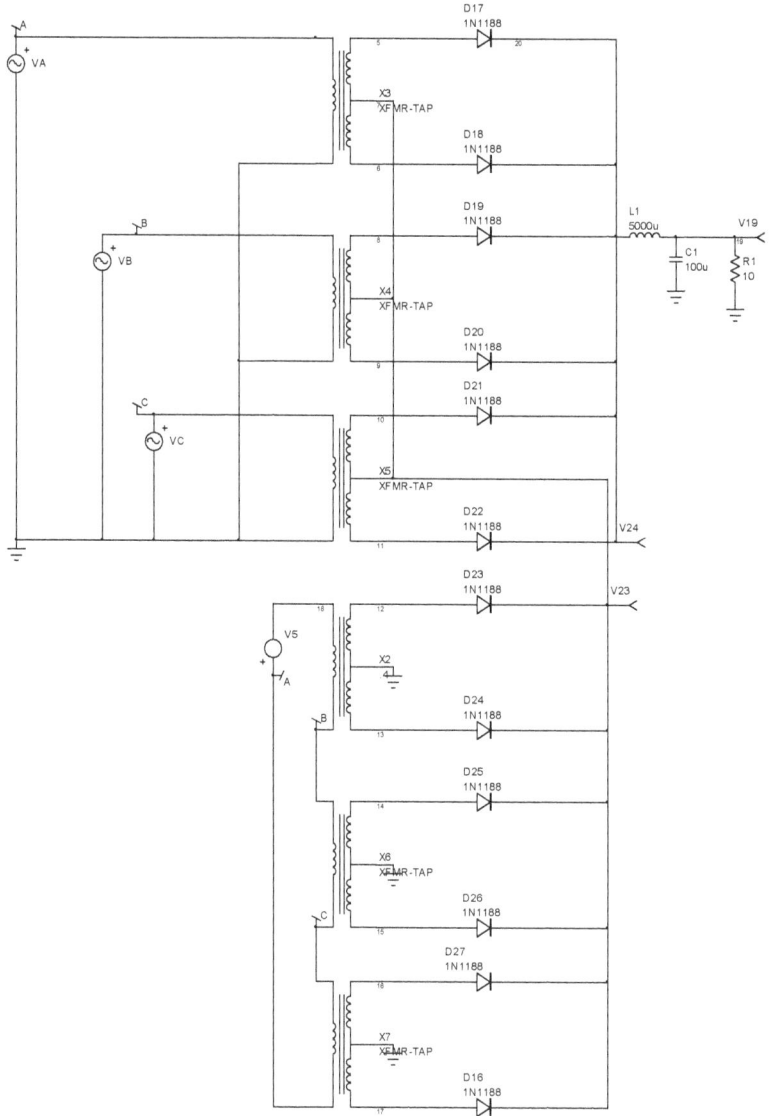

Figure 8.4

Three Phase Delta/Wye Rectifier Filter

```
THREEPHASE.cir
.TRAN 10U 100M 20m 100u
.OPTIONS abstol=1E-8 itl4=10000 method=GEAR
.OPTIONS gmin=1E-10 icstep=40
.PRINT   TRAN V19
.PRINT   TRAN V24
.PRINT   TRAN V23
V1 1 A
X2 18 B 12 0 13 XFMR-TAP { RATIO=.577 }
X6 B C 14 0 15 XFMR-TAP { RATIO=.577 }
X7 C A 16 0 17 XFMR-TAP { RATIO=.577 }
R1 19 0 10
X3 1 0 5 7 6 XFMR-TAP { RATIO=1 }
X4 B 0 8 7 9 XFMR-TAP { RATIO=1 }
X5 C 0 10 7 11 XFMR-TAP { RATIO=1 }
L1 20 19 5000u
V5 A 18
C1 19 0 100u
V2 A 0 SIN 0 163 60 0
V3 C 0 SIN 0 163 60 11.111m
V4 B 0 SIN 0 163 60 5.555m
D16 17 7 DN1188
D17 5 20 DN1188
D18 6 20 DN1188
D19 8 20 DN1188
D20 9 20 DN1188
D21 10 20 DN1188
D22 11 20 DN1188
D23 12 7 DN1188
D24 13 7 DN1188
D25 14 7 DN1188
D26 15 7 DN1188
D27 16 7 DN1188
.END
```

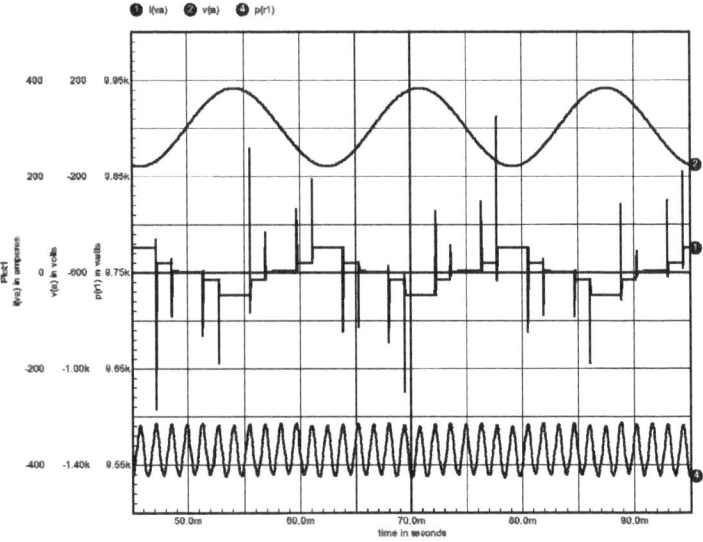

Figure 8.5

Three Phase Delta / Wye Rectifier Filter Waveforms

The results in Figure 8.5 show the input voltage input current and output voltage. The ripple frequency is 12 times the input frequency and the power factor is approximately 0.82. The harmonic content is greatly reduced from the single phase rectifier circuit as can be seen in the Fourier results below.

256

FOURIER COMPONENTS OF TRANSIENT RESPONSE I(VA)

DC COMPONENT = 6.282716E-02

HARMONIC NO	FREQUENCY (HZ)	FOURIER COMPONENT	NORMALIZED COMPONENT	PHASE (DEG)	NORMALIZED PHASE (DEG)
1	6.000E+01	3.974E+01	1.000E+00	-1.771E+02	0.000E+00
2	1.200E+02	5.768E-02	1.451E-03	-1.277E+02	2.266E+02
3	1.800E+02	1.352E+01	3.401E-01	8.444E+00	5.399E+02
4	2.400E+02	3.121E-02	7.854E-04	-7.946E+01	6.291E+02
5	3.000E+02	4.405E-01	1.108E-02	4.597E+00	8.903E+02
6	3.600E+02	1.389E-01	3.496E-03	2.320E+01	1.086E+03
7	4.200E+02	4.967E-01	1.250E-02	1.796E+02	1.420E+03
8	4.800E+02	1.634E-01	4.111E-03	-1.346E+02	1.283E+03
9	5.400E+02	4.799E+00	1.208E-01	2.251E+01	1.617E+03

TOTAL HARMONIC DISTORTION = 3.613245E+01 PERCENT

The requirements of EN61000-3-2 dictate a much higher power factor and reduced harmonic content. These requirements are generally met by use of active power factor correction. Active power factor correction utilizes electronics to force the input current to look like a reflection of the input voltage (i.e. resistive). The result of this type of correction typically results in power factor of greater than 0.98 and harmonic distortion of less than 3%.

Discontinuous Flyback Power Factor Corrector

The discontinuous flyback converter is the simplest topology that can be used to provide power factor correction. The peak input current of the discontinuous flyback converter, with a fixed duty cycle and fixed frequency, is defined by:

$$Ipk = \frac{Vin}{Lpri} \cdot ton$$

And the average current is related to the peak current as:

$$Iavg = \frac{Ipk}{2} \cdot Duty$$

By substitution:

$$Iavg = \frac{1}{2} \cdot \frac{Vin}{Lpri} \cdot ton \cdot Duty$$

Showing that if L_{PRI}, t_{ON} and Duty are all fixed, then the average input current is proportional to the input voltage, resulting in an ideal power factor of unity. An example of the flyback power factor corrector is shown in Figure 8.6.

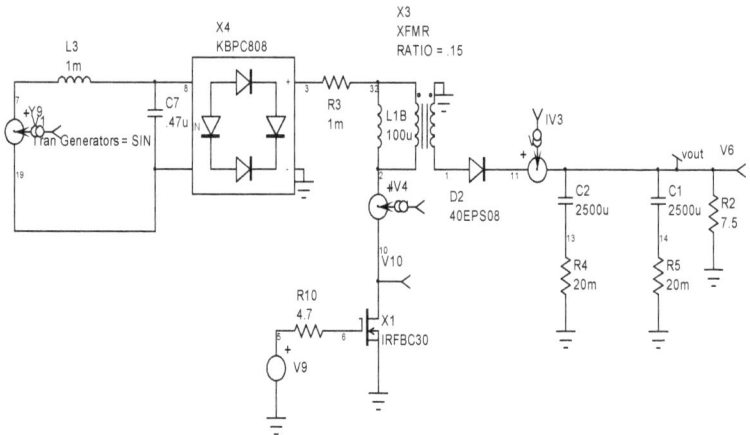

```
FlybackPFC.cir
.TRAN .2U 20m 0 5u UIC
.FOUR 60 I(V1)
.OPTIONS abstol=1E-8 itl4=1000 method=GEAR
.OPTIONS gmin=1E-10
.PRINT   TRAN V10
.PRINT   TRAN V6
.PRINT   TRAN IV4
.PRINT   TRAN IY9
.PRINT   TRAN IV3
R2 vout 0 7.5
R3 3 32 1m
L1B 2 32 100u
V4 2 10
X1 10 6 0 IRFBC30 {   }
D2 1 11 40EPS08
V1 7 19 DC=163 SIN 0 163 60
C2 vout 13 2500u IC=28
C1 vout 14 2500u IC=28
V3 11 vout
R4 13 0 20m
R5 14 0 20m
X4 8 19 3 0 KBPC808 {   }
X3 32 2 0 1 XFMR { RATIO=.15 }
C7 8 19 .47u
L3 7 8 1m
V9 5 0 PULSE 0 12 0 .01u .01u 4u 10u
R10 5 6 4.7
.END
```

Figure 8.6

Discontinuous Flyback Power Factor Corrector

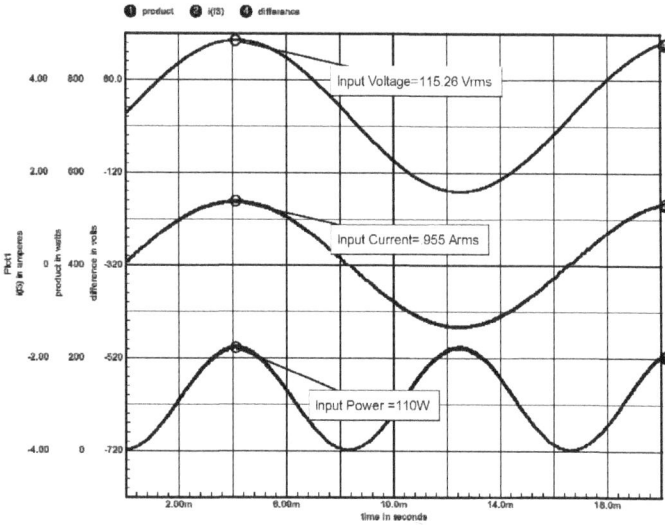

Figure 8.7

PFC Voltage, Current and Power

```
FOURIER COMPONENTS OF TRANSIENT RESPONSE I(V1)

DC COMPONENT = -3.182485E-04

HARMONIC   FREQUENCY   FOURIER     NORMALIZED   PHASE       NORMALIZED
   NO         (HZ)     COMPONENT   COMPONENT    (DEG)       PHASE (DEG)
    1       6.000E+01  1.351E+00   1.000E+00   -1.070E+02   0.000E+00
    2       1.200E+02  7.732E-05   5.725E-05    9.343E+01   3.074E+02
    3       1.800E+02  6.267E-03   4.640E-03   -1.408E+02   1.801E+02
    4       2.400E+02  4.218E-04   3.123E-04   -8.227E+00   4.197E+02
    5       3.000E+02  5.012E-03   3.711E-03   -8.097E-01   5.341E+02
    6       3.600E+02  1.544E-04   1.143E-04   -1.407E+02   5.012E+02
    7       4.200E+02  2.933E-03   2.171E-03    1.147E+02   8.636E+02
    8       4.800E+02  1.761E-04   1.304E-04   -5.726E+01   7.986E+02
    9       5.400E+02  2.073E-03   1.535E-03   -9.416E+01   8.687E+02

TOTAL HARMONIC DISTORTION = 6.519727E-01 PERCENT
```

The results show unity power factor and 1.28% total harmonic distortion. This is an ideal case and nonlinearities in the inductance as well as small variations in duty cycle and or frequency will increase the distortion to some degree, however this is a viable circuit especially at lower power levels. The limitations are

260

generally related to the poor ratio of peak to average current and utilization of the power transformer. These are the same general issues that result in the standard flyback converter. The flyback power factor corrector can also be simulated using state space models as shown in Figure 8.8. There are a few benefits to using the state space model including faster simulation times and the ability to measure the loop gain response.

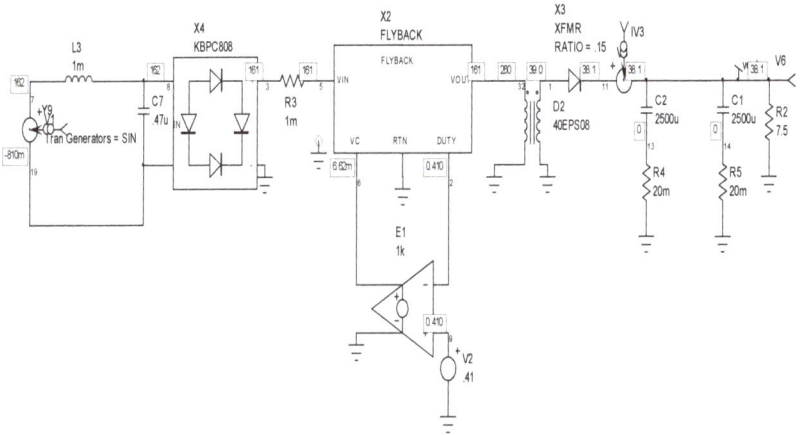

```
Flyback PFC State Space.Cir
.TRAN 2u 20m 0 UIC
.PROBE
.OPTION ITL4=2500 GMIN=1n ABSTOL=.01u UNTOL=10u RELTOL=.01
.FOUR 60 I(V1)
X2 5 0 6 32 2 FLYBACK Params: L=100u NC=1 F=100k EFF=1 RB=1m
E1 6 0 9 2 1k
R3 3 5 1m
D2 1 11 40EPS08
V1 7 19 DC=163 SIN 0 163 60
C2 12 13 500u ; IC=50
R1 vout 4 1m
L4 12 vout 1u
C1 vout 14 500u
U3 11 12
R4 13 0 20m
R5 14 0 20m
X4 8 19 3 0 KBPC808
V2 9 0 DC=.41
X3 32 0 1 0 XFMR Params: RATIO=.15
C7 8 19 .47u
L3 7 8 1m
U8 4 0 DC=28
.END
```

Figure 8.8

State Space Flyback Power Factor Corrector Schematic

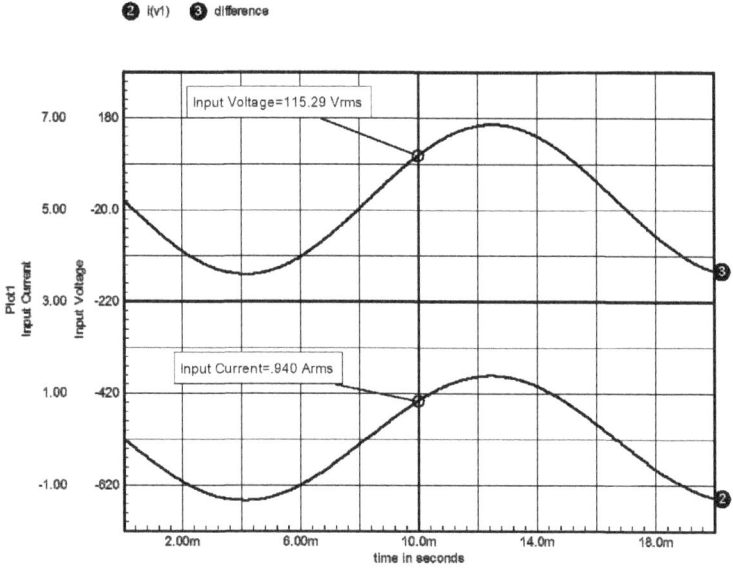

Figure 8.9

Discontinuous Flyback Power Factor Corrector Results

Critical Conduction Power Factor Corrector

One of the major hindrances of the boost converter is the output rectifier diode. The diode must have a high enough voltage rating to support the output voltage and is abruptly switched with the output current flowing through it. This leads to a very high loss in both the rectifier and the MOSFET switch. Technology continuously works to improve these high voltage diodes; however another option is becoming more widespread. This is the critical conduction boost PFC, which operates at the continuous and discontinuous boundary. This is achieved by the use of a zero-crossing detector which determines the point at which the inductor current has reduced to near zero. At this point the MOSFET can be turned on with a minimal recovery effect in the output rectifier, significantly reducing the losses in both the MOSFET and the diode. Critical conduction PFC controllers are presently available from several manufacturers. Two of the most popular are the MC33262 from

On Semiconductor and the TDA4863 from Infineon.

A simplified SPICE model of a critical conduction mode boost PFC is shown in Figure 8.10.

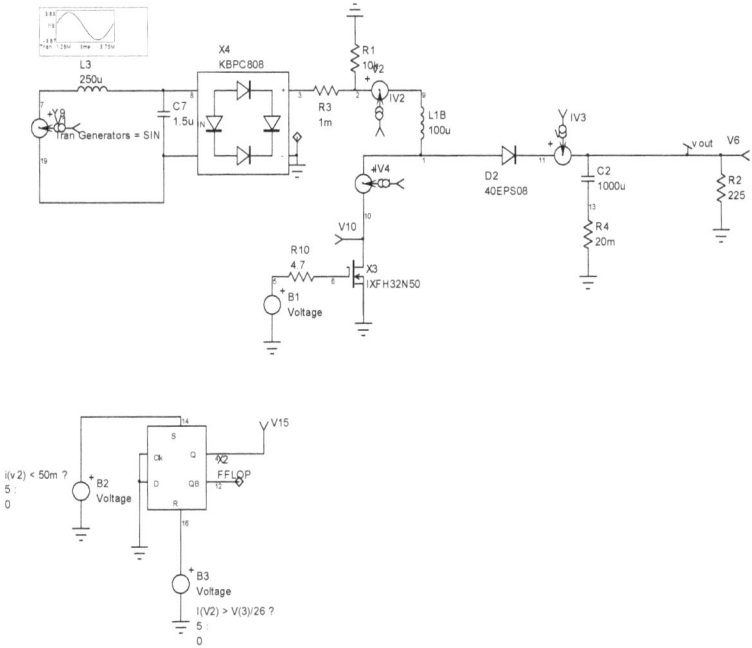

```
Critical PFC1.cir
.TRAN 1U 3.75m 1.25m .01u UIC
.PROBE
.FOUR 400 I(U1)
R2 vout 0 225
U2 2 9
R3 3 2 1m
L1B 1 9 100u
U4 1 10
EB3 16 0 Value={IF(I(U2)>U(3)/26 , 5 , 0)}
D2 1 11 40EPS08
U1 7 19 DC=163 SIN 0 163 400
C2 vout 13 1000u IC=250
R1 2 0 10k
U3 11 vout
R4 13 0 20m
X3 10 6 0 IXFH32N50
X4 8 19 3 0 KBPC808
EB150 Value={IF(V(4) > 2.5 , 15 , 0)}
EB2 14 0 Value={IF (I(U2)<50m , 5 , 0)}
RT14 14 0 1G
X2 0 0 16 14 12 4FFLOP
C7 8 19 1u
L3 7 8 100u
R10 5 6 4.7
.END
```

Figure 8.10

Critical Conduction Boost Power Factor Corrector

In this simulation, the latch is set when the current in the inductor falls to 50mA. The latch is reset when the Inductor current reaches a level that is proportional to the rectified input voltage ($V_{RECT}/26$).

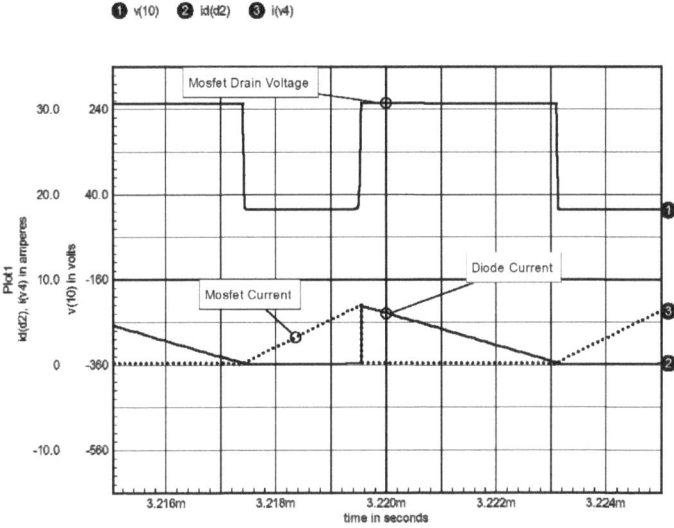

Figure 8.11

Critical Conduction Boost Waveforms

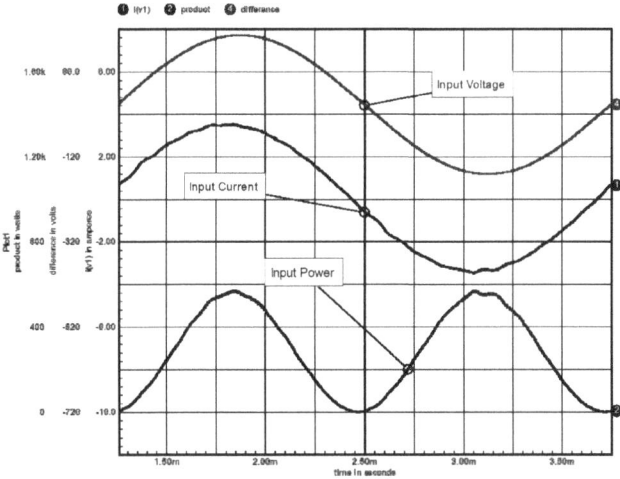

Figure 8.12

Critical Conduction Boost Input Current

FOURIER COMPONENTS OF TRANSIENT RESPONSE I(V1)
DC COMPONENT = 9.193709E-06

HARMONIC NO	FREQUENCY (HZ)	FOURIER COMPONENT	NORMALIZED COMPONENT	PHASE (DEG)	NORMALIZED PHASE(DEG)
1	4.000E+02	3.421E+00	1.000E+00	6.626E+00	0.000E+00
2	8.000E+02	1.849E-04	5.405E-05	1.742E+02	1.609E+02
3	1.200E+03	3.140E-02	9.178E-03	1.769E+02	1.570E+02
4	1.600E+03	2.670E-04	7.804E-05	-9.829E+01	-1.248E+02
5	2.000E+03	4.432E-03	1.296E-03	-1.743E+02	-2.075E+02
6	2.400E+03	6.726E-05	1.966E-05	6.698E+01	2.722E+01
7	2.800E+03	4.988E-03	1.458E-03	1.774E+02	1.310E+02
8	3.200E+03	9.157E-05	2.677E-05	-1.508E+02	-2.038E+02
9	3.600E+03	3.411E-03	9.971E-04	1.764E+02	1.168E+02

TOTAL HARMONIC DISTORTION = 9.436542E-01 PERCENT

Boost Mode Power Factor Corrector

One of the most popular PFC topologies is the boost topology. The most popular controllers for boost PFC circuits are the UC3854 series of highpower factor preregulators, manufactured by Texas Instruments.

Although several attempts have been made to model the UC3854, I have not seen any non-state space transient SPICE models available for this device that function properly and give the right answers. This primarily due to the overall complexity of the device and the nature of its operation, which results in very long simulation times at a fairly high switching frequency rate. The need to simulate for multiple periods results in a very large number of transient iterations or calculations.

The model used in the simulation shown in Fig. 8.13 is a state space average model, included in the Power IC Model Library for Pspice and available from AEi Systems (www.aeng.com). Even though the model is created with state space techniques, you can perform many types of transient analyses with it. Figure 8.14 shows the steady state input voltage, current, power, and total harmonic distortion.

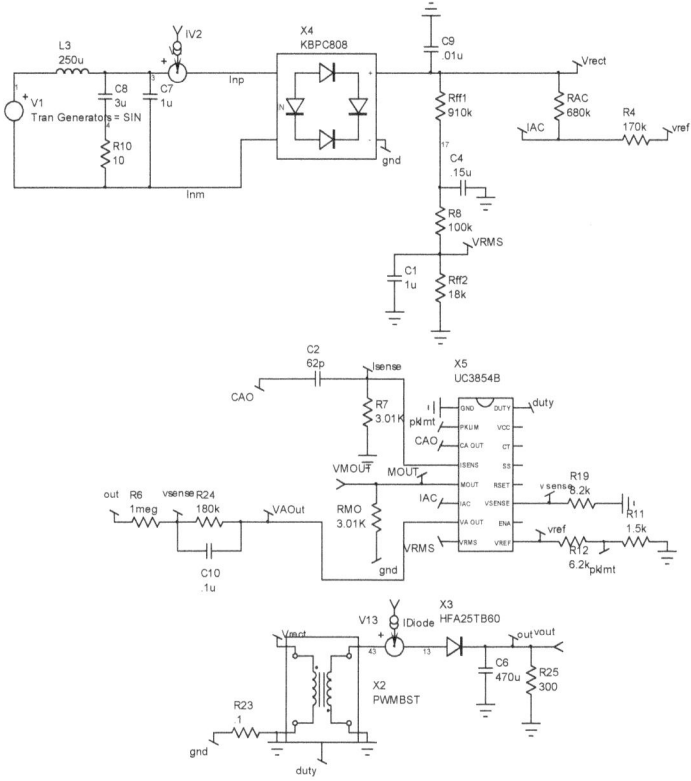

Figure 8.13

Boost Power Factor Corrector

```
UC3854StateSpace.cir
.TRAN 1u 250m 230m 10u UIC
.FOUR 60 I(V2)
.OPTIONS abstol=1E-8 itl4=1000 .OPTIONS method=GEAR vsectol=.5E-6
.OPTIONS gmin=1E-10 reltol=0.005
.PRINT  TRAN IV2
.PRINT  TRAN VMOUT
.PRINT  TRAN vout
.PRINT  TRAN IDiode
V1 1 Inm DC=90 SIN 0 150 60 0 0 0
X4 Inp Inm Vrect gnd KBPC808 {  }
C7 3 Inm 1u
L3 1 3 250u
C8 3 4 3u
R10 4 Inm 10
Rff1 Vrect 17 910k
Rff2 VRMS 0 18k
RAC Vrect IAC 680k
R4 IAC vref 170k
R6 out vsense 1meg
R11 0 pklmt 1.5k
X3 13 out HFA25TB60 {  }
V2 3 Inp
C1 VRMS 0 1u IC=1
X5 0 pklmt CAO Isense MOUT IAC VAOut VRMS vref vsense duty UC3854B {  }
R24 vsense VAOut 180k
RMO MOUT gnd 3.01K
C10 vsense VAOut .1u IC=0
C2 CAO Isense 62p IC=0
R7 0 Isense 3.01K
R8 17 VRMS 100k
C4 17 0 .15u IC=7
R12 pklmt vref 6.2k
R19 vsense 0 8.2k
C9 Vrect 0 .01u
R23 0 gnd .1
X2 Vrect 0 43 0 duty PWMBST {  }
C6 out 0 470u IC=375
R25 out 0 300
V13 43 13
.END
```

FOURIER COMPONENTS OF TRANSIENT RESPONSE I(V2)

DC COMPONENT = 1.039190E-04

HARMONIC NO	FREQUENCY (HZ)	FOURIER COMPONENT	NORMALIZED COMPONENT	PHASE (DEG)	NORMALIZED PHASE (DEG)
1	6.000E+01	6.002E+00	1.000E+00	-1.343E-01	0.000E+00
2	1.200E+02	2.381E-04	3.967E-05	-5.550E+01	-5.523E+01
3	1.800E+02	1.400E-01	2.332E-02	-1.757E+02	-1.753E+02
4	2.400E+02	1.094E-04	1.822E-05	-7.497E+01	-7.443E+01
5	3.000E+02	3.560E-02	5.930E-03	-1.776E+02	-1.770E+02
6	3.600E+02	8.766E-05	1.460E-05	-8.850E+01	-8.770E+01
7	4.200E+02	2.760E-02	4.599E-03	-1.772E+02	-1.762E+02
8	4.800E+02	7.394E-05	1.232E-05	-1.015E+02	-1.004E+02
9	5.400E+02	2.400E-02	3.998E-03	-1.775E+02	-1.762E+02

TOTAL HARMONIC DISTORTION = 2.482531E+00 PERCENT

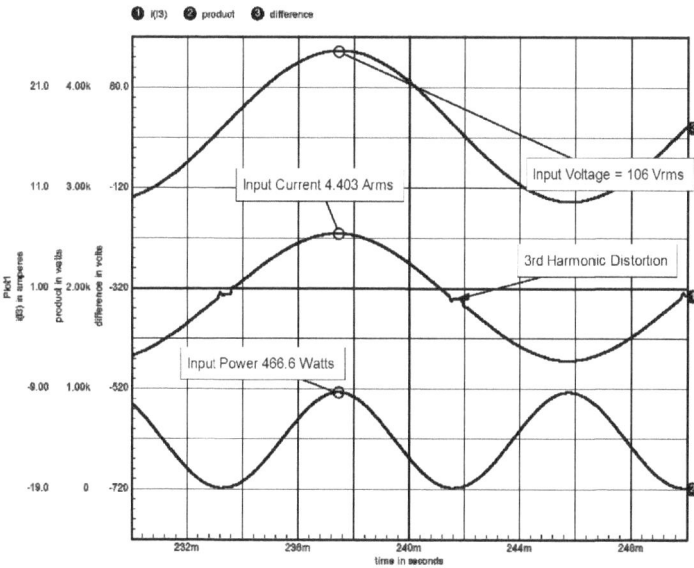

Figure 8.14

Boost Power Factor Corrector Results

Chapter 9

Improving Simulation Performance

SPICE IS AN evolving program. Software manufacturers are constantly adding new features and extensions in order to enhance the program and its interface. They are also striving to increase the simulation speed. The arrival of more powerful hardware dramatically improved simulation speed. Despite these achievements, we seem to be caught in an unending cycle. Hardware and software improvements allow more sophisticated modeling, which slows simulation speed and demands increased processing power. Fortunately, the end user has benefited greatly by this cycle. Just a few years ago, a long transient cycle-by-cycle simulation of a SMPS was impractical. Today, these simulations can be performed in a matter of minutes. This chapter provides information that will help you increase simulation speed and productivity when using SPICE. Here are some basic hints:

- Build models as your design progresses. Begin with simple models, and make them only as complex as they need to be.

- Limit the complexity of the model to the parameters which you need to measure. For example, if you are only performing DC measurements, then you don't need to calculate the charge storage parameters.

- Try to understand the features and limitations of the models that you are using.

- Use the transient statement parameters and simulator options effectively. The RELTOL option and the Tmax and Tstep parameters have dramatic effects upon the speed of the simulation (See Chapter 10).

- Maximize the use of subcircuits. If, for example, you commonly use series resistance for capacitors, create a subcircuit in order to hide its complexity and provide faster schematic entry.

- Use state machine models in order to simulate extensive digital (synchronous) circuits.

- Use UIC and initial conditions in order to reduce simulation time by starting the simulation near the desired operating conditions.

Building Circuit Models

The most effective use of SPICE occurs during the development of a project. Typical uses of SPICE during the early design stages might be to evaluate high level system specifications or very low level circuit concepts like the basic operating characteristics of key building blocks. Very simple circuit representations and coarse tolerances may be used at this point in order to quicken simulations and provide the desired results.

Simplifying Your Models

Reduction of the model complexity is one of the simplest ways to provide dramatic speed improvements. As a general rule, you should model only the circuit elements and complexities that are required for your design.

For example, if you are interested in evaluating the ripple and switch currents of a power converter, you should not include the control circuitry. The control circuitry does not enhance the simulation, and its added circuit complexity will needlessly slow the simulation. MOSFETS or transistors can usually be replaced by simplified representations such as switches or behavioral models. These first order models will have a negligible contribution to the simulation accuracy of the ripple voltage. In fact, the pulse width modulator models in the Power Supply Designer's Library from Intusoft have two levels of complexity. The Powernd.Lib file contains simple output driver models, while the Power.Lib file contains complex models. The simple models replace the output driver stage with a logic level output (B element If-then-else expression). The resulting simulation speed improvement is significant.

The following example uses the power stage of a SEPIC converter in order to show the degree of improvement you may obtain by using various .Options parameters. Eight simulations were performed with different options and MOSFET representations. In one simulation, a power MOSFET subcircuit model was used. In another simulation, a simple switch (voltage controlled resistor) subcircuit was used. Each simulation ran for 2 ms (Tstop). The simulation time, peak-to-peak ripple voltage, peak switch (or MOSFET) current, and the RMS switch (or MOSFET) current were recorded.

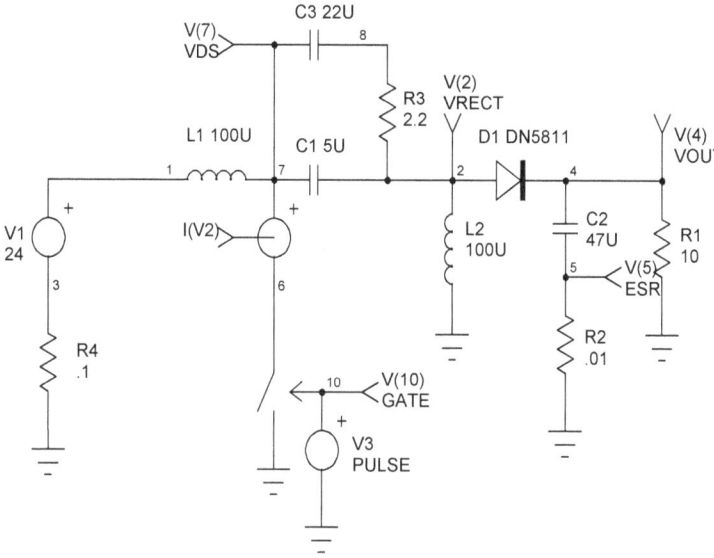

Figure 9.1

**Circuit using a Switch (Voltage Controlled Resistor)
Subcircuit for the MOSFET Representation**

The circuit in Figure 9.1 uses a switch subcircuit to represent the
MOSFET. The circuit in Figure 9.2 is an identical circuit, but
contains the MN6763 Power MOSFET model.

273

```
SEPIC1.cir
.PROBE
.TRAN .2u 2m 1900u .1u UIC
.OPTIONS RELTOL=.001
C2 4 5 47U IC=24
C3 7 8 22U IC=24
R1 4 0 10
R2 5 0 .01
R3 8 2 2.2
R4 3 0 .1
L1 1 7 100U IC=2
L2 0 2 100U IC=3
X1 6 0 10 SWITCH
U1 1 3 DC=24
U2 7 6
D1 2 4 DN5811
U3 10 0 PULSE 0 15 .1U .1U .1U 5U 10U
C1 7 2 5U IC=24
.END
```

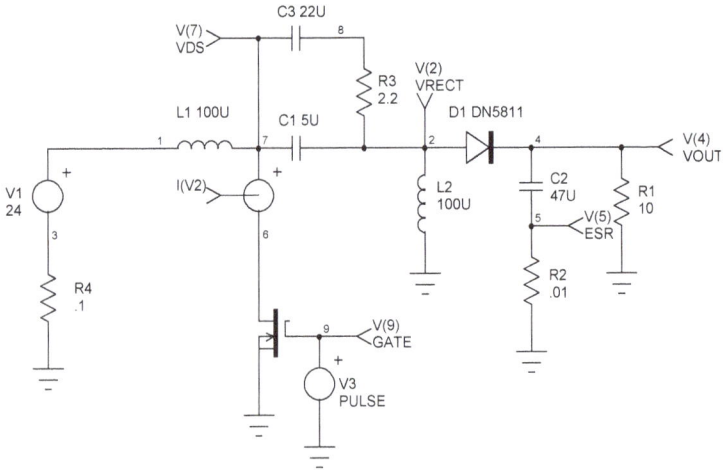

sepic2.ga

Figure 9.2

Circuit using a Power MOSFET Subcircuit

All of the simulations were performed with IsSpice 7.51 on a 75 MHz Pentium® computer with 16 MB of RAM, running under Windows 3.11.

The results are as follows:

Switch Type	SWITCH SUBCIRCUIT			
RELTOL	0.001	0.01	0.01	0.01
Tstep	.1u	0.1u	.1u	.2u
Tmax	.2u	.2u	none	none
Time - seconds	35.40	34.70	14.38	13.68
Ripple - mv$_{p-p}$	299.20	297.50	338.90	344.00
Peak Switch Current - Amps	6.22	6.22	6.23	6.23
RMS Switch Current - Amps	3.65	3.65	3.60	3.71

Switch Type	MN6763 MOSFET			
RELTOL	0.001	0.01	0.01	0.01
Tstep	.1u	0.1u	.1u	.2u
Tmax	.2u	.2u	none	none
Time - seconds	191.50	54.70	34.88	33.95
Ripple - mv$_{p-p}$	296.30	298.90	300.50	297.10
Peak Switch Current - Amps	6.07	6.34	6.36	6.36
RMS Switch Current - Amps	3.57	3.50	3.59	3.55

A typical graph of the ripple voltage and switch current for the first column of each simulation series is shown in Figures 9.3 and 9.4.

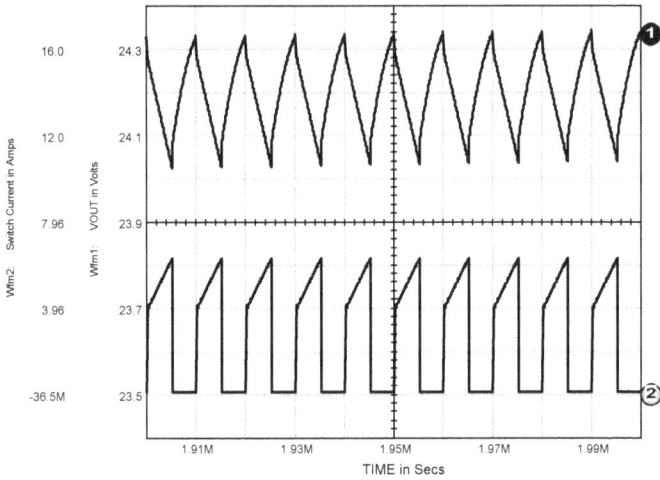

Figure 9.3

Ripple Voltage using the Switch Subcircuit

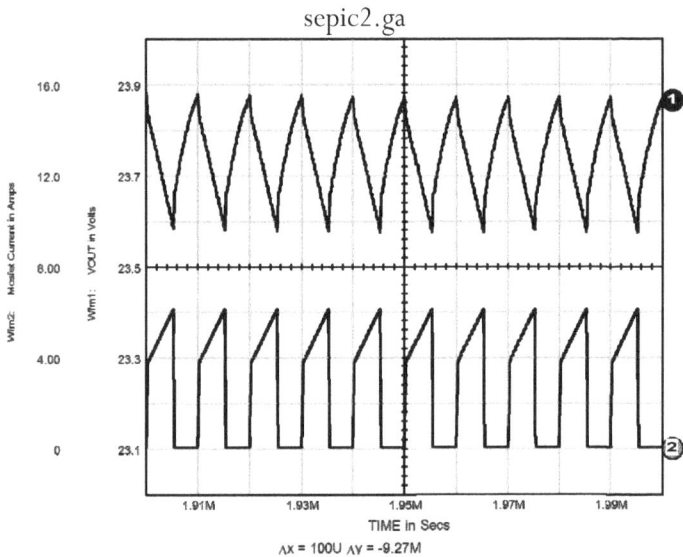

Figure 9.4

Ripple Voltage using the MN6763 MOSFET Subcircuit

In the case of the switch subcircuit model, the error in the ripple voltage is due to a "ring" on the upper and lower peaks of the waveform. This appears to be related to aliasing of the waveform. A tell-tale sign of aliasing can be spotted if the waveform is clipped when is should be smooth. Here are some solutions to the aliasing problem:

- Tighten the maximum timestep control (reduce Tmax)

- Take more data points (reduce Tstep)

- View the non-interpolated simulation data, as opposed to the interpolated .PRINT data which is based on the actual calculated timepoint values.

Another possible cause is the spurious oscillations that can appear when trapezoidal integration is used. A solution to this phantom ringing problem is the use of the Gear integration method rather than the default Trapezoidal integration method. In general, the Gear method, in conjunction with a slightly reduced RELTOL value, yields simulation speeds which are similar to those of the Trapezoidal method. Although the Gear integration method is somewhat slower, fewer timepoints will be rejected and therefore the total number of required timepoints will be reduced.

PSpice uses a modified trapezoidal Gear method that is a combination of trapezoidal and Gear integration. This algorithm is always in effect and will tend to produce a response that is somewhere between what SPICE 3 will provide for either pure trapezoidal or pure Gear integration.

The Gear integration method and the most liberal parameters (the last column) were selected, and the two circuits were simulated again. The results are provided below.

Switch Type	Switch Subcircuit	MN6763 MOSFET
RELTOL	0.01	0.01
Tstep	.2u	.2u
Tmax	none	none
Method	Gear	Gear
Time - seconds	16.97	230.30
Ripple - mv_{p-p}	299.10	296.90
Peak Switch Current - Amps	6.22	6.08
RMS Switch Current - Amps	3.68	3.60

The simulation times were slightly longer, but the results were much more accurate, especially with respect to the ripple voltage.

As you can see from the results, there is a significant difference in simulation speed between the runs with the switch subcircuit model and the runs with the MOSFET model. The effects of tolerances, simulator options and Gear integration are evident. The fastest simulation ran 13 times faster than the slowest simulation.

Based on these measurements, as well as many other simulations, the following recommendations are offered as a starting point for the transient simulation of power switching circuits are shown below.

Recommended Transient Parameters

Coarse Analysis
RELTOL=.01
Method=Gear
ABSTOL/VNTOL = 8 orders of magnitude below the maximum circuit current and voltage
Tstep=1/(25*Switching Frequency)
Tmax=1/(10*Switching Frequency)
Fine Analysis
RELTOL=.001
ABSTOL/VNTOL=Default
Tstep=1/(100*Switching Frequency)
Tmax=1/(25*Switching Frequency)

Each circuit was simulated using the recommended parameters. The results are as follows:

Switch Type	Switch Subcircuit	MN6763 MOSFET
Time - seconds	14.10	171.50
Ripple - mv$_{p-p}$	299.28	296.82
Peak Switch Current - Amps	6.22	6.08
RMS Switch Current - Amps	3.71	3.60

Output Stage Complexity

The SEPIC converter model was completed via the addition of the control circuitry. The purpose of the analysis was to determine the output's transient response when the circuit was subjected to a load step from 2.4 Amps to 1.4 Amps, and from 1.4 Amps to 2.4 Amps.

Since we are not particularly interested in the dynamics of the MOSFET, the switch subcircuit was used in order to increase the simulation speed. The schematic for the model is shown in Figure 9.5.

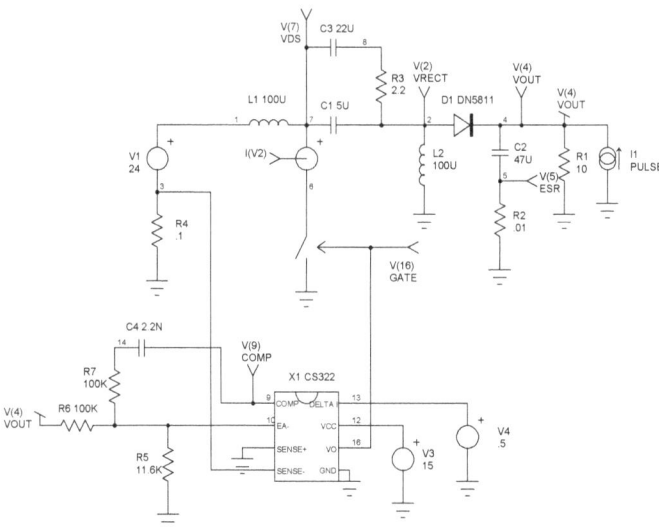

The results of the transient step load response are shown in Fig. 9.6 for two versions of the CS322 controller model: one using a detailed output driver structure and one using a simplified behavioral output driver model. In the full-driver version of the CS322, the output stage is constructed using transistors and diodes.

```
SEPIC:  SEPIC CONVERTER
.PROBE
.TRAN .2U 2M 1M .5U UIC
* U(4)=UOUT
* U(2)=URECT
* U(7)=UDS
* U(5)=ESR
* U(11)=GATE
* U(9)=COMP
.PRINT TRAN  U(4)  U(2)  U(7)  I(U2)
.PRINT TRAN  U(5)  U(11)  U(9)
L2 0 2 100U IC=2.5
C1 7 2 5U IC=24L2 0 2 100U IC=2.5
C1 7 2 5U IC=24
U1 1 3 24
D1 2 4 DN5811
C2 4 5 47U IC=24
R1 4 0 10
U2 7 6
R2 5 0 .01
C3 7 8 22U IC=24
R3 8 2 2.2
X1 9 10 0 3 0 11 12 13 CS322
U3 12 0 15
R4 3 0 .1
U4 13 0 .5
R5 10 0 11.6K
R6 4 10 100K
R7 10 14 100K
C4 14 9 2.2N
I1 0 4 PULSE 0 1 1010U 1U 1U 400U
X2 6 0 11 SWITCH
L1 1 7 100U IC=2.5
.END
```

Figure 9.5

SEPIC Converter Circuit and Netlist

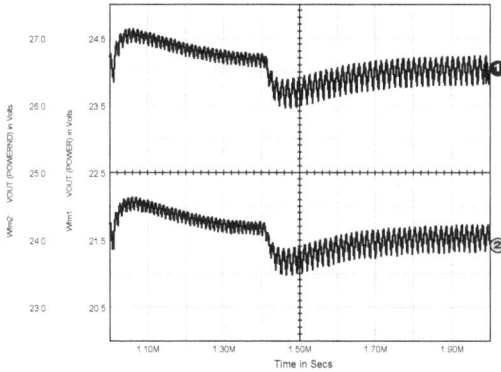

Figure 9.6

SEPIC Converter Transient Response

The behavioral version essentially uses a simple voltage-controlled voltage source as the output signal driver. A summary of the results is shown below.

Library	Full Model	Behavioral Models
Time (s)	798.00	168.45
Total iterations	174694.00	40804.00
Time points	36133.00	12157.00
Memory used (MB)	10.52	6.77

As you can see from the data above, the reduced driver complexity results in a considerably faster simulation. The exact output driver model is therefore recommended only when the output driver and switching MOSFET characteristics are of interest. In all other instances, the reduced complexity version achieves significant speedup with a minimal loss of accuracy.

.OPTIONS

An experiment was conducted in order to determine the effect of tolerances upon the simulation speed and accuracy of transient simulations. The results were both interesting and surprising, and led to a method which significantly improves simulation speed without sacrificing accuracy.

Several dozen circuits were selected, and initial simulations were performed. The simulation times and output results were recorded. Various tolerances, the quantity of saved data, and the graphics resolution were altered, and the simulations were performed again.

The following were determined to be the most significant contributors to simulation speed and accuracy. They are listed in order of decreasing sensitivity. Please note that the following list is based upon many parameters, and may have a varying degree of effect on your simulations.

- Internal tolerance defaults

- External tolerance values

- Real time waveform display

- Amount of data saved (assuming virtual RAM was not needed)

The following table lists the initial and final results of four simulations:

Circuit	UPS	SEPIC	FWD	CS322
Initial Simulation Time - Secs	217.50	188.60	406.10	214.53
Final Simulation Time - Secs	119.00	100.52	304.60	127.00
% Speed Improvement	45.29	46.70	24.99	40.80

Note: The FWD circuit did not show as much of an improvement as the other circuits because many of the .Options parameters were already being used.

The table below provides the average improvement for each modification to the simulation:

Modification	Improvement
Changed TRTOL to 100 (when used with TMAX)	25%
Changed ABSTOL to 0.01µSec and VNTOL to 10u	10%
No marching waveform display	5%
Removed PRINT statements for all vectors except those which were required and increased TSTEP	5%

The results of the final simulation were nearly identical to those of the initial simulation and no accuracy was sacrificed.

State Machine Models

State Machine models are a new addition to SPICE. They allow very large blocks of digital circuitry to be modeled easily and simulated quickly. The IsSpice state machine model is written in an AHDL language based on C [5,36]. Those SPICE simulators that have incorporated the public domain XSPICE extensions from the Georgia Institute of Technology will have access to this state machine element. The behavior of each state machine is defined in a separate ASCII text file. You may have as many state machines in the circuit as desired.

An example of a sine wave ROM, which is located in Chapter 7 of this book, demonstrates the speed improvement brought about by the use of the state machine (nearly a five-fold improvement over the simulation using discrete gates).

For more information on state machine modeling, see [5].

Hardware Considerations

SPICE is one of the most demanding applications that you can run—from both a memory and computational standpoint. In general, SPICE simulations of a design under investigation are run literally hundreds of times. Therefore, any improvement in simulation speed, whether from transient settings, .OPTION settings, or computer performance, is multiplied many times. If time is worth money, a user of SPICE is justified in having the fastest PC available on the market at the time.

Longer simulation times, tighter simulation tolerances, more saved data, or smaller time steps will increase the memory requirements considerably.

It is not unreasonable to use several gigabytes of RAM. If a simulation requires more RAM than is available in your computer, it will automatically use swap space on the hard disk. Although this allows the simulation to be completed, the access time of the hard disk is considerably slower than that of the RAM.

If you see that the hard disk is active during the course of a simulation, it is a good indication that your system would benefit from additional RAM.

Chapter 10

Solving Convergence and Other Simulation Problems

Simulation Convergence—Quick Fix

IF YOU ENCOUNTER a convergence problem, change the .OPTIONS settings you are using to the following:

- ABSTOL = 0.01µ   (Default=1p)

- VNTOL = 10µ   (Default=1µ)

- GMIN=0.1n   (Default=1p)

- RELTOL = 0.05   (Default=0.001)

- ITL4 = 500   (Default=10)

These settings will cure most simulation convergence problems unless there is an error in your circuit description.

Repetitive or Switching Simulations

Switching simulations refer to simulations that have a significant number of repetitive cycles, such as those found in SMPS simulations. SMPS simulations can experience a large number of rejected time points. Rejected time points are due to the fact that PSpice has a dynamically varying time step that is controlled by constant tolerance values (RELTOL, ABSTOL, and VNTOL). An event that occurs during each cycle, such as the switching of a power semiconductor, can trigger a reduction in the time step value. This is caused by the fact that PSpice attempts to maintain a specific accuracy and adjusts the time step in order to accomplish this task. The time step is increased after the event, until the next cycle, when it is again reduced. This time step hysteresis can cause an excessive number of unnecessary calculations. To correct this problem, we can regress to a SPICE 2 methodology and force the simulator to have a fixed time step value.

To force the time step to be a fixed value, set the TRTOL value to 25, i.e. .OPTIONS TRTOL=25. The default value is 7. The Trtol parameter controls how far ahead in time SPICE tries to jump. The value of 25 causes PSpice to try to jump far ahead. Then set TMAX (maximum allowed time step) in the .TRAN statement to a value that is between 1/10 and 1/100 of the switching cycle period. This has the opposite effect; it forces the time step to be limited. Together, they effectively lock the simulator time step to a value that is between 1/10 and 1/100 of the switching cycle period and eliminate virtually all of the rejected time points. These settings can result in over a 100% increase in speed!

Note: In order to verify the number of accepted and rejected time points, you may issue the .OPTIONS ACCT parameter and view the summary data at the end of the output file.

If this does not help the simulation converge, proceed to the next section that has more details.

Simulation Convergence

The answer to a nonlinear problem, such as those in the SPICE DC and transient analyses, is found via an iterative solution. For example, PSpice makes an initial guess at the circuit's node voltages and then, using the circuit conductances, calculates the mesh currents. The currents are then used to recalculate the node voltages, and the cycle begins again. This continues until all the node voltages settle to values that are within specific tolerance limits. These limits can be altered using various .OPTIONS parameters such as RELTOL, VNTOL, and ABSTOL.

If the node voltages do not settle down within a certain number of iterations, the DC analysis will issue an error message such as "No convergence in DC analysis," "Singular matrix," "GMIN stepping failed," or "Source stepping failed." PSpice will then halt the run because both the AC and transient analyses require an initial stable operating point in order to proceed. During the transient analysis, this iterative process is repeated for each individual time step. If the node voltages do not settle down, the time step is reduced and PSpice tries again to determine the node voltages. If the time step is reduced beyond a specific fraction of the total analysis time, the transient analysis will issue the error message "Time step too small," and the analysis will be halted.

Convergence problems come in all shapes, sizes, and disguises, but they are usually related to one of the following:

- Circuit topology

- Device modeling

- Simulator setup

The DC analysis may fail to converge because of incorrect initial voltage estimates, model discontinuities, unstable/bistable operation, or unrealistic circuit impedances. Transient analysis failures are usually due to model discontinuities or unrealistic circuit, source, or parasitic modeling. In general, you will have problems if the impedances, or impedance changes, do not remain reasonable. Convergence problems will result if the impedances in your circuit are too high or too low.

The various solutions to convergence problems fall under one of two types. Some are simply band aids that merely attempt to fix the symptom by adjusting the simulator options. Other solutions actually affect the true cause of the convergence problems.

The following techniques can be used to solve a majority of convergence problems. When a convergence problem is encountered, you should start at solution 0 and proceed with the subsequent suggestions until convergence is achieved. The sequence of the suggestions is structured so that they can be incrementally added to the simulation. The sequence is also defined so that the initial suggestions will be of the most benefit. Note that suggestions that involve simulation options may simply mask the underlying circuit instabilities. Invariably, you will find that once the circuit is properly modeled, many of the "options" fixes will no longer be required!

General Discussion

Many power electronics convergence problems can be solved with the .OPTIONS GMIN parameter. GMIN is the minimum conductance across all semiconductor junctions. The conductance is used to keep the matrix well conditioned. Its default value is 1E-12mhos. Setting GMIN to a value between 1n and 10n will often solve convergence problems. Setting GMIN to a value greater than 10n may cause convergence problems.

GMIN stepping is an algorithm in PSpice and SPICE 3 that greatly improves DC convergence. This algorithm uses a constant minimal junction conductance that keeps the sparse matrix well conditioned and a separate variable conductance to ground at each node, which serves as a DC convergence aid. The variable conductances cause the solution to converge more quickly. They are then reduced, and the solution is re-computed. The solution is eventually found with a sufficiently small conductance. Then the conductance is removed entirely in order to obtain a final solution. This technique has proven to work very well, and PSpice selects it automatically when convergence problems occur. The suggestion of increasing the .OPTIONS GMIN value to solve DC and operating point convergence problems is performed automatically by this new algorithm. GMIN may still be increased (relaxed) for the entire AC or transient simulation by setting an alternate .OPTIONS GMIN value.

PSpice does not always converge when relaxed tolerances are used. One of the most common problems is the incorrect use of the .OPTIONS parameters. For example, setting the tolerance option, RELTOL, to a value greater than 0.01 will often cause convergence problems.

Setting the value of ABSTOL to 1μ will help in the case of circuits that have currents larger than several amperes. Again, do not overdo this setting. Setting ABSTOL to a value that is greater than 1μ may cause more convergence problems than it will solve.

After you have performed a number of simulations, you will discover the options that work best for your circuit. Very often, various options will be needed as the circuit topology is developed. Invariably, you will find that after you have debugged your circuit representation, and if your components are well modeled, most of the options can be removed.

If all else fails, you can almost always get a circuit to simulate in a transient simulation if you begin with a zero voltage/zero current state. This makes sense if you consider the fact that the simulation always starts with the assumption that all voltages and currents are zero. The simulator can almost always track the nodes from a zero condition. Running the simulation will often help uncover the cause of the convergence failure.

The above recommendation is only true if your circuit is constructed properly. Most of the time, minor mistakes are the cause of convergence problems. Error messages will help you track down the problems; however, a good technique is to scan each line of the netlist and look for anomalies. It may be tedious, but it is a proven way to weed out mistakes.

Not all convergence failures are a result of the PSpice software! Convergence failures may identify many circuit problems. Check your circuits carefully, and do not be too quick to blame the software.

DC Convergence Solutions

- Check the circuit topology and connectivity.

Common Mistakes and Problems

- Make sure that all the circuit connections are valid. Also, verify component polarity.

- Check for syntax mistakes. Make sure that you used the correct SPICE units (i.e. MEG instead of M(milli) for 1E6).

- Make sure that there is a DC path from every node to ground.

- Make sure that voltage/current generators use realistic values, especially for rise and fall time.

- Make sure that dependent source gains are correct, and that E and G element expressions are reasonable. If you are using division in an expression, verify that division by zero cannot occur or protect against it with a small offset in the denominator.

Increase ITL1 to 400 in the .OPTIONS Statement

Example: .OPTIONS ITL1=400

This increases the number of DC iterations that PSpice will perform before it gives up. In all but the most complex circuits, further increases in ITL1 will not typically aid convergence.

Add .NODESETs

Example: .NODESET V(6)=0

View the node voltage/branch current table in the output file. PSpice produces one even if the circuit does not converge. Add .NODESET values for the top-level circuit nodes (not the subcircuit nodes) that have unrealistic values. You do not need to nodeset every node. Use a .NODESET value of 0V if you do not have a better estimation of the proper DC voltage. Caution is warranted, however, for an inaccurate .NODESET value may cause undesirable results.

Add Resistors and use the OFF Keyword

Example: D1   1   2   DMOD OFF
RD1 1 2 100MEG

Add resistors across diodes in order to simulate leakage. Add resistors across MOSFET drain-to-source connections to simulate realistic channel impedances. This will make the impedances reasonable so that they will be neither too high nor too low. Add ohmic resistances (RC, RB, RE) to transistors. Use the .OPTIONS statement to reduce GMIN by an order of magnitude.

 Next, you can also add the OFF keyword to semiconductors (especially diodes) that may be causing convergence problems. The OFF keyword tells PSpice to first solve the operating point with the device turned off. Then the device is turned on, and the previous operating point is used as a starting condition for the final operating point calculation.

Use PULSE Statements to turn on DC Power Supplies

Example: VCC 1 0 15 DC
 …becomes VCC 1 0 PULSE 0 15

This allows the user to selectively turn on specific power supplies. This is sometimes known as the "pseudo-transient" startup method. Use a reasonable rise time in the PULSE statement to simulate realistic turn on. For example,

V1 1 0 PULSE 0 5 0 1U

…will provide a 5-V supply with a turn-on time of 1 μs. The first value after the 5 (in this case, 0) is the turn-on delay, which can be used to allow the circuit to stabilize before the power supply is applied.

Add UIC (Use Initial Conditions) to the .TRAN Statement

Example: .TRAN .1N 100N UIC

Insert the UIC (use initial conditions) keyword in the .TRAN statement. UIC will cause PSpice to completely bypass the DC analysis. You should add any applicable .IC and IC (initial conditions) statements to assist in the initial stages of the transient analysis. Be careful when you set initial conditions, for a poor setting may cause convergence difficulties.

AC Analysis Note: Solutions 4 and 5 should be used only as a last resort, because they will not produce a valid DC operating point for the circuit (all supplies may not be turned on and circuit may not be properly biased). Therefore, you cannot use solutions 4 and 5 if you want to perform an AC analysis, because the AC analysis must be preceded by a valid operating point solution. However, if your goal is to proceed to the transient analysis, then solutions 4 and 5 may help you and may possibly uncover the hidden problems that plague the DC analysis.

Transient Convergence Solutions

• Check circuit topology and connectivity.

• Set RELTOL=0.01 or 0.005 in the .OPTIONS statement.

Example: .OPTIONS RELTOL=0.01

This option is encouraged for most simulations, because reducing RELTOL can increase the simulation speed by 10% to 50%. Only a minor loss in accuracy usually results. A useful recommendation is to set RELTOL to 0.01 for initial simulations and then reset it to its default value of 0.001 when you have the simulation running the way you like it and a more accurate answer is required. Setting RELTPOL to a value less than 0.001 is generally not required.

- Set ITL4=500 in the .OPTIONS statement.

Example: .OPTIONS ITL4=500

This increases the number of transient iterations that SPICE will attempt at each time point before it gives up. Values that are greater than 500 or 1000 will not usually bring convergence.

- Reduce the accuracy of ABSTOL/VNTOL if current/voltage levels allow it.

Example: .OPTION ABSTOL=1N VNTOL=1M

ABSTOL and VNTOL should be set to about 8 orders of magnitude below the level of the maximum voltage and current. The default values are ABSTOL=1p and VNTOL=1μ. These values are generally associated with IC designs.

- Realistically model your circuit; add parasitics, especially stray/junction capacitance.

The idea here is to smooth any strong nonlinearities or discontinuities. This may be accomplished via the addition of capacitance to various nodes and verifying that all semiconductor junctions have capacitance. Other tips include the following:

- Use RC snubbers around diodes.

- Add capacitance for all semiconductor junctions (3pF for diodes and 5pF for BJTs if no specific value is known).

- Add realistic circuit and element parasitics.

- Watch the real-time waveform display and look for waveforms that transition vertically (up or down) at the point during which the analysis halts. These are the key nodes that you should examine for problems.

- If the .MODEL definition for the part does not reflect the behavior of the device, use a subcircuit representation. This is especially important for RF and power devices such as RF BJTs and power MOSFETs. Many model vendors cheat and try to "force fit" the SPICE .MODEL statement in order to represent a device's behavior. This is a sure sign that the vendor has skimped on quality in favor of quantity. Primitive level 1 or 3 .MODEL statements *cannot* be used to model most devices above 200MHz because of the effect of package parasitics. And .MODEL statements *cannot* be used to model most power devices because of their extreme nonlinear behavior. In particular, if your vendor uses a .MODEL statement to model a power MOSFET, throw away the model. It is almost certainly useless for transient analysis.

- Reduce the rise/fall times of the PULSE sources.

Example: VCC 1 0 PULSE 0 1 0 0 0
    ....becomes   VCC 1 0 PULSE 0 1 0 1U 1U

Again, we are trying to smooth strong nonlinearities. The pulse times should be realistic, not ideal. If no rise or fall time values are given, or if 0 is specified, the rise and fall times will be set to the TSTEP value in the .TRAN statement.

- Add UIC to the .TRAN line.

Example: .TRAN .1N 100N UIC

If you are having trouble getting the transient analysis to start because the DC operating point cannot be calculated, insert the UIC keyword in the .TRAN statement (skip initial transient solution). UIC will cause PSpice to completely bypass the DC analysis. You should add any applicable .IC and IC (initial conditions) statements to assist in the initial stages of the transient analysis. Be careful when you set initial conditions, for a poor setting may cause convergence difficulties.

- If your simulator supports it, change the integration method to Gear.

Example: .OPTIONS METHOD=GEAR

This option causes SPICE 3 to use Gear integration to solve the transient equations, as opposed to the default method of trapezoidal or modified trapezoidal integration. The use of the Gear integration method should be coupled with a reduction in the RELTOL value. This will produce answers that approach a more stable numerical solution. Trapezoidal integration tends to produce a less stable solution that can produce spurious oscillations. Gear integration often produces superior results for power circuitry simulations, because high-frequency ringing and long simulation periods are often encountered.

Modeling Tips

Device modeling is one of the hardest steps encountered in the circuit simulation process. It requires not only an understanding of the device's physical and electrical properties, but also a detailed knowledge of the particular circuit application. Nevertheless, the problems of device modeling are not insurmountable. A good first-cut model can be obtained from data sheet information and quick calculations, so the designer can have an accurate device model for a wide range of applications.

Data sheet information is generally very conservative, yet it provides a good first-cut of a device model. To obtain the best results for circuit modeling, follow the rule: "Use the simplest model possible." In general, the SPICE component models have default values that produce reasonable first-order results. Here are some helpful tips:

- Do not make your models any more complicated than they need to be. Overcomplicating a model will only cause it to run more slowly and will increase the likelihood of an error.

- Remember: modeling is a compromise.

- Do not be afraid to pull apart your circuit and test individual sections or even models, especially the ones you did not create.

- Create subcircuits that can be run and debugged independently. Simulation is just like being at the bench. If the simulation of the entire circuit fails, you should break it apart and use simple test circuits to verify the operation of each component or section.

- Document the models as you create them. If you do not use a model often, you might forget how to use it.

- Be careful when you use models that have been produced by hardware vendors. Many have limitations on the operating point bounds for which they can be used.

- Semiconductor models should always include junction capacitance and the transit time (AC charge storage) parameters.

- If the .Model definition for a large geometry device does not reflect the behavior of the device, use a subcircuit representation.

- Be careful when using behavioral models for power devices. Many models are not thoroughly tested and work at one operating point but are highly inaccurate at other operating points.

- **And lastly, there is no substitute for knowing what you are doing!!**

References

General

[1] Meares, L.G.; Hymowitz C.E., *Simulating with Spice*, Intusoft, San Pedro, CA, 1988.

[2] Muller, K.H., *A SPICE Cookbook*, Intusoft, San Pedro, CA, 1990.

[3] Meares, L.G.; Hymowitz C.E., *Spice Applications Handbook*, Intusoft, San Pedro, CA, 1990.

[4] Intusoft Newsletters, various dates from 1986 to present.

[5] *PSpice A/D Reference Guide*, product version 10.0, June 2003.

[6] Quarles, T.L., *Analysis of Performance and Convergence Issues for Circuit Simulation*, ERL Memo M89/42, University of California, Berkeley, CA, Apr. 1989.

[7] *Berkeley SPICE Version 2G User's Guide*, Aug. 1981.

[8] Berwick, J., *SPICE Simulation Aids Power Factor Corrector Design*, Power Conversion & Intelligent Motion, February, 1994, 20(2), pp. 19-20, 22, 24-26.

[9] Ben-Yaakov, S., *The Unified Switched Inductor Model*, Proceedings of the 17th Convention of Electrical and Electronics Engineers in Israel, IEEE, New York, 1991, pp. 320-323.

[10] Middlebrook, R.D., *Power Electronics: Topologies, Modeling, and Measurement*

[11] IEEE International Symposium on Circuits and Systems, vol. 1, IEEE, New York, 27-29 April 1981, pp. 230-238.

[12] Hymowitz, C.E., Intusoft Modeling Corner: A SPICE Generic Model for IGBTs, *Intusoft Newsletter*, June 1992.

[13] Petrie, A.F.; Hymowitz, C.E., *A SPICE model for IGBTs*, Proceedings of the Applied Power Electronics Conference, 1995, pp. 147-152.

[14] Kawaguchi, Y.; Terazaki, Y.; Nakagawa, A., *Subcircuit SPICE Modeling of a Lateral IGBT for High Voltage Power IC Design*, IEEE International Symposium on Power Semiconductor Devices and ICs, 1995, pp. 346-349.

[15] Shen, Z.; Chow, T.P., *Modeling and Characterization of the Insulated Gate Bipolar Transistor (IGBT) for SPICE Simulation*, Devices and ICs: Proceedings of the International Symposium on Power Semiconductor Devices and ICs, IEEE Service Center, Piscataway, NJ, 1993, pp. 165-170.

[16] Dutta, R.; Tsay, C.; Rothwarf, A.; Fischl, R., *Physical and Circuit Level Approach for Modeling Turn-Off Characteristics of GTOs*, IEEE Transactions on Power Electronics, November 1994, 9(6), 560-566.

[17] Hamill, D.C., *Gyrator-Capacitor Modeling: A Better Way of Understanding Magnetic Components*, IEEE Service Center, Piscataway, NJ, 1994, pp. 326-332.

[18] Chen, J.E.; Rodriguez, F.D., *SPICE Modeling of a Resolver-to-Digital Converter for Closed Loop Simulations of Brushless DC Motors*, Proceedings of the Intersociety Energy Conversion Engineering Conference, vol. 1, 1991, pp. 224-229.

[19] Shenai, K., *A Circuit Simulation Model for High-Frequency Power MOSFETs*, IEEE Transactions on Power Electronics 6(3), pp. 539-547, July 1991.

[20] Chandra, H.N.; Thottuvelil, V.J., *Modeling and Analysis of Computer Power Systems*, IEEE Service Center, Piscataway, NJ, 1989, pp. 144-151.

[21] Liffring, M.E.; Spier, R.J., *Simulating Discrete Semiconductors with Differing Junction Temperatures on SPICE*, Proceedings of the

Intersociety Energy Conversion Engineering Conference, 1989, **3**(4), 457-461.

[22] Filseth, E.; Jachowski, M., *SPICE Extensions Dynamically Model Thermal Properties*, EDN, 14 Apr. 1988, 33(8), 169-180.

[23] Amin, A.M.A.; Steelman, J.E.; Ranade, S., *Adaptive Harmonic Cancellation: SPICE Model and Results*, IEEE Service Center, Piscataway, NJ, 1986.

[24] Huliehel, F.; Ben-Yaakov, S., *Low Frequency Sampled Data Models of Switched Mode DC-DC Converters*, IEEE Transactions on Power Electronics, 1991, 6, 55-61.

[25] Ben-Yaakov, S., *A Unified Approach to Teaching Feedback in Electronic Circuit Courses*, IEEE Transactions on Education, 1991, 34, 310-316.

[26] Tsafrin, H.; Ben-Yaakov, S., *The Dynamic Response of PWM DC-DC Converters with Input Filters*, IEEE Applied Power Electronics Conference (APEC), Boston, 1992, pp. 764-771.

[27] Monteith, D., *Using SPICE2 in Computer-Aided Design of Energy Conversion Electronics*, 21st Intersociety Energy Conversion Engineering Conference, 25-29 Aug. 1986.

[28] Severns, R.; Bloom, G., *Modern DC-to-DC Switchmode Power Converter Circuits*, Van Nostrand Reinhold, New York, 1985.

[29] Griffin, R., *SPICE Modeling for Switching Power Converters with Crossover Between Continuous and Discontinuous Conduction Modes*, PEC 1988, pp. 19-35.

[30] Keller, R., *Closed-loop Testing and Computer Analysis and Design of Control Systems*, Electronic Design, 22 November 1978, pp. 132-138.

[31] Lauritzen, P.; Yee, H., *SPICE Models for Power MOSFETS: An Update*, APEC'88, pp. 281-289.

[32] Cordonnier, C. *SPICE Model for TMOS Power MOSFETs*, Motorola Application, Note AN1043, 1989.

[33] Ridley, R.B.; Lee, F.C., *Practical Nonlinear Design Optimization Tool for Power Converter Components*, PESC 1987, pp. 314-323.

[34] Yang, P., *Simulation and Modeling*, IEEE Circuit and Devices Magazine, Sept. 1991, pp. 9-37.

[35] Choudhury, U., *Sensitivity Analysis in SPICE 3*, Master's Thesis, University of California, Berkeley, Dec. 1988.

[36] Cox, F.; Kuhn, W.; Murray, J.; Tynor, S., *Code Level Modeling in XSPICE*, Proceedings of the 1992 International Symposium on C&S, San Diego, CA, May 1992.

Average/State Space Modeling and Simulation

[37] Bass, R.M.; Heck, B.S.; Khan, R.A., *Average Modeling of Current-mode Controlled Converters: Instability Predictions*, International Journal of Electronics, Nov. 1994, 77(5), 613-628.

[38] Vorperian, V., *Simplified Analysis of PWM Converters using Model of PWM Switch. II. Discontinuous Conduction Mode*, IEEE Transactions on Aerospace and Electronic Systems, May 1990, 26(3), 497-505.

[39] Cheng, R.-J.; Hu, Z.-H., *A New Average Model of Switching Converters*, 1988 IEEE International Symposium on Circuits and Systems, 7-9 June 1988, vol. 2, IEEE, New York, pp. 1147-1150.

[40] Rim, C.T.; Joung, G.B.; Cho, G.H., *A Practical Switch Based State-Space Modeling of DC-DC Converters*, Proceedings of TENCON 87: 1987 IEEE Region 10 Conference Computers and Communications Technology Toward 2000, vol. 3, IEEE, New York, 1987, pp. 1006-1010.

[41] Olivier, E.; Rognon, J.P.; Perret, R., *Application of the Average Circuit Method to the Modeling of AC to DC Converters*, IEEE, New York, 1985, pp. 1281-1287.

[42] Polivka, W.M.; Chetty, P.R.K.; Middlebrook, R.D., *State Space Average Modeling of Converters with Parasitics and Storage Time Modulation*, IEEE Power Electronics Specialists Conference, 16-20 June 1980, IEEE, New York, pp. 119-143.

[43] Ben-Yaakov, S.; Rahav, G., *Average Modeling and Simulation of Series-Parallel Resonant Converters by SPICE Compatible Behavioral Dependent Sources*, IEEE, New York, 1996. pp. 116-120.

[44] Kang, Y.; Lavers, J.D., *Automatic Generation of SPICE-compatible Behavior Models for Computer Simulation of DC-DC Converters*, IEEE Workshop on Computers in Power Electronics 1994, IEEE, Piscataway, NJ, , pp. 73-78.

[45] Lee, Y.-S.; Cheng, D.K.W.; Wong, S.C., *A New Approach to the Modeling of Converters for SPICE Simulation*, IEEE Transactions on Power Electronics, Oct. 1992, 7(4), 741-753.

[46] Moussa, W.M.; Morris, J.E., *Comparison between State Space Averaging and PWM Switch for Switch Mode Power Supply Analysis*, Proceedings of the 1990 IEEE, Southern Tier Technical Conference, 1990, pp. 15-21.

[47] Monteith, D.O., Jr.; Salcedo, D., *Modeling Feedforward PWM Circuits using the Nonlinear Function*, 10th International Solid-State Power Electronics Conference, Published by Power Concepts, Ventura, CA, 1983.

[48] Ben-Yaakov, S., *SPICE Simulation of PWM DC-DC Converter Systems: Voltage Feedback, Continuous Inductor Conduction Mode*, IEE Electronics Letters, Aug. 1989, *25*(16),1061-1063.

[49] Ben-Yaakov, S.; Edry, D.; Amran, Y.; Shimony, O., *SPICE Simulation of Quasi-resonant Zero-current-switching DC-DC Converters*, IEE Electronics Letters, June 1990, 26(13), 847-849.

[50] Ben-Yaakov, S.; Rot, Y.; Avirav, Y.; Cohen Z.-A., *Electronic Circuit Simulation in Engineering Education: Theoretical Considerations and Practical Implementation*, EC Newsletters, 1990, 2(2), 7-14.

[51] Ben-Yaakov, S., *SPICE Simulation of Quasi-resonant Zero-current-switching DC-DC Converters*, IEEE Electronics Letters, 1990, 26, 847-848.

[52] Kimhi, D.; Ben-Yaakov, S. *A SPICE Model for Current Mode PWM Converters Operating under Continuous Inductor Current Conditions*, IEEE Transactions on Power Electronics, 1991, 6(2), 281-286.

[53] Amran, Y.; Huliehel, F.; Ben-Yaakov, S., *A Unified SPICE Compatible Average Model of PWM Converters*, IEEE Transactions on Power Electronics, 1991, 6.

[54] Ben-Yaakov, S.; Gaaton, Z., *Unified SPICE Compatible Model of Current Feedback in Switch Mode Converters*, IEE Electronics Letters, 1992, **28**, 1356-1357.

[55] Ben-Yaakov, S., *Modeling the Switch of PWM Converters*, IEEE Transactions on Aerospace and Electronic Systems, 1992, **28**, 921-922.

[56] Ben-Yaakov, S.; Vardy, D.; Gaaton, Z., *A Unified Model of Current Feedback in Switch-mode Converters*, International Symposium of Circuits and Systems (ISCAS), San Diego, 1992.

[57] Edry, D.; Hadar, M.; Ben-Yaakov, S., *A SPICE Compatible Model of Tapped-inductor PWM Converters*, IEEE Applied Power Electronics Conference (APEC), Orlando, 1994.

[58] Ben-Yaakov, S., *Average Modeling of PWM Converters by Direct Implementation of Behavioral Relationships*, IEEE Applied Power Electronics Conference (APEC), San Diego, 1993, pp. 510-516.

[59] Edry, D.; Ben-Yaakov, S., *Dynamics of the Capacitive-loaded Push-pull Parallel-resonant Converter: Investigation by a SPICE Compatible Average Model*, IEEE Applied Power Electronics Conference (APEC), Orlando, 1994, pp. 1035-1041.

[60] Ben-Yaakov, S.; Adar (Edry), D., *Average Models as Tools for Studying the Dynamics of Switch Mode DC-DC Converters*, IEEE Power Electronics Specialists Conference (PESC), Taipei, 1994, pp. 1218-1225.

[61] Middlebrook, R.; Cuk, S., *A General Unified Approach to Modeling Switching-converter Power Stages*, IEEE Power Electronics Specialists Conference (PESC) record, 1976, pp. 18-34.

[62] Middlebrook, R.; Cuk, S., *A General Unified Approach to Modeling Switching DC-to-DC Converters in Discontinuous Conduction Mode*, IEEE Power Electronics Specialists Conference (PESC), 1980, pp. 36-57.

[63] Bello, V., *Computer Aided Analysis of Switching Regulators using SPICE2*, IEEE Power Electronics Specialists Conference (PESC) record, 1980, pp. 3-11.

[64] Bello, V., *Computer Program adds SPICE to Switching-regulator Analysis*, Electronic Design, 5 March 1981, pp. 89-95.

[65] Bello, V., *Using the SPICE2 CAD Package for Easy Simulation of Switching Regulators in both Continuous and Discontinuous Conduction Modes*, Proceedings of the 8th National Solid-State Power Conversion Conference (Powercon 8), Apr. 1981, pp. H3.1-H3.14.

[66] Bello, V., *Using the SPICE2 CAD Package to Simulate and Design the Current mode Converter*, Proceedings of the 11th National Solid-State Power Conversion Conference (Powercon 11), April, 1984.

[67] Meares, L., *New Simulation Techniques using SPICE*, IEEE Applied Power Electronics Conference (APEC), Apr. 1986, pp. 198-205.

[68] Chen, J.; Rodriquez, R., *Duo-Mode Non-Linear State Space Averaged SPICE Model of a Current Mode Buck Converter*, IEEE Applied Power Electronics Conference (APEC), 1988, pp. 53-58.

[69] Thottuvelil, J., et al., *Linear Averaged and Sampled Data Models for Large Signal Control of High Power Factor AC-DC Converters*, IEEE Power Electronics Specialists Conference (PESC), June 1990.

[70] Vorperian, V., et al., *Nonlinear Modeling of the PWM Switch*, IEEE Transactions on Power Electronics, Apr. 1989, Vol 4, #2.

[71] Meares, L., *Modeling Pulse Width Modulators*, Intusoft Newsletter, Aug. 1990, pp. 2-9.

[72] Vorperian, V., *Simplify your PWM Converter Analysis using the Model of the PWM Switch*, VPEC Current, Fall 1988.

[73] Vorperian V., *Simplified Analysis of PWM Converters using the Model of the PWM Switch*, parts I and II, Transactions on Aerospace and Electronic Systems, May 1990, 26(3), 490-505.

[74] Vorperian, V., *Simplify PWM Converter Analysis using a PWM Switch Model*, Power Conversion International Magazine, March 1990, pp. 8-16.

[75] Ridley, R., *New Simulation Techniques for PWM Converters*, Proceedings of the Applied Power Electronics Conference (APEC), 1993, pp. 517-523

Magnetics Design and Modeling

[76] Meares, L.G.; Hymowitz, C.E.; Martinelli, R., *Magnetics Designer User's Guide*, Intusoft, San Pedro, CA, 1996.

[77] Martinelli, R., *Designing High Frequency Transformers using Computer Aided Techniques*, Powertechnics Magazine, Jan. 1988.

[78] Meares, L.; Hymowitz, C.E., *Improved Spice Model Simulates Transformers Physical Processes*, EDN, 19 Aug. 1993.

[79] Watson, J.K., *Applications of Magnetism*, John Wiley and Sons, New York, 1980.

[80] Members of the Staff of the Department of Electrical Engineering Massachusetts Institute of Technology, *Magnetic Circuits and Transformers*, John Wiley and Sons, New York, 1947.

[81] Cherry, E.C., *The Duality Between Interlinked Electric and Magnetic Circuits and the Formation of Transformer Equivalent Circuits*, Proceedings of the Physical Society, 1949, 62B, 101-111.

[82] Peters, D.; Maka, T., *An Analytical Procedure for Determining Equivalent Circuits of Static Electromagnetic Devices*, IEEE Transactions on Industry and General Applications, 1966, 2(6), 456-460.

[83] Duaharjre, A.; Middlebrook, R.D., *Modeling and Estimation of Leakage Phenomena in Magnetic Circuits*, Proceedings of the IEEE Power Electronics Specialists Conference (PESC), 1986, pp. 213-226.

[84] Starr, F.M., *Equivalent Circuits - I*, Transactions of the AIEE, June 1932, 51, 287-298.

[85] El-Hamamsy, A.; Chang, E. I., *Magnetics Modeling for Computer-Aided Design of Power Electronics Circuits*, Proceedings of the IEEE Power Electronics Specialists Conference (PESC), 1989, pp. 635-645.

[86] Hamill, D., *Lumped Equivalent Circuits of Magnetic Components: The Gyrator-Capacitor Approach*, IEEE Transactions on Power Electronics, April 1993, 8(2), 97-103.

[87] Hamill, D., *Gyrator-Capacitor Modeling: A Better Way of Understanding Magnetic Components*, IEEE Applied Power Electronics Conference (APEC) proceedings, 1994, pp.326-332, 0-7803-1456-5/94

[88] Urling, A. M.; Niemela, V. A.; Skutt, G. R.; Wilson, T. G., *Characterizing High-frequency Effects in Transformer Windings—A Guide to Several Significant Articles*, IEEE Power Electronics Specialists Conference (PESC) record, June 1989, pp.373-385.

[89] Dowell, P.L., *Effects of Eddy Currents in Transformer Windings*, Proceedings of IEE, Aug. 1966, 113(8), 1387-1394.

[90] Venkatraman, P.S., *Winding Eddy Current Losses in Switch Mode Power Transformers due to Rectangular Wave Currents*, Proceedings of the 11th National Solid-State Power Conversion Conference (Powercon 11), 1984, pp. A1.1-A1.11.

[91] Severns, R.P., *A Simple, General Method for Calculating HF Winding Losses for Arbitrary Current Waveforms*, Proceedings of the High Frequency Power Converter Conference (HFPC), Toronto, 1991.

[92] Owen, H. A.; Niemela, V. A.; Wilson, T. G., *Enhanced Cross-Coupled-Secondaries Model for Multiwinding Transformers*, Proceedings of the IEEE Power Electronics Specialists Conference, 1992, pp. 1269-1276.

[93] Niemela, V. A.; Owen, H. A.; Wilson, T. G., *Frequency-Independent-Element Cross-Coupled-Secondaries Model for Multiwinding Transformers*, Proceedings of the IEEE Power Electronics Specialists Conference (PESC), 1992, pp. 1262-1268.

[94] Collins, J., *An Accurate Method for Modeling Transformer Winding Capacitances*, IEEE IECON proceedings, vol. 2, Nov. 1990, pp. 1094-1099.

[95] Carsten, B., *High Frequency Conductor Losses in Switchmode Magnetics*, Proceedings of the High Frequency Power Converter Conference (HFPC), May 1986, pp. 155-176.

[96] Ferreira, J., *Improved Analytical Modeling of Conductive Losses in Magnetic Components*, IEEE Transaction on Power Electronics, 1994, 9(4), 127-131.

[97] El-Hamamsy, S.-A.; Chang, E.I., *Magnetics Modeling for Computer-Aided Design of Power Electronics Circuits*, IEEE Service Center, Piscataway, NJ, 1989, pp. 635-645.

[98] Edry, D.; Ben-Yaakov., *A SPICE Compatible Model of Magamp Post Regulator*, IEEE Applied Power Electronics Conference (APEC), Boston, 1992, pp. 793-800.

[99] Thottuvelil, J., *Using SPICE to Model the Dynamic Behavior of DC-to-DC Converters Employing Magnetic Amplifiers*, IEEE Applied Power Electronics Conference (APEC), 1990. Applied Power Electronics Conference

[100] MacLean, D., *The SPICE Simulation of a Piecewise-Linear Electrical Model of a Saturating Magnetic Device with Hysteresis*, IECEC 1987, pp. 640-645.

[101] Takach, M.; Lauritzen, P., *Survey of Magnetic Core Models*, Proceedings of the Applied Power Electronics Conference, 1995, pp. 560-566.

[102] Hymowitz, C., *Simulating Nonlinear Magnetics*, Intusoft Newsletter, June 1995.

[103] Dixon, L., *An Electrical Circuit Model for Magnetic Cores*, Unitrode Corp., Oct. 1994.

[104] Hsu, S.P.; Middlebrook, R.D.; Cuk, S., *Power Conversion International Magazine*, February 1982, p. 68.

Other General References

[105] Basso, C.P., *Switch-Mode Power Supply SPICE Cookbook*, 1st ed., McGraw-Hill, New York, 2001.

[106] Christiansen, D.; Jurgen, R.K.; Fink, D.G., *Electronics Engineers' Handbook*, McGraw-Hill, 4th ed., 1996.

Endnotes

[1] *PSpice A/D Reference Guide*, product version 10.0, June 2003.

[2] Yang, P., *Simulation and Modeling*, IEEE Circuit and Devices Magazine, Sept. 1991, pp. 9-37.

[3] Meares, L.; Hymowitz, C.E., Improved Spice Model Simulates Transformers Physical Processes, EDN, 19 Aug. 1993.

[4] Ben-Yaakov, S. and Adar (Edry), D., *Average Models as Tools for Studying the Dynamics of Switch Mode DC-DC Converters*, IEEE Power Electronics Specialists Conference (PESC), Taipei, 1994, pp. 1218-1225.

[5] Berwick, J., *SPICE Simulation Aids Power Factor Corrector Design*, Power Conversion & Intelligent Motion, February 1994, 20(2), pp. 19-20, 22, 24-26.